BEYOND
REDUCTIONISM

Gateways for Learning and Change

Neil Douglas
Terry Wykowski

S^t_L

St. Lucie Press

Boca Raton   London   New York   Washington, D.C.

Library of Congress Cataloging-in-Publication Data

Douglas, Neil, 1962–
   Beyond reductionism : gateways for learning and change / Neil
Douglas, Terry Wykowski.
      p.   cm.
   Includes bibliographical references and index.
   ISBN 1-57444-263-5 (alk. paper)
   1. Organizational learning.   2. Organizational change.
I. Wykowski, Terry.   II. Title.
HD58.82.D68   1999
658.4'06--dc21   98-17559
                                                                      CIP

© 1999 by CRC Press LLC
St. Lucie Press is an imprint of CRC Press LLC

No claim to original U.S. Government works
International Standard Book Number 1-57444-286-57
Library of Congress Card Number   99-17559
Printed in the United States of America   1 2 3 4 5 6 7 8 9 0
Printed on acid-free paper

Coventry University

Preface

Misapprehension of the nature of change, the poor quality of discourse and the lack of purposeful behavior converge to trap organizations and their leaders in patterns of superficial learning and reductionism. Reductionism is seen as the fallacy of modern life and the collective mind set that fuels under-performance and the failure of organizations to achieve their potential.

This book takes a critical look at behavior in late 20th century organizations. It argues, however, that the dynamics conspiring to restrain the efforts of individuals, leaders and members of groups and teams transcend personal attributes and leadership styles. These dynamics are rooted in the nature of work and institutions and the histories and cultures of the organizations themselves. This book is about strategies for overcoming these dynamics; it is about creating the foundations for learning in organizations where learning is perceived as the basis and the consequence of change.

Part One, comprised of Chapters 1 and 2, provides the analytical grounding for the book and introduces key concepts. Chapter 1 develops perspectives on learning and change and describes three core constraints on learning and effective change. In Chapter 2, three principles, designed as gateways through the constraints, are introduced and integrated. The model from Chapter 2 provides the framework for integration and the structure for Parts Two, Three and Four by applying the principles to the three dimensions of life in organizations: individuals, leaders and groups.

Change occurs one person at a time. Any successful effort to enhance learning and improve performance begins with individuals as individuals. Part Two applies the three principles to individuals in Chapters 3, 4, and 5. The leader's responsibility is to create a learning environment — a culture which fosters purposeful behavior and creative discourse. The principles, applied to leaders in Chapters 6, 7, and 8 of Part Three, characterize a leader for all seasons. A critical mass of change at the level of the individual, shaped and molded by leaders and expressed in group action defines effective organizational change. The principles are applied to groups in Chapters 9, 10 and 11 of Part Four.

We came to our joint consulting practice and the writing of this book from very different places. One of us comes from an objectively focused background in systems engineering and senior management; the other from a more subjectively oriented background in psychology and organizational behavior. Our cross tutoring, our experience and the reflection associated with writing this book have developed in both of us a deep sense of the dual nature of reality in organizations. A central premise of this book is that an especially negative aspect of reductionism results from de-linking the objective and subjective realities of organizational life. The central principle and the gateway through reductionism, which seeks to blend and balance objective and subjective factors, underpins this book.

The Authors

The authors have combined the experiences and learnings from their management consulting practice with those of their separate careers to produce this book. The perspectives of Neil Douglas having been a CEO and general manager and Terry Wykowski with a social and behavioral sciences background have been blended with solid research and application to develop the major themes of the book. Together the authors have undertaken and completed projects encompassing culture and change management coupled with strategic realignment, leadership development and executive tutorials, and teambuilding for achievement of objective results. Client organizations include multinational companies, hospitals, high technology firms and academic institutions.

Neil Douglas has a background in information technology and management at all levels. He was a Chief Information Officer, a Senior Vice President for a large organization and served as President of two high technology companies. His research and consulting assignments in Organizational Behavior utilize his extensive background in leading change as a senior executive.

Terry Wykowski was educated at the graduate and post graduate levels in both the United States and at the University of Oxford in England. She has an extensive background in Organizational Behavior and Psychology. Her work background includes internal and external consulting in change management and training; she has led consulting assignments for large organizations in the U.S. and in Europe.

Testimonials

"I am delighted to introduce *Beyond Reductionism: Gateways for Learning and Change*. It is a most stimulating and novel approach to the subject. I anticipate that it will be a highly influential work."

— **Dr. Rory F. Knight**, Dean,
Templeton College, University of Oxford

"A truly timely and insightful analysis of prevailing change management practices and assumptions. The authors skillfully integrate objective structure-oriented models with the powerful relational dynamics of organizational cultures that influence and drive successful organizational performance. Seriously researched and documented methodologies validate this counter-reductionism paradigm of leadership. Leaders and professionals will find *Beyond Reductionism* an intriguing, unconventional and practical approach to the challenges of effective learning and change."

— **Dr. Roger W. Birkman**, Chairman of the Board,
Birkman International, Inc., and author of *True Colors*

"Finally a text that digs beneath the veneer of management fads to deal with complex and sometimes intractable issues in leadership, organizational behavior and organizational performance. A refreshing text that doesn't simply state the obvious and does not seek organizational performance improvement through simplification, rather by acknowledging and dealing directly with inherent organizational complexity. Overall, a thoughtful, insightful, instructive and well-researched text. A significant addition to the management literature that should serve both the thoughtful practitioner and the practical academician."

— **Dr. Osama Mikhail**, Chief Strategic Officer,
St. Luke's Episcopal Health System and Professor,
Management and Policy Sciences,
University of Texas, School of Public Health

"Leading organizations through change, sustaining change and building an organizational culture that supports flexibility and encourages a level of comfort with ambiguity are the major challenges in healthcare today. *Beyond Reductionism: Gateways for Learning and Change* provides a framework that will help leaders to tailor strategies for their unique situations and develop learning organizations that embrace logical and well directed change. Leaders will be well prepared for the millennium by this innovative book."

— **Diana Browning**, Senior Vice President
for Hospital and Ambulatory Operations,
City of Hope National Medical Center
and Beckman Research Institute

"In my view, the specific uses of groups to enhance the efficacy of institutional knowledge in *Beyond Reductionism* provides a new perspective. Few authors writing in the area of leadership capture the nuances of group dynamics that impact group formation, functioning and effectiveness. This text contributes to the field of group dynamics and the processes associated with learning in groups."

— **Dr. Elizabeth A. Smith**, Vice President, Summit Resources,
Visiting Assistant Professor in Industrial/Organizational Psychology,
University of Houston and author
of *Creating Productive Organizations: The Productivity Manual*

"I found this work to contain many valuable insights for leaders as they grapple with escalating changes that surround us all."

— **David LeVrier**, Vice President,
Human Resources, Hines Interests

Beyond Reductionism: Gateways for Learning and Change presents challenges to leaders and professionals in all types of organizations to examine and improve performance from within. Applying the perspectives presented by Neil Douglas and Terry Wykowski in existing organizations is sure to expose ideas for change and improve teamwork."

— **J. Curtis Grindal**, President,
Transworld Exploration and Productions, Inc.

"Douglas and Wykowski have a very interesting and provocative approach to organizations and organizational behavior. I am sure that after careful study of *Beyond Reductionism* and serious reflection on their own organizations, managers will better understand the dynamics of the year 2000 environment. They have insightfully pointed the way for organizations to grow and prosper. By learning and changing, organizations can move beyond box-type thinking to a more creative pursuit.

Their strategies of management and leadership should be stimulating to leaders struggling for solutions to complex organizational and environmental challenges. The blend of subjective and objective guidance they provide highlights the difficult balance successful leaders must maintain. To insure that an organization meets its potential, leaders are required to seek a new view and way of thinking, behaving and managing. I am confident that *Beyond Reductionism* will open the eyes of many to a different and better means of achieving organizational success."

— **Dr. Kelley Moseley**, Professor and Director,
Health Care Administration, Texas Woman's University

Acknowledgments

We would like to thank the people on whose broad shoulders we stood to write this book. They include Chris Argyris, Peter Berger, Roger Birkman, Mary Douglas, Michael Earl, Andy Grove, Charles Handy, Rom Harre, Miles Hewstone, David Hodges, Robert Kegan, John Laverty, Thomas Luckman, Peter Senge, and Ed Shein. The late Dan Gowler, when he was a Fellow at Templeton College at the University of Oxford, taught, modeled and inspired critical thinking. He did this with a unique blend of passion, rigor, gentleness and compassion. His support and superior intellect made a permanent mark on Terry's life and work, and Dan's efforts through his patient tutoring and words of wisdom were passed on to Neil. Dan's positive influence lives on in both our work and writings. His wife and partner, Karen Legge, continues their work in developing unique insights in the field of organizational behavior.

Templeton College's Centre for Management Studies and Pembroke College at the University of Oxford provide the substance for a spirit of lifetime learning that lives on and is reflected in this book. The Templeton College Library was utilized extensively; their people and resources were invaluable. Our discussions with Templeton College Fellows, especially Rory Knight, Roger Undy, Nick Woodward, Janine Nahapiet, Rosemary Stewart and Sue Dobson, were enlightening and much appreciated.

We thank our clients for their courage in pursuing their organizational purpose and especially for those clients that supported us in the writing of this book.

There were several people who reviewed our book and gave us critiques, stories and suggestions. These colleagues and friends include Sandy Birtwistle, Chuck Hewitt, Bob Lee, Elizabeth Smith and Ted Zipf.

Ray Anthony, an accomplished author and consultant himself, is acknowledged with getting us to write in the first place. He bombarded us with encouragement, methodology and even publishers to make sure we wrote.

Glenn MacRill painstakingly provided the technical skill and artistic support for the figures and models in our book and his expertise in practical computer technology and communication was of great help.

We appreciate the expertise, advice and support of Drew Gierman, Marie Etzler, and Pat Roberson and their colleagues at CRC Press.

We thank our families for their patience and support. Thank you, Jim Wykowski, for giving us the space (literal and psychological) to devote ourselves to writing and consulting during these past few years and for the great parties when we completed this book. A special thanks to Grace Douglas for her prayers.

Ken Shelton, Editor of *Executive Excellence*, once described us as "The Odd Couple." Given that truth of our different styles and personalities, we must acknowledge each other as co-authors and business partners for completing this book and still working together. Our modus operandi with each other is one of cross-tutoring and continues to be a source of mutual growth, intellectual stimulation and accomplishment.

Contents

PART FOUR: GROUPS

Dedication

This book is dedicated to Toni and Tony, Terry's parents, whose endless and invigorating belief in our work has inspired us to go where we never thought we could.

Jennifer and Tony, Neil's children, who have grown up to be all he dreamed they would be and more.

ANALYSIS OF CONSTRAINTS AND DEVELOPMENT OF GATEWAYS FOR LEARNING AND CHANGE

Introduction

Leadership as an occupation and an art would seem to have reached a high state of development in late 20th century organizations. If the standard for leadership, however, is improved organizational performance resulting from the behavior and interventions of leaders, it is not clear that such a perception is justified. Many leaders will argue that the good performance of their organizations is a consequence of their efforts and in a few cases they will be right. Many leaders will also not agree that standards for leadership are low. Irrespective of popular conceptions as well as the self-perceptions of leaders, our experience leads us to this belief: leadership that truly adds value is rare. This belief does not deny the success of many organizations but asks to what degree such success is due to structural factors and the efforts of individuals in contrast to the initiatives and behavior of leaders. Looking good as an organization in good times may not be a sign of good leadership. We could even suggest that organizational success often seems to occur in spite of the efforts of leaders.

Good leadership is important in good and bad times for different reasons. When economies and markets are growing and opportunity seems to lie around every corner, the standard for good leadership should be achieving potential and not merely looking good. In difficult times, standards tend to be less ambiguous and often include survival. While most leaders hope to lead successfully through both good and bad times, existing leadership models and practices do not equip them for success and the character of life in organizations constrains them.

At the heart of these prevailing practices and cultural influences is reductionism. While reductionism is not a term in common usage in the language of management studies, no other term so precisely names the factors and circumstances that define this phenomenon. Reductionism is a process that reduces complex data and events to simple terms, especially to overly-simple terms. Reductionism means reducing how we think about the whole to the components of the whole and the analysis of systems to their constituents. While our use of the term is disparaging, reductionism may or may not produce negative consequences. Breaking big problems into small pieces can be useful, even necessary, in developing viable and incremental solutions. Understanding constituents can often lead to understanding the larger entity. Our anxiety about reductionism is when the consequences of it produce false perceptions and conclusions, a loss of perspective and a loss of a sense of the whole. In a pejorative sense, reductionism can be seen as simplistic, immature, conceptually crude and intellectually half-baked.

Reductionism is ubiquitous in organizations, and not surprisingly, in the larger domain of society. If reductionism is a constraint on achievement of potential in organizations, it is a constraint on authenticity, social progress, justice, equity, general well-being and meaningful existence in the surrounding culture. Reductionism defines many of the dilemmas and paradoxes of life. British business author and consultant Charles Handy has pointed to reductionism as the "sin of modern life" and as "missing the meaning and message of the forest in a minute examination of its trees."[1] Work is reduced to creating the capacity to consume; education is reduced to training for work; religion is reduced to appealing to the greatest numbers; sport is reduced to business and product promotion;

popular entertainment and journalism are reduced to ratings based on creating sensation. In political life, discourse is reduced to the lowest common denominator. The best people seem not to rise to the top; we're disillusioned and discontented with politics and we're not quite sure why we are.

Reductionism in organizational life is seductive. Members of organizations, especially leaders, need to feel and be seen as productive and in control of organizational processes. The temptation is great, therefore, to bring attention to bear on that which can be quantified and controlled in some way whether or not the thing in question has any meaning for the organization. Examples of reductionism in organizations and in the practice of managing them are plentiful and will be referenced throughout this book. Whenever emphasis and focus shift from important organizational outcomes to processes, reductionism is in play. Creating advanced communications systems without enhancing the information content of what's being communicated is reductionism. In organizations, enriching human dynamics for the inherent value of doing so is reductionism. Focusing on cutting cost and on next quarter's performance to the detriment of growth and strategic interests is reductionism. Applying reengineering, as a machine-related metaphor to human processes, is reductionism. (Although the original conception of reeingineering was integrative and comprehensive.)

Reductionism is so pervasive, we are led to wonder if it defines the limits of leadership potential; more broadly, does it define the limits of human potential? Perhaps reductionism is the ultimate collective defense mechanism, the cure for our existential angst. Reductionism moves us to perceptions of certainty in the midst of uncertainty; it protects us from threat to the perceptions and beliefs we're comfortable with. Whether or not reductionism is a deeply embedded limitation of potential, it is clear to us that to move beyond it is a stretch of intellect and will. We are equally certain that any proposed model of leadership for the new millennium must aim to escape its grip and our misplaced pride in it.

The consequences of reductionism for organizations are superficial learning and an underdeveloped ability to adapt to changing circumstances. This book proposes to elevate leadership standards, to raise the bar, so to say, through a non-reductionist paradigm centered on creating the foundations for enhanced learning and beneficial change. The concentric circles in Figure 1 represent the overall structure of the proposed paradigm and that of the book as well. "Learning" and "Change" are the targets and are featured at the center of the figure. Beneficial change is seen as the analog of effective learning and both are seen as the aim of leadership. "Purposeful Behavior" and "Creative Discourse" are foundational; they are seen as the preconditions or the antecedents of learning

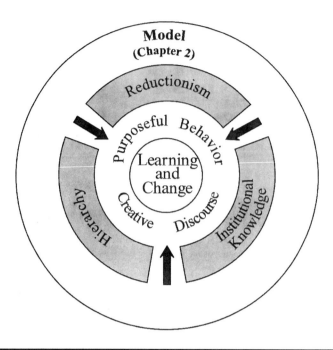

Figure 1   Leadership Paradigm

and change. The book argues, however, that there are constraints which act as barriers to achievement of the preconditions and therefore to learning and change. "Reductionism" is seen as the central constraint. The other constraints of "Hierarchy" and "Institutional Knowledge" are animated by the effects of reductionism. Hierarchy refers to layers of authority and bureaucracy which persist in organizations despite what we're told by leaders. Institutional knowledge refers to the crystallized assumptions that drive cultural behavior.

Perspectives on learning and change and their antecedents are developed in Chapter 1. The constraints, how they operate and how they interrelate are also described in this chapter. In Chapter 2, three principles designed as gateways through the constraints are introduced and integrated in the model referenced as the outer ring in Figure 1. The model from Chapter 2 provides the structure for Parts Two, Three and Four of the book by applying the principles to the three dimensions of life in organizations: individuals, leaders and groups.

Chapter 1

Constraints on Organizational Learning and Change

Anticipatory Summary

Much of value is lost in the gap between the reality and the potential of achievement in organizations. Why is it so difficult to change and close the gap? The dynamics that conspire to restrain change and the efforts of leaders seem to transcend leadership styles and simplistic approaches. These dynamics appear to be rooted in the nature of work and institutions and the histories and cultures of the organizations themselves. This book is about learning to change and changing so that learning becomes a way of life in organizations; its aim is to reduce the dimensions of the gap between reality and potential.

1.1   Perspectives on Change and Learning

■ The key concepts in our definition of organizational learning are these: reality and our experience of it, the basic assumptions (institutional knowledge) we hold both individually and collectively, actions or the consequences of our assumptions, and efficacy (the ability of our assumptions to produce desired effects).

- Since how we perceive change and how we behave within the context of change are the central issues in learning, the nature of change itself is influential.
- Learning is seen as the basis and consequence of change.
- Change and the appropriate learning response to it are framed by a sustained sense of purpose and the creation of results related to purpose. The ability to transcend defensive and flawed perceptions, perceive reality accurately and consistently communicate within a model of truth are collateral requirements.

1.2   Constraints on Change and Learning

- Misapprehension of the nature of change, the poor quality of discourse and the lack of purposeful behavior trap organizations and their leaders in patterns of superficial learning and reductionism.
- The key to understanding how a culture of learning can be brought about and sustained lies in understanding the constraints on such a culture.
- The core set of constraints are reductionism, hierarchy, and institutional knowledge.

1.2.1   Reductionism

Reductionism is characterized as over-simplification and a failure to fully comprehend the nature of life in organizations. Reductionism is seen as the fallacy of modern life and the mentality that fuels under-performance.

1.2.2   Hierarchy

Why, in the face of what managers say and general agreement that excessive hierarchy is a counter force to effective organizational behavior, does it persist and thrive?

1.2.3   Institutional Knowledge

Culture exists on two planes or in two dimensions — behavior and the knowledge that sets behavior in motion. Institutional knowledge largely constitutes the motivating dynamics of institutionalized conduct or culture-driven behavior.

1.3   *Priming Organizations for Learning and Change*

- The preconditions or antecedents for organizational learning and change are these: *purposeful behavior* and the ability to engage in *productive* and *creative discourse.*
- Three principles, introduced in the next chapter, are developed as gateways through the constraints to the preconditions for learning and change.

Constraints on Organizational Learning and Change

Much of value is lost in the gap between how organizations perform and how they could perform — between the reality and the potential of achievement. What occupies this space are jobs not created, cures for diseases not discovered, economic gains not realized, opportunities for innovation and service quality lost, human potential wasted, improvements in quality of life not achieved and differences not reconciled. As leaders, we must have a deep sense that these losses are worth our concern. We keep trying to change ourselves, our employees, our team members, our organizations towards improvement. We try to respond to change and to generate change to achieve the potential of our organizations. With so much at stake and the apparent motivation to change, unanswered questions persist:

> Why is it so difficult to bring about useful and enduring change?
> Why do so many highly promoted change undertakings fail?
> Why do some organizations appear to have it and then lose it? What is it they had? What is it they lost?
> Paradoxically, why do the organizations that most need to change experience the greatest difficulty in doing so?

Many leaders seem to move in synchrony from one change-oriented management trend to another. The latest trend, often a reincarnation of an old one with a new name, is adopted and pursued until it goes out of fashion, at which time a successor is embraced and the cycle begins again. Through all of this motion and activity, very little seems to change. We're familiar with an organization that has moved from continuous quality improvement to business process reengineering to lateral restructuring to reorientation around core competencies to customer service without achieving any real change in the character and level of performance of the organization. The last initiative we're aware of in this organization was focused on communicating and promoting the hoped for results of these earlier efforts with slick brochures and press releases based on the notion that if we say it's real persuasively enough, it will be seen as real and might actually become so. While it is not our aim to criticize any useful approach to change in organizations, the dynamics that conspire to restrain change and the efforts of leaders clearly seem to transcend leadership styles and reductionist or overly simplistic approaches. These dynamics appear to be rooted in the nature of work and institutions and the histories and cultures of the organizations themselves.

We believe that effective change in organizations is a process in contrast to the traditional view of change as an event followed by another state of business as usual. Effective and enduring change, therefore, is seen as the analog to effective organizational learning. This book is about learning to change and changing so that learning becomes a way of life in organizations. It is, more specifically, about building the foundations for learning and, in the process, positioning for effective change by creating a learning culture. This book is not about change in a generic sense. It is also not about learning as a given or self-evident good, but is, instead, about the linking of learning and change as pragmatically good. It does not assume that fundamental and broadly based change is needed in every situation. Rather, it assumes that effective change is a steady state proposition in good organizations and that effective learning is the engine that drives such change. The aim is to reduce the dimensions of the gap between reality and potential — to create and maintain the ability to change when change would be useful while maintaining the good sense not to change when change would be counter to the organization's best interests.

Since beneficial change and effectual learning are essentially the same, the foundations or preconditions for change and learning are the same. We contend that, at the most fundamental level, the preconditions for organizational learning and change are these: *purposeful behavior* and the ability to engage in *productive* and *creative discourse*. Organizations are by definition purposeful. Purposeful behavior on the part of organization members would seem to be a given — in our experience, it is not. Change efforts often assume lives of their own, leading down paths that either obscure or contradict purpose. Individuals involved in such efforts tend to succumb to temptations to focus on the trappings, i.e., on activities that monitor, measure, control, and report. These efforts often fall into the agendas of self- and narrowly interested people. Without alignment around what is beneficial and useful and the collective motivation to achieve results related to a common purpose, there can be no purposeful behavior, and therefore, no effective change or learning.

In a parallel sense, without the ability to communicate within a standard of *valid* information, resultant patterns of discourse will inevitably mask the truth and drive ineffectual learning and change. Since information is defined to be the communication of knowledge and intelligence, the term "valid information" would seem to be redundant. It is not redundant, however; *valid* is a crucial modifier and refers to relevant, accurate, complete and non-contradictory information. The attention given to communication in organizations is too frequently centered on form and not on substance and content. We are consistently struck by how artifacts, noise, obfuscations and banality frame discourse among individuals in organizations. It is our loss and to our detriment, individually and collectively, that the current age has taken shape as the "information age" and not the "valid information age." T. S. Eliot said, "Humankind cannot bear very much reality."[2] Our experience validates Eliot's phrase. If the quality of information we communicate to each other is to be elevated and if learning and effective change is to be enhanced as a result of such elevation, however, our ability to bear reality will have to be challenged and strengthened.

1.1   Perspectives on Change and Learning

The term "organizational learning" seems to have some vague appeal for many people in organizations, but when asked to explain what they think it means, they tend to be at a loss to do so. Learning, in fact, has multiple meanings. We say that we learn a skill. We learn the lines of a play; we learn to dance and ride a bicycle. We come to realize, through learning, that certain patterns of behavior produce beneficial consequences for us. We all learn as individuals and as collections of individuals. If we didn't learn, we couldn't adapt to organizational life and no organization could survive beyond its first mistake. What exactly, then, is meant by "organizational learning," and more specifically, what do *we* mean when we use the term? Our meaning is pragmatic; it refers to human processes that create important and beneficial consequences for organizations. Our definition connects answering a question or solving a problem with action. It means modifying perception and behavior based on consciously evaluating experience. Action is then taken based on the understanding and wisdom brought about by this analysis within a relevant period of time. It is confusing and misleading to speak of creating organizational learning as if such a capacity didn't exist. Our meaning, then, is associated with improving the capacity of individuals, groups and thus organizations to learn and embedding such elevated capacity in the cultures of organizations.

The key concepts in our definition of organizational learning are these: reality and our experience of it, the basic assumptions we hold both individually and collectively, actions or the consequences of knowledge, and efficacy. The core questions are what sense do we make of circumstances and the playing out of events in the stream of time and what actions do we take in response to and in anticipation of these circumstances and events? In our search for a substantial and operative meaning of organizational learning, we have evolved the following definition on three levels:

1. The ability to comprehend internal and external reality and the connections between these aspects of reality
2. The ability to recognize and understand the basic assumptions operating within the culture of an organization and the ability to identify the differences between assumptions that are congruent with reality and those that are not
3. The ability to change the assumptions that need to be changed and to leave alone those that do not

Since how we perceive change and how we behave within the context of change are the central issues in learning, the nature of change itself is influential.

Charles Handy in his book, *The Age of Unreason*, explores the nature of change.[3] He distinguishes between continuous change and discontinuous change. Continuous change is linear, incremental, gradual, predictable and controllable. Handy states, "The past is the guide to the future." Under continuous change, with minor and fully understood adjustments, reality and our experience of it will play out in approximately the same way in the future as they did in the past. Continuous change suggests that our basic assumptions will continue to be valid and that the future is a straight line projection from where we are in the present. In contrast, discontinuous change is transformative and disjunctive; it is nonlinear, nonincremental, nongradual, not part of a pattern and not fully predictable. The past is, at best, only a partial guide to the future. Under discontinuous change, reality and our experience of it will be different. Our assumptions will become incongruent with reality and therefore invalid. We are accustomed to thinking about change related to societies, economies and the sweep of history in these terms. It is, nevertheless, surprising when discontinuous change occurs in our own time, even at this macro or global level. While virtually all the West's strategic thinkers saw change related to the Soviet Union and its relationship with the West as continuous, discontinuity emerged. The USSR collapsed and the age of bi-polarity ended. In our own micro-worlds, the dynamics of continuity and discontinuity affect our day to day lives and the functioning of our organizations. The status quo holds sway for an organization until markets change, new products and competitors appear or the economy cycles into another phase. The presentation of new problems in our work groups, even the presentation of a new set of personalities causes continuity to shift to discontinuity. Even though discontinuity seems to be ever more prevalent in modern life, we are usually not prepared for it while we tend to be always ready for change of a continuous sort.

The efficacy of learning and the nature of change are inextricably bound; we could also assert that the nature of learning and the efficacy of change are similarly bound. Chris Argyris, a founding father of organizational learning, has described two modes of learning that pertain to both organizations and individuals. Single-loop learning implies that assumptions (or governing values) are held constant and that thought and action vary only within the set of existing assumptions. Double-loop learning, on the other hand, holds fundamental assumptions up for evaluation and reformulation.[4] Continuous change suggests the appropriateness and efficacy of single-loop learning. Single-loop learning deals with the presenting problem and does not ask why does this problem exists in the first place. Actions may be modified but assumptions are held constant when single-loop learning is occurring. Single-loop learning is clean and orderly; it is compatible with planning, analysis, structure and clear organizational roles. Single-loop learning is learning within a subject matter context. As work becomes more specialized, we tend to be trained for single-loop learning; as organizations become more differentiated, we tend to get better and better at it. Perhaps our preference for and our skill in single-loop learning can be traced to the myths of antiquity and is deeply ingrained in our Western sensibility. The original meaning of the ultimate source of the old English "leornian" — to learn — was "furrow" or "track." "'Lira', a Latin cognate of learn, retains the ancestral meaning 'furrow' or 'tract'."[5] If we cease to follow the track (analogous to our basic assumptions), not only do we stop learning, but we are also in danger of graver consequences.

Single-loop learning holds assumptions constant, hastens changes in action and behavior and progresses continuously along an established track. Learning of a different nature is required when there is no track or when the track may lead somewhere we don't want to go. Under discontinuous change, the status quo no longer represents the basis for the way forward. The necessary mode of learning under conditions of discontinuity has been called by Argyris double-loop learning. Rather than simply responding to the presenting problem, double-loop learning brings forth questions such as: why does the problem exist in the first place? Are the governing conditions responsible for our producing unintended consequences? Double-loop learning challenges fundamental assumptions and makes them subject to change. While single-loop learning is clean and orderly, double-loop learning tends to be rather messy and untidy and not amenable to formulaic approaches. If single-loop learning is compatible with textbook analysis, planning and structure, double-loop learning is in accord with openness, flexibility and comfort with uncertainty. We tend not to be well trained for double-loop learning; we find it difficult and often painful. Double-loop learning may be counterintuitive for most of us, but increasingly, long term success for individuals and organizations depends on our ability to learn to do it and to become comfortable with the ambiguity that surrounds it.

We want answers. Whether our answers take the form of a sophisticated analysis or the simple answers to the innocent questions of a child, we want reality to be continuous. When we treat legitimate discontinuity as continuity, however, we misperceive reality and make wrong choices. The consequences of single-loop learning within a context of discontinuous change vary in significance between meager effectiveness in routine problem solving and failure to adapt to important market, economic and technological circumstances. Planning and forecasting processes inevitably treat discontinuity as continuity. The only thing we know for sure about the future is that it won't play out the way we think it will. Niels Bohr, the renowned physicist, said, "Prediction is very difficult, especially about the future." Thomas J. Watson, President of IBM in 1948, said, "I think there is a world market for about five computers."[6] We earnestly undertake formal strategic and business planning processes by freezing assumptions and projecting the future for five or more years in the certain knowledge that our projections will be wrong.

When we treat continuity as discontinuity, we make unsustainable sacrifices in efficiency. The application of double-loop learning when single-loop learning is called for brings about squandered effort. Questioning and rethinking assumptions that are either perfectly valid or irrelevant within the presenting problem or context is an indefensible application of energy and time. Looking at change as an abstraction, the case can be made for either the continuous nature or the discontinuous nature of all change. Pragmatically speaking, such arguments have little meaning. Both perspectives are valid and produce real consequences in the lives of people and organizations. It is generally true that the closer (in terms of time and space) that we get to any set of circumstances, the more change associated with those circumstances seems continuous. Conversely, the farther away we move from any set of circumstances, the more those circumstances seem to be governed by discontinuity. In the practical regard of change and our appropriate learning response to it, the essential issue is one of perspective framed by a sustained sense of purpose and the creation of results related to purpose. Whether we take a short term and narrow view of circumstances or a longer term and broader view depends on the impact of such a view on the results or the consequences of effort related to purpose. The necessary perspective relates first to the character of change confronting the organization, incorporates a proper balance in modes of learning and extends to actual responses to and generation of change. The ability to transcend defensive and flawed perceptions, perceive reality accurately and consistently communicate within a model of truth are collateral requirements. These themes will be explored throughout this book.

1.2   Constraints on Change and Learning

The fundamental assumptions that underpin the rationale and existence of organizations and the management of them are that organizations are purposeful and that many heads are better than a few. We believe the key to understanding how beneficial change and a culture of learning can be brought about and sustained in organizations lies in understanding the constraints on purposeful behavior and on truthful and creative discourse. Of all the factors that restrain purposeful behavior and effective communication in organizations, we have identified three that comprise a core set of constraints; these are reductionism, hierarchy, and institutional knowledge. These constraints tend to be part of the fabric of organizational life, our patterns of socialization, education and work and the practice of management. Each of these constraints is influential and potent in its own way and they come together to militate against purposefulness and productive interaction. It is a great irony that the conception of the *organization* as a means of achieving particular aims has evolved under the influence of these constraints in the direction of limiting the achievement of aims.

1.2.1 Reductionism

We defined reductionism in the introduction to this chapter. The general definition pertains to a process that reduces complex data or phenomena to inappropriately simple terms. Thomas Kuhn distinguished normal from paradigm-breaking science; from the perspective of "normal" science, William J.M. Hrushesky writing in *Perspectives in Biology and Medicine* provides a penetrating insight: "The vivid, ubiquitous illusion that the disassembly and resultant destruction of that which we seek to understand brings us closer to our goal, permeates postmodern science. It is the greatest of the four endogenous impediments to knowledge. (These are inertia, dualism, linearity and reductionism.) Unbounded reductionism is the staunchest of the four vestal virgins guarding the temple of the trivial from creativity." He goes on to say, "Reductionism, has become a religion, and the rate of growth of both knowledge and understanding has diminished."[7] (Parenthetical comments are those of the authors.)

The classic definition of reductionism refers to the attempt to reduce one science to another by demonstrating that the key terms of the one are definable in the language of the other and that the conclusions of the one are derivable from the propositions of the other. Theorists and practitioners of the social sciences, including management, have been infatuated with the rigor and empiricism of the hard sciences for decades. Even in the interest of discovery of new perspectives, reductionism is in play when we try to reduce organizational analysis and management studies to hard science and engineering models. This is an especially ironic circumstance given that "paradigm-breaking" science itself has moved beyond the tight predictability and determinism of cause and effect while those who would force management and organizational analysis into scientific and engineering metaphors have not.

Reductionism can be seen as the dark side or the downside of the Enlightenment. The Enlightenment, or the Age of Reason, is the Eighteenth-century European philosophical movement that has shaped, in one way or another, intellectual life in the West for the last 250 years. The Enlightenment was a reaction to superstition and ignorance and set the stage for the blooming of science and discovery. Reason and the scientific method were the centerpieces of the Enlightenment. The theory that all knowledge originates in experience, or empiricism, framed the essence of the Enlightenment; belief in the possibilities of reason to beneficially shape human progress animated it. Science and experience, however, have taught us that classical empiricism alone cannot answer all of our questions — that the unknown and the unknowable are aspects of reality that we can't escape. Pure science has begun to take account of this natural revelation; most of the rest of us have not. In the present age, which we might call the post-enlightenment or even the counter-enlightenment, we are locked into the extremes of the Enlightenment — we seem to have pushed the paradigm into the region of nonsense.

Reductionism is underpinned by notions of tangible expression and quantification. Meaning and reality are expressed in measurement and physical evidence. If the object of any interest can be experienced, counted, displayed and compared, it has value; if tangible expression is difficult or if the object is inherently ambiguous, any perception of value is diminished. This sense of value in itself is not corrupting unless the perception of value shifts from that which has significance to that which can be merely counted.

Reductionism, unbridled by an overarching sense of purpose, exerts an enormous and generally negative influence in organizations. The essence of reductionism is to become oriented to that which can be easily understood and expressed simply because it can be easily understood and expressed, not because it matters. Reductionism masks the truth and separates people from purpose. It thwarts communication and learning and makes us think we understand when we don't. Any attempted change within the framework of this erroneous understanding will inevitably lead to failure. William Whyte, in *Social Theory for Action*, talks about the consequences for learning: "If you think you know something that 'ain't so,' then you continue to act on this misconception, in spite of increasing failures and frustrations. As humans generally do not abandon a theory simply through the discovery of its faults but tend to persist in error until they envision at least the glimmerings of a more adequate theory, the learning process can be long and painful."[8]

The most acutely felt aspect of reductionism in organizations and one which will become a point of focus in this book pertains to how that which is perceived as rational and objective is sharply demarcated from that which is seen as emotional and subjective. Organizations exist for objective reasons and objective reality frames their existence. However organizations are collections of human beings who have emotions, needs, imaginations, biases, idiosyncrasies and egos. Organizations, therefore, embrace a reality that is both objective and subjective. Misperceptions and loss of perspective related to the whole of organizational circumstances are the result of emphasis on objective factors to the exclusion or under-valuation of subjective ones, and sometimes the other way around. Objectivity and subjectivity are different views of the same reality — as two sides of the same coin. We will argue throughout this book that there is a dialectical relationship — a relationship of mutual cause and effect — between objectivity and subjectivity in organizations and that understanding this relationship and acting within the framework of such understanding is a central precondition to learning and beneficial change. Reification is a term that sheds additional light on this aspect of reductionism.

Reification is the process of regarding something abstract as a material or concrete thing. It is the apprehension of human phenomena in non-human terms; it is reductionism in the extreme. Social reality is complex, contradictory, paradoxical and ambiguous. Organizations, as expressions of social reality, are abstractions and embrace this untidy reality. To treat this world as tangible, objective and concrete is to reify it and to misperceive it. Reification lies at the heart of mechanistic views of organizations, resultant objectification in the extreme and hierarchy. Through reification, human beings are capable of producing a reality that denies their own humanity.

1.2.2 Hierarchy

Hierarchical structures, layers of authority and the bureaucracy that attaches to these structures and patterns are clearly out of favor. Hierarchy has been discredited in terms of how we speak about it if not in terms of what we do and how we continue to order life in our organizations. Modern management theory, popular books, journal articles and high profile executive development programs all point to the virtues of non-hierarchical and organismic forms. Mechanistic structures and hierarchical systems of control are almost universally denounced as inappropriate in the present age. The nature of the present age itself, described as the information or post-industrial or post-modern age, makes rigid and legalistic forms of organizational arrangement appear to be anachronistic. It is anything but a unique insight that hierarchy, beyond some minimal level, is a restraint on good performance and significant achievement. There is, however, a gap between what we know and espouse and what we do. Why, in the face of rhetoric and general agreement that hierarchy is a counter force to effective organizational behavior, does it persist? Why, when organizational layers are removed, usually with great and self-congratulatory fanfare, do they creep back in and reappear? What is it that keeps us so deterministically connected to hierarchy?

Differentiation of tasks, job specialization, division of labor and notions of economy of scale are factors that lead to organizations with many parts and members. Some method of coordination and integration is obviously required. The conventional practice of management could have evolved in the direction of development and translation of common cause or purpose and creation of systems of accountability for producing results related to purpose. Instead, leaders of organizations, as Robert Merton observed in his article, "Bureaucratic Structure and Personality,"[9] have opted for coordination through mechanistic structures and processes designed to bring about reliable and predictable behavior. The function of coordination has largely, therefore, been satisfied through authority-based hierarchies for control, guidance and communication. Edgar Schein offered a definition of an organization, acknowledged to be preliminary and incomplete, in his book *Organizational Psychology.*[10] "An organization is the planned coordination of the activities of a number of people for the achievement of some common, explicit purpose or goal, through division of labor and function, and through a hierarchy of authority and responsibility." This definition, or something very much like it, is the accepted view of organizations and the emphasis continues to be on "hierarchy of authority and responsibility" and on reliability and predictability.

Hierarchy can be a profound manifestation of reductionism. The nature of hierarchy, comprising aspects of control, the social and economic order, and culture, suggests something about its appeal and durability. Control, or more accurately the perception of control, is associated with mechanistic views of organizations. If leaders view the components of their organizations as cogs in a wheel or as a collection of interacting machines, the illusion of controlling them in a self-determining way is a natural extension. In their article "The Meaning of Management and the Management of Meaning," Gowler and Legge develop the theme of management-as-hierarchy as an expression of meaning about the social order. "The sovereignty of management is generally regarded as in some way given and the fatalistic acceptance of this by actors (within organizations) has led to the idea that the sovereignty of management in an industrial hierarchical organization is some kind of truism."[11] (Words in parentheses are those of the authors.) The attributes of sovereignty, privilege and economic status of management are embodied in hierarchy; elitism, as manifested in power, status and prestige, attaches to one's place in the hierarchy. Whereas patterns of empowerment and accountability for results or outcomes are difficult to bring about, the creation of hierarchy based on tasks and activities is remarkably easy. Any perceived void in coordination and control is filled by a layer in the hierarchy. Leaders creating subordinate layers also gain by causing a perception of their own elevation, and in the process, establish distance between themselves and real work. Finally, communities of interest based on tasks and occupational groupings catalyze and sustain well-developed hierarchies. As tasks become more refined and differentiated, our training for the task becomes more intense and our belonging to the task supersedes our belonging to the larger organization. These task-based hierarchical units then begin to take on a separate and independent life, in perception if not in reality.

Hierarchy is a constraint on change and learning because it obscures purpose and the efforts of leaders even though it is intended to do the opposite. If hierarchy evolves based on functions or tasks, some purpose will exist in the minds of people, but it is not likely to be the same purpose as that which exists in the minds of the leaders. Hierarchy brings about an orientation to narrow sub-goals (often conflicting with the goals of the larger organization) and sub-optimization. The degree of orientation and optimization to sub-goals appears to vary directly with the number of layers separating the unit and the level at which organizational purpose is comprehended. Hierarchy plays an important role in the phenomenon of negative or diminishing returns to scale — that most unpleasant circumstance defined by lower levels of productivity and output driven by higher levels of resource and activity. Hierarchy sets up political dynamics. It puts up walls and segregates people; it slots them into predetermined ways of perceiving and being perceived. Hierarchy fuels notions of turf or territoriality and provokes defensiveness in response to perceived threats to territory. Such defensive norms close down valid and effective communication. Max Weber, German sociologist and influential contributor to the study of organizational behavior, argued that the "ideal bureaucracy" was an example of both scientific rationality and efficiency. Even Weber, however, cautioned that bureaucracy itself could become an entrapment leading to an "iron cage of bureaucratic rationality."[12]

Hierarchy persists and thrives in most organizations even though we know, at least at some level, that it is not in our collective best interests. We talk about flattening structures. We redraw charts and move boxes around. Yet, the underlying reasons for hierarchy remain unrecognized and unchanged. Feeling and seeming to be in control causes managers to feel and to seem to be effective. As we have seen, well-developed hierarchies support the illusion of control and the self-perceived well-being of managers. The uncomfortable truth, at a more fundamental level, is that managers have a lot at stake in perpetuating hierarchy. Rewards, status and perceptions of success continue to accrue to organizational members who are well placed in hierarchical terms. One of the basic assumptions that drives behavior continues to be that one succeeds by having many subordinate people and multiple subordinate layers. We're aware of an illustrative situation in an organization we know. Two of three peer-level managers were promoted to the position of vice president. The promoted managers were line managers with multiple vertical layers reporting to them comprising a large number of employees. The third manager, who was not promoted and did not have a large number of direct reports, was responsible for results in a major segment of the company's market and worked in a lateral and collaborative mode with many parts of the organization. Before the promotion of the two managers, the three of them were assigned their roles with the assurance that they were peers and that collaboration and results would be the criteria for promotion. Following the promotions, the third manager was disillusioned and disheartened especially considering that this manager had a greater impact on organizational success than the other two. The message clearly seemed to be: this is what we say but when the time for change and action arrives, this is what we do!

1.2.3 Institutional Knowledge

The culture of an organization or any group has been defined by Edgar Schein as, "A pattern of shared basic assumptions that the group learned as it solved its problems of external adaptation and internal integration, that has worked well enough to be considered valid and, therefore, to be taught (consciously or not) to new members as the correct way to perceive, think and feel in relation to those problems."[13] (Parenthetical comments are those of the authors) Culture has a potent capacity to influence purposeful behavior and achievement of organizational potential. The influence of culture may operate for good or ill. To the extent that culture is not understood, i.e., when basic assumptions about the organization, its markets, its members, its environment are tacit, unexamined and unchallenged, the actions of the organization will be controlled to a far greater extent by its culture than by its leaders or anything else. Culture exists on two planes or in two dimensions — behavior and the knowledge that sets behavior in motion. Behavior is the aspect of culture that we see. Behavior is what people do and is represented in the symbolic and physical manifestations of deeply held assumptions. Knowledge refers to these assumptions which tend to be taken for granted. Basic assumptions, in this sense, are similar to what Chris Argyris has identified as "theories-in-use," and defined as "the implicit assumptions that actually guide behavior, that tell group members how to perceive, think about and feel about things."[14]

The term "institutional" is used as a modifier of "knowledge" to suggest the embedded, unalterable and crystallized nature of the basic assumptions that drive behavior in organizations. These assumptions pertain to external and internal environments, social and technical processes and human nature. At the core of institutionalization is habitualized behavior. Institutionalization is defined as "a continuing social situation in which the habitualized actions of two or more individuals interlock."[15] Habitualization carries with it the important gain that choices are narrowed enabling actions to be reproduced with an economy of effort. Experience is encapsulated in institutional knowledge; it serves as a guide to the future and helps to mitigate uncertainty. Institutional knowledge largely constitutes the motivating dynamics of institutionalized conduct or culture-driven behavior. Institutional knowledge tends to be stable, durable and highly resistant to change. It embodies sets of assumptions that have taken on a life of their own and operate outside of awareness. The essential mechanism of control exerted by institutional knowledge results from internalizing hardened and thickened assumptions by individuals. As the subjective natures of individuals are altered by institutional knowledge, any attempt to change basic assumptions will represent a challenge and a threat to the sense-making and meaning-making of individuals. The components of institutional knowledge represent the building blocks of culture, and all too often, are expressions of reductionism; to underestimate the enduring quality of institutional knowledge is to misapprehend how learning and change can be brought about.

As complex and subtly catalytic as institutional knowledge is, it is well understood from various perspectives including that of Schein as a social psychologist. The process of institutionalization and internalization by individuals explains its pervasiveness, durability and usefulness. The sociologists Berger and Luckman, argue that all human activity is subject to habitualization and habitualization is at the core of institutionalization. The assumptions that flow from activity that is recurrent and has become ingrained carry the important psychological gain that choices are unconsciously narrowed enabling actions to be produced with an economy of effort. It is almost as if people do not see the choices.[16] Mary Douglas, an anthropologist, describes the terms introduced by Ludwick Fleck in the 1930s: the "thought collective" and the "thought style." "The individual within the collective is never or hardly ever conscious of the prevailing thought style which almost always exerts an absolutely compulsive force upon his thinking, and with which it is not possible to be at variance.[17] Thomas Kuhn, writing from the perspective of the philosophy of science, described his insights regarding the nature of scientific progress and introduced the term "paradigm." For Kuhn, paradigm represents the institutionalized assumptions/knowledge that relate to "normal science" within any discipline at any point in time. "The scientific community is largely bound by the presuppositions it holds, such premises in turn providing the rules discerning the perceptual limits of problems and solutions."[18]

Physicist David Bohm is interested in understanding and fostering dialogue across paradigms or among individuals whose thinking tends to be circumscribed by different sets of assumptions. He uses the term "tacit infrastructure" to name these sets of interlocking assumptions or components of institutional knowledge.[19] Frank Blackler, in a contributing chapter to the 1992 book, *Rethinking Organization*, describes a theory proposed by Roberto Unger for a more integrative approach to organizational and social change:

Writing from a Political Science perspective, Unger's key theoretical concept is the notion of 'formative context'. Through this he focuses on the arrangements and beliefs that people take for granted, and on the ways in which they identify and pursue their interests. Such assumptions are pervasive in their effects for they give coherence and continuity to the roles that people enact in everyday life. Normally unrecognized by those who are affected by them, formative contexts are an accepted set of pragmatic institutional and imaginative assumptions that guide the ways in which interests are defined and problems are approached.[20]

The "institution-in-the-mind" is the term fashioned by Shapiro and Carr to express their psychologically-based perspective on institutional knowledge. Shapiro, a psychoanalyst, and Carr, an Anglican priest, are associated with the Tavistock Institute of London. Their insights are especially attuned to how shared or collective interpretations of organizational life become subjective in the minds of organization members:

The organization is composed of the diverse fantasies and projections of its members. Everyone who is aware of an organization whether a member of it or not, has a mental image of how it works. Though these diverse ideas are not often consciously negotiated or agreed upon among the participants, they exist. In this sense, all institutions exist in the mind, and it is in interaction with these in-the-mind entities that we live. Of course, all organizations also consist of certain real factors, such as people, profits, buildings, resources and products. But the meaning of these factors derives from the context established by the institution-in-the-mind.[21]

"Basic assumptions," "tacit infrastructure," "thought style," "paradigm," "institution-in-the-mind," "formative context" — all of these terms refer to institutional knowledge as seen through different lenses and understood in different frameworks and this, as we have come to understand culture, is the essence of it.

1.3 Priming Organizations for Learning and Change

A common feature of the constraints is that each is deeply systemic or structural in nature. The interconnectedness of these constraints brings about another level of systemic influence. For example, the process of reductionism fuels the development of hierarchy and institutional knowledge sets up its tenacious resistance to change. Institutional knowledge develops in phase with the emergence of objective reality in organizations. The conversion of institutional knowledge to subjective reality for individuals seals the continuation of reductionism and hierarchy. Reductionism, hierarchy and institutional knowledge are conspirators in the process of obscuring objective purpose. These systemic influences are powerful and suggest that a kind of determinism is at work rendering fundamental change impossible. However, there is cause for hope, when we bring to mind that society and our organizations are human products. If we construct our social settings, given the motivation, the skills and the tools, we can reconstruct them and make them better. Applying the three principles introduced in the next chapter as gateways through the constraints to the preconditions comprise the requisite skills and tools. The metaphor of priming an organization for learning and change captures and ties together the notions of constraints, principles and the preconditions. To prime an organization is to first apply the principles to the constraints as in sanding and repairing damaged surfaces, removing rust and chipped paint, and then exercising the preconditions as in applying a coat of primer to which the finished surface of learning and effective change can adhere.

References

1. Handy, C., *The Age of Unreason,* Harvard Business School Press, Boston, 1989.
2. Eliot, T. S., "East Coker," from *Collected Poems 1909–1962,* Harcourt Brace Jovanovich, San Diego, 1970, 182.
3. Handy, C., *The Age of Unreason,* Harvard Business School Press, Boston, 1989.
4. Argyris, C., *Overcoming Organizational Defenses: Facilitating Organizational Learning,* Allyn & Bacon, Boston, 1990.
5. *Webster's Word Histories,* Merriam-Webster, Inc., Springfield, MA, 1989.
6. Starbuck, W. H., Acting First and Thinking Later: Theory Versus Reality in Strategic Change, *Organizational Strategy and Change,* Jossey-Bass, 1985.
7. Hrushesky, W. J. M., Triumph of the trivial, *Perspectives in Biology and Medicine,* The University of Chicago, Spring 1998, 41, 3.
8. Whyte, W. F., *Social Theory for Action: How Individuals and Organizations Learn to Change,* Sage Publications, Newbury Park, 1991, 17.
9. Merton, R., Bureaucratic Structure and Personality, *Social Forces,* 18, 1940.
10. Schein, E. H., *Organizational Psychology,* 3rd ed., Prentice-Hall, Englewood Cliffs, 1988.

11. Gowler, D. and Legge, K., The Meaning of Management and the Management of Meaning: a view from social anthropology, *Perspectives on Management,* Oxford University Press, Oxford, 1983.
12. Brown, C., Organization Studies and Scientific Authority, *Rethinking Organization: New Directions in Organizational Theory and Analysis,* Sage Publications, London, 1992.
13. Schein, E. H., *Organizational Culture and Leadership,* 3rd ed., Jossey-Bass, San Francisco, 1992, 12.
14. Argyris, C., *Overcoming Organizational Defenses: Facilitating Organizational Learning,* Allyn & Bacon, Boston, 1990, 22.
15. Berger, P. L. and Luckman, T., *The Social Construction of Reality: A Treatise in the Sociology of Knowledge,* Penguin, 1966, 75.
16. Berger, P. L. and Luckman, T., *The Social Construction of Reality: A Treatise in the Sociology of Knowledge,* Penguin, 1966, 75.
17. Fleck, L., *The Genesis and Development of a Scientific Fact,* (1935), University of Chicago Press, Chicago, translation, 1979.
18. Kuhn, T. S., *The Structure of Scientific Revolutions,* 2nd ed., University of Chicago Press, Chicago, 1970.
19. Bohm, D. and Peat, F. D., *Science, Order and Creativity,* Phantom, New York, 1987.
20. Blackler, F., Formative Contexts and Activity Systems: Postmodern Approaches to the Management of Change, *Rethinking Organization: New Directions in Organizational Theory and Analysis,* Sage Publications, London, 1992, 278.
21. Shapiro, E. R. and Carr, A. W., *Lost in Familiar Places: Creating New Connections Between the Individual and Society,* Yale University Press, New Haven, 1991, 69.

Chapter 2

Three Principles as Gateways for Learning and Change

Anticipatory Summary

These principles form gateways through the constraints on purposeful behavior and effective discourse and create the potential to bring about beneficial change through learning:

Principles	Constraints
• Achieve an Operative Balance of Objective and Subjective Factors	• Reductionism
• Delegate Only Around Purpose	• Hierarchy
• Enhance the Efficacy of Institutional Knowledge	• Institutional Knowledge

2.1   Principle No. 1: Achieve an Operative Balance of Objective and Subjective Factors

■ Organizations are human constructions and can be said to possess both objective and subjective realities.

■ This principle addresses the aspect of reductionism associated with the failure to understand and reconcile these realities.

■ It provides a gateway through reductionism by aiming to exploit the potentially productive clash of these opposites.

2.2   Principle No. 2: Delegate Only Around Purpose

■ Hierarchy in organizations is natural and useful to the extent that it doesn't yield a life of its own.

■ Delegation is the driver and substance of hierarchy.

■ Hierarchy itself, then, is not the essential matter. The issue is rather the basis of delegation, i.e., the foundation for entrusting and empowering others.

2.2.1 A Working Definition of Purpose

2.2.2 Purposeful Delegation

■ Highly evolved structures that obscure and convolute purpose through multiple layers are the norm.

■ Patterns of delegation based on purpose will naturally and inevitably flatten structures and remove the damaging effects associated with hierarchies.

2.3   Principle No. 3: Enhance the Efficacy of Institutional Knowledge

■ This principle is concerned with change and with culture, especially the aspect of culture represented by latent attitudes, beliefs and knowledge.

■ Behavior change is perceived as consequential to shifts in the "silent language" or in the terms of this principle, institutional knowledge.

■ The key words in this principle are "enhance" — "to alter and improve" — and "efficacy" — in this case, referring to the power of institutional knowledge to produce an effect.

2.4   An Integrative Model for Learning and Change

■ The model integrates constraints and mitigating principles with application of these principles; it bridges theoretical insights and practical application.

2.4.1 Dynamic Theme

■ The model is mediated by the Dynamic Theme which refers specifically to the dual nature of reality in organizations, the relationship between the extremes of these realities and the mechanics of transition between the extremes.

2.4.2 Application of the Principles

■ The principles are connected to practice by way of the three organizational dimensions of Individuals, Leaders and Groups:
  ■ *Individuals:* A critical mass of change in individuals is a precondition for enhanced learning and effective organizational change.
  ■ *Leaders:* The essential function of synthesizing objective factors and organizational behavior, as well as change and learning, is informed by the conjunction of a leader's personal characteristics with the structures and culture of an organization.
  ■ *Groups:* The composite and emergent motivations, perceptions, needs and defenses create dynamics that either support purposeful group behavior and achievement or lend themselves to dysfunction.
■ The application of the principles within the context of Individuals, Leaders and Groups provides the structure and the basis for Parts Two, Three and Four of this book.

Three Principles as Gateways
for Learning and Change

A new President and CEO was appointed in an organization we know. This organization, while highly regarded and successful in the past, now faces the need to change to meet new market and economic challenges. According to all indications, this leader is not only committed to change, but also has the instincts and the skills to bring it about. What he inherited was an organization similar to many today, challenged to make changes that were overdue yesterday and to react in the present like an organization of tomorrow. Like many leaders, he is confronted with formidable forces that will close down change and pull the organization, like gravity, back to business as usual. All three constraints — "reductionism," "hierarchy" and "institutional knowledge" — are deeply embedded and operating fully in this organization. They threaten, sometimes subtly, sometimes overtly, sometimes consciously, often unconsciously, to sabotage the best of his intentions and plans. At a time when he needs the leaders in the organization to challenge their assumptions, break with the past and work together to develop a viable way forward, the organization is in the grip of these constraints. Reductionism is present in the stream of management interventions embraced and later discarded that fail to address fundamental issues and divert energy and attention from more comprehensive solutions. The constraint of hierarchy is being played out with leaders defending their turf and jockeying to maintain their positions irrespective of whether or not the existing structure is congruent with the needs of the organization. Institutional knowledge is operating through the basic assumptions that continue to drive the behaviors, decisions and the pattern of relationships of this organization. Even though subordinates are saying what this leader wants to hear, they are stuck in the midst of these constraints and their actions are likely to belie their words.

We were asked to recommend a new structure for this organization. Instead of offering our version of the *ideal structure*, our advice was to confront the fundamental constraints by reshaping the organization around the following three principles:

1. *Achieve an Operative Balance of Objective and Subjective Factors*
2. *Delegate Only Around Purpose*
3. *Enhance the Efficacy of Institutional Knowledge*

These three key principles consistently emerge as *antidotes* to counteract the negative effects of the three constraints. Taken individually and together, the three principles relate to the constraints in a direct way: for "reductionism" as a constraint, *Achieve an Operative Balance of Objective and Subjective Factors* surfaces; for "hierarchy," the principle *Delegate Only around Purpose* emerges; the principle, *Enhance the Efficacy of Institutional Knowledge* results from the need to transform "institutional knowledge" from a constraining to a facilitating force.

We believe these principles are fundamental and form gateways through the constraints on purposeful behavior and effective discourse, creating the potential to bring about beneficial change through learning.

2.1   Principle No. 1: Achieve an Operative Balance of Objective and Subjective Factors

Human beings embody natures that are both objective and subjective. While organizations cannot be said to have minds of their own, organizations are human constructions and can therefore, be said to also possess both objective and subjective realities. Organizations exemplify material or objective reality expressed in terms of facilities, product and service mix, cost structure, market share, strategy, earnings, etc. In the domain of subjectivity, organizations also represent collective perceptions, ways of thinking, motivations, attitudes and beliefs. This principle addresses the aspect of reductionism associated with the failure to understand and reconcile these realities. Moreover, it provides a gateway through reductionism by aiming to exploit the potentially productive clash of these opposites.

There are two major points of focus as we introduce this principle. The first of these relates to how an appropriate balance of objective and subjective factors influences both the ability to create a clear purpose and the ability to establish and sustain effective patterns of delegation around such purpose (the substance of Principle Number 2). The second point of focus concerns how such a balance affects the ability to comprehend and alter institutional knowledge (the subject of the Principle Number 3). This principle is concerned with building the capacity to grasp reality more fully and to act within such understanding. This first principle acts as a fulcrum through which leverage is created by way of the other two principles.

To fail to acknowledge that our subjective natures play a significant role in how we perceive reality and ultimately how we act is to invite ineffective working relationships, non-purposeful behavior and inhibited learning. An interpretation of this principle, however, as an intent to create warm, conflict-free, feeling-driven organizations would be completely in error. The intent rather is to create an organizational climate that fosters attitudes, values, mindsets and beliefs that drive behavior which supports the achievement of objective aims. The key word is balance — suggesting a sustained orientation to objective factors while working to mitigate the negative aspects of subjectivity and to enhance its positive potential. Metaphorically, we can envision objective factors as one blade of a pair of scissors and subjective factors as the other blade. Employed separately, neither blade is effective; utilized together, the two blades can trim and shape circumstances to produce beneficial results.

While organizations largely appear to be objectively driven and oriented, frequently to the extreme, managers working within organizations tend to go back and forth between objective and subjective approaches to problems and issues. At any given moment, the orientation is usually one way or the other reflecting a tension that appears to be something like the repellent forces of two magnetic poles — with objectivity represented at one pole and subjectivity at the other. Rather than grasping the essential reality that both objective and subjective aspects of any issue or problem exist inseparably, managers frequently envision an either/or approach and tend to focus on objective factors or subjective ones to the complete exclusion of the other. Reductionism is usually associated with what we might call over-objectivity. It applies, however, to both over-subjectivity and over-objectivity. Overemphasis on either becomes reductionism bringing about a loss of perspective of the whole and an impaired ability to achieve results. In the extreme, wearing the indicators of one's personality type on a badge (produced by several popular psychometric instruments) so that everyone will understand everyone else's psyche is as subjectively reductionist as the efficient measurement of countable yet irrelevant units of production is objectively so.

2.1.1 Objectivity in Organizational Life

Managers expect objectivity of themselves and are usually expected by others to be so inclined. Objectivity or the appearance of it tends to be dominant over time. Objectivity plays out, on the surface, as detachment from human factors — as minimizing the role of subjectivity in the encounters of individuals in organizations. Good managers are pictured as tough and bottom-line oriented, concentrating on what can be measured, that which is rational and tangible. The formal training of managers emphasizes analysis, systems and objective processes. Objectivity drives economic analysis and recently popular management practices such as restructuring or downsizing and process redesign. In our experience, when the effectiveness of a working group or team breaks down or doesn't develop, the usual cry is, "We must separate process from content!" — meaning that we must get on with the objective charge of the group and not muddle things up with human dynamics or subjective factors.

Such assertions expose a deeply rooted inability to comprehend or an unwillingness to acknowledge how subjective factors influence the creation of objective results and, in fact, why subjective factors are matters of concern in the first place. Recently in a large organization, we suggested to a senior manager that objective goals should frame the teambuilding he felt obliged to pursue for one of his departments. He didn't agree and responded that, "we'll go ahead with teambuilding, dealing with the soft stuff, and then we'll get down to the real business of sorting out the objective results we want to produce." To illuminate this point of view, he used a sports metaphor that went something like this, "you might do teambuilding with a football team off the field, but when you get on the field you have to be concerned about the serious (and objective) business of playing football." To paraphrase his meaning, teamwork might be useful on the sidelines but not on the playing field.

In order to not leave an impression that we are at odds with objectivity, we must assert that the production of objective results is the reason that organizations exist in the first place — to meet objectively defined needs, to remain objectively viable and to grow in measurable and concrete terms.

2.1.2 Subjectivity in Organizational Life

In good times or bad, subjective issues are always present whether consciously acknowledged or not and managers are always dealing with subjectivity whether they intend to or not. When conscious and intended subjectivity enters the field of organizational life, it is usually in the form of a focus on values and other "soft" virtues. Books, articles and developmental programs espousing the paramount role of human potential, participation, loyalty, empowerment and even orchestrated confrontation in organizational success move in and out of favor. In our work with leaders of organizations, we find that most of them cycle in and out of engagement with such approaches. In the current period, which has been called "post-re-engineering," an orientation to softer management approaches seems to be regaining some influence. In their hearts, however, objectively driven managers tend to view such subjectivity as touchy-feely and disconnected with economic reality. When economic hard times occur, orientations to subjective factors quickly fade with the embarrassing residue of mission statements asserting that "people are our greatest assets."

In summary, this principle is concerned with the ability to persistently and under all circumstances maintain a focus on objective factors while simultaneously understanding and dealing with subjective ones. Ultimately, the subjective factors will either facilitate or inhibit the achievement of objective results. Objectivity and subjectivity are highly conditioned by each other. The subjective factors that have a bearing on the accomplishment of objective results encompass how we perceive reality, how we think, what motivates us, how we attribute causes to circumstances, what triggers our defenses and how we behave. Whenever we encounter objective success, we find individuals who find meaning in what they do and that meaning motivates them and enables them to learn and become aligned with organizational purpose. Whenever we encounter objective failure, we invariably find defensive behaviors that thwart learning and change and patterns of attribution and thought that generate faulty perceptions.

2.2   Principle No. 2: Delegate Only Around Purpose

Human rationality and capacity are bounded. Organizations, as institutional forms, come together to deal with inherent human limitation through division of labor and structured relationships. Hierarchy and bureaucracy usually ensue, and as we have seen, hierarchy can constrain achievement. The work of organizations, however, tends to get done even if not optimally. In modern knowledge-intensive organizations, networks of relatively informal relationships seem to drive creativity and production, often in spite of formal structures. Since hierarchy in some form appears to be inescapable, imprinting the principle *Delegate Only Around Purpose* into an organization's pattern of working relationships will mitigate the restraining effects of hierarchy.

Hierarchy in organizations is natural and useful to the extent that it doesn't yield a life of its own — a life which may or may not operate in concert with the larger purpose of the organization. Delegation is the driver and substance of hierarchy. Hierarchy itself then is not the essential matter. The issue rather is the basis of delegation, i.e., the foundation for entrusting and empowering others. In our experience, hierarchy tends to be driven by patterns of delegation based on tasks or functions as opposed to responsibility for results related to purpose — a circumstance which, in most organizations, accounts for the restraining nature of hierarchy.

2.2.1   A Working Definition of Purpose

It has become commonplace, yet no less valid, to suggest that a strong sense of purpose lies at the heart of all great accomplishments. Purpose is a straightforward concept, and its meaning is no more complex than "an object to be attained" according to *The Oxford Concise Dictionary*. As the construct around which alignment, commitment and achievement in organizations can be developed, however, a more specific and expansive definition is required. Further, to meet the requirements of this principle, purpose must relate to the whole of the organization and, at the same time, be comprehended and framed as the basis for action by all levels of the organization.

Our definition begins with and builds on the notion that purpose is what an organization aims to accomplish. Purpose relates to the organizational objectives or ends expressed in actionable and comprehensible terms that both reflect the aspirations of the various segments of the organization and can be translated up and down and across the organization. Purpose exists at multiple levels within an organization — at the highest level and at the level of each operating or supporting unit. At any level, purpose must have an external focus, i.e., organizations must reach outside themselves to those they serve — their customers (both internal and external), patients, markets, communities, etc.

While vision and mission statements are aspects of purpose and usually answer the questions "what is our reason to be" and "what are our highest aspirations," they are not enough. Expressions of vision and mission appropriately tend to be inspirational, and they should provide a foundation, a solid base upon which purpose can be fully articulated and translated with relevance and consistency throughout an organization. These expressions, however, are incomplete; they do not inform decision making, priority setting and resource allocation. Rather, fully articulated purpose at any organizational level is a distillation of concrete, objective outcome goals underpinned by mission and vision. The achievement of such goals must be commonly understood in measurable or otherwise observable terms. Purpose will reflect discrimination or choices having been made among a larger set of alternative outcomes based on the principle of potential leverage with respect to vision and mission. Purpose must also enable the selection of actions and initiatives in lieu of others throughout an organization. What employees can grasp and operationalize are translations of purpose up and down the organization that guide them in doing their jobs, direct them in selecting tasks and courses of action with accountability to produce results that are tied to the overall organizational purpose. Ideally, if left leaderless for a while, these employees could continue to do their jobs by staying focused on purpose. Purpose must be inclusive of what the various constituencies and stakeholders feel are meaningful about their work providing the logical and animating construct around which organizational energy may be productively applied.

According to our understanding of purpose as an impelling and catalyzing concept, the following tests may be applied:

- Is purpose consistent with the higher order motives of the organization (usually expressed in vision and mission)?
- Does purpose have a pragmatic orientation, i.e., is it an expression of external consequences of effort as opposed to the effort itself?

- Given that resources are always limited, does purpose enable trade-off decisions to be made among competing alternatives?
- Is the achievement of purpose generally recognizable, i.e., is achievement measurable or at least unambiguous in terms of observable effects?

Our definition of purpose should not be confused with strategic plans as such plans are typically developed. Too often, these plans reflect the results of a process that has become irrelevant yet self-perpetuating. Such plans tend to represent the unreconciled and contradictory notions of strategy of the various segments of the organization. We believe that the organizational energy consumed by developing strategic plans in the conventional sense would be far more usefully applied to developing a dynamic sense of strategic direction consistent with the definition of purpose offered in this chapter.

The key aspects of our definition of purpose to bear in mind as we introduce the second principle, *Delegate Only Around Purpose,* are 1) the orientation to the whole, and 2) the focus on objective results that relate to the whole. The notion of purpose as the basis of delegation is concerned with the consequences of the work of organizational units linked as directly as possible with the consequences of the effort of the larger organization and with the accountability for achievement within that context. In other words, if an organization's purpose embodies such factors as product or service innovations with attendant market consequences, earnings, balance sheet effects, customer satisfaction, patient outcomes, etc., the associated patterns of purposeful delegation must relate only to producing results that bear directly on these desired outcomes. For example, the engineering department in an oil field equipment manufacturing company must deliver and test designs for equipment that customers want, need and will buy. Any activity not related to this purpose is of secondary importance at best and irrelevant at worst. Similarly, the clinical service departments of a hospital exist to have a beneficial impact on patient outcomes and support the mission of the larger institution. When these departments operate out of some narrow and parochial purpose with their own agenda, extraneous bureaucratic structures and disconnectedness with larger purpose proliferate and intensify.

2.2.2 Purposeful Delegation

It is self-evident that clarity of purpose is required in order for purpose to become the basis of delegation. Facilitating the creation of this clarity is, in our view, the first duty or obligation of leadership at all levels. The act or the process itself of developing and articulating purpose addresses issues of common cause and interdependence and begins to deal with territoriality and self-interest. Purpose sets the stage. It provides the opportunity for motivation to emerge — motivation to achieve objective results that have meaning for the larger organization. Having created clarity of purpose, achievement with respect to purpose becomes the focus of interest, and the creation of patterns of purposeful delegation becomes an issue of great significance. To entrust roles and resources to others — to empower others to act is the process by which the energy, expertise and vision of one is multiplied. It is in its most basic form how leadership is enacted or, more precisely, how personal and leadership leverage is created.

While this principle relates to organizational structure, it does so only in a secondary or derivative way. This principle primarily relates to motivation. If we aim to mitigate the constraining effects of hierarchy on purposeful behavior, a new sense of the meaning of accountability and good performance is necessary. The motivation to succeed in narrow spheres must be supplanted by patterns of motivation for collaboration to achieve objective results that have meaning for the larger enterprise. Task or function-based hierarchical structures are unfortunately very easy to produce; therefore, highly evolved structures that obscure and convolute purpose through multiple layers are the norm. Patterns of delegation based on purpose will naturally and inevitably flatten structures and remove the damaging effects associated with hierarchies. To delegate around purpose is difficult; it takes a great deal of effort, thought and courage. The standard templates of organizational structure have to be thrown away. In this process, well established and comfortable boundaries of turf, status, perquisites and prerogatives have to be dismantled and reassembled. Leaders should be especially attentive when managers are delegating to managers, i.e., when delegation is occurring at levels intermediate to the level where work is going on. Entire functions and layers must be challenged for their contribution to purpose. If a clear connection with purpose can't be made, the layer or the function in question probably should not exist.

In our experience, examples of sustained delegation around purpose are rare. As an illustration, we will describe an organization that we know well that experienced a period of change and remarkable progress attended by purposeful delegation only to revert to a function-based hierarchy with consequential loss of opportunity. The organization in question was mature and successful in a market ripe for significant change and reordering. At this point in the life of the organization, a new and visionary CEO arrived on the scene in a highly visible, energetic and challenging way. He transformed this organization from one of status quo inclinations to a progressive and forward looking one. He identified key leaders within the organization and recruited others — all of whom were change and opportunity minded. They participated in shaping the transformation and were committed to it. This small core leadership group represented various levels in the organization with the common attribute that all were accountable for outcomes related directly to the agreed upon way forward — the purpose. Each of these leaders was able to translate the larger purpose of the organization into terms that had meaning for the units they led and influenced. Through redesigned patterns of resource allocation, acquisitions and restructuring, the organization became positioned to become the market leader, which it had not been, and more significantly, to shape the market itself. Unprecedented growth occurred for about two years.

Support for the CEO and the new leadership team was not universal. From the outset of the transformation process, the established functional managers found themselves on the outside looking in. The traditionalists saw risk and potential doom in the transformation and relentlessly clamored to be let in, and although not saying so, to go back to the old ways. The CEO eventually weakened. He began to empower managers who were not aligned with the new direction and the transformation was over. The core leadership group grew from 8 to more than 20 people. Patterns of delegation reverted to a task and function basis, and the organization was back to business as usual.

The growth of the organization stalled. The CEO and virtually all of the original core leadership group left the organization. The organization survives today. It is not the market leader, however, and like its competitors, merely reacts to market forces. The organization did not achieve its potential greatness; it could have shaped the market but instead it became a passive traditional player like everyone else. Energy and attention were dissipated by the pressure of the hierarchical and functional traditions. In the end, the organization essentially lost its way — it lost its sense of purpose.

2.3   Principle No. 3: Enhance the Efficacy of Institutional Knowledge

Culture is a currently popular term in the vocabulary of organizational change. Strictly speaking, the concept of culture embodies both behavior and the knowledge that drives behavior, i.e., underlying attitudes, beliefs and values. A formal definition of culture includes the words "integrated pattern of human knowledge, belief and behavior," further, "customary beliefs, social forms and material traits of a social group". According to anthropologist, Edward Hall, culture refers to customs, i.e., practices and behaviors but also to "ways of organizing life, of thinking and of conceiving the underlying assumptions about social life and man himself."[1] It is clear to us that culture representing both behavior and knowledge is an appropriate context for thinking about the social structures representative of modern organizations.

In our experience and in our scope of awareness of current practices, however, culture change is usually taken to mean behavior change. The focus of change undertakings is most often on form, that is to say, on behavior. This principle is concerned with change and with culture but our primary orientation is to the aspect of culture represented by latent attitudes, beliefs and knowledge. Behavior change, therefore, while seen as necessary in any change process, is perceived as consequential to shifts in what Hall, calls the "silent language" or in the terms of this principle, "institutional knowledge."

The mechanics of control of institutional knowledge are discussed in Chapter 1 where institutional knowledge is introduced and described as a constraint on purposeful organizational behavior. The essential point intrinsic to this principle is that institutional knowledge is powerful and exacts a hold on us. Experience is encapsulated in institutional knowledge; it serves as a guide to the future and helps to mitigate uncertainty. By knowledge, we refer specifically to assumptions — assumptions about markets, social structures, production processes — about what is good and bad and the nature of man/woman. Knowledge also refers to conventions, rules, norms, values, beliefs and myths. By institutional, we mean that which has become crystallized and therefore objective — that which appears as given, self-evident and unalterable. Institutional knowledge represents what Berger and Luckman describe in their book, *The Social Construction of Reality*, as "the motivating dynamics of institutionalized conduct" or behavior.[2]

How we think is driven by the assumptions we hold or, perhaps more accurately, by the assumptions that hold us! While institutional knowledge produces varied and plentiful effects, it is highly resistant to change. Since institutional knowledge tends to be regarded as objective truth, challenges to it are usually suspect and viewed as effrontery. For Mary Douglas writing in *How Institutions Think*, "Institutions have the pathetic megalomania of the computer whose whole vision of the world is its own program." She goes on to argue that "the hope of intellectual independence is to resist, and the necessary first step in resistance is to discover how the institutional grip is laid upon our mind."[3] A cogent example relates to the health care industry in the United States. Consumers and providers of healthcare services in the U.S. have lost control to brokers and inter-mediaries. Healthcare providers did indeed lose touch with their markets. They were lulled into a false sense that existing patterns in healthcare economics and systems of delivery would continue indefinitely. Since at least 1975, concerted efforts have been made to introduce classical notions of market sensitivity and corporate adaptation into healthcare organiza-tions. Our perception is that interlocking stocks of institutional knowledge effectively prevented the assimilation of these simple principles. The institutions themselves, their associated physician communities and their administrators, or more accurately, the collective assumptions of these entities conspired, without really knowing it, to maintain the status quo in the face of developing demands for change. The cultural effect mani-fested in collective behavior was a sustained look inward and an orien-tation to doing the same things better. The real consequence, in spite of much rhetoric concerning change, was a profound loss of opportunity — a loss of ability to rationally allocate resources, to provide broadly-based accessibility and to sustain self-determination.

Institutional knowledge is not single dimensional in organizational life. It would be a mistake to conclude that the stock of knowledge pertaining to the whole of the organization or the institution in question comprised the extent of our concern in introducing this principle. In fact, multiple stocks of knowledge can be at work and either at odds or in concert with each other within the framework of any organization. In addition to the organization itself, stocks of knowledge pertaining to professions or dis-ciplines, industries or industry segments, even "schools of thought" can be in play representing interlocking stocks of knowledge coming together to produce consequences that may be altogether unintended.

The discovery of institutional knowledge at any level is not easy. It requires reflection, honest assessment, openness to challenge and the persistence to keep digging until the discovery rings with clarity and truth. As a part of a strategic planning process in an organization we know, senior managers were polled to discover their perceptions of the organi-zation's core competencies. Based on their collective perceptions, core competencies were identified and used to frame and describe the orga-nization's strengths on which to build and grow. As impressive as the core competencies sounded, the evidence suggested that they were not valid — that the managers confused who they would like to be with who they were. While the public image might be enhanced by the statement of idealized core competencies, an actual change would not be likely to occur because the assumption was that change had already occurred.

There are positive as well as negative aspects to institutional knowl-edge. It is argued by some that institutions "encode information" — that institutions themselves (in a virtually automatic way) make routine decisions, solve routine problems and do a lot of regular thinking on behalf of individuals.[4] It is self-evident that efficiency, i.e., economy of thought and effort, is clearly served by institutionalization — specifically by institutional knowledge. Working within the context of institutional knowledge, assumptions are given and performance can be optimized. On the other hand, when there are no stable assumptions, even the simplest action requires evaluation. The absence of any stable assumptions suggests that the environment is completely chaotic and disordered. S. N. Woodward, in his article, "The Myth of Turbulence," describes how the perception of turbulence in environments is often a justification for poor performance — "a metaphor for conditions with which organizations have difficulty coping." The perception of turbulence suggests that all assumptions must always be up for evaluation. Woodward paraphrased Plato, "the unexamined turbulence is not worth living with." He goes on to argue that this notion deflects attention from real and particular problems resulting in failure to solve problems and exploit opportunities. Finally, Woodward asserts: "The fact that I see a turbulent environment and you see an ordered one probably indicates that you are winning and I am losing."[5]

The good news is that institutional knowledge, as the embodiment and collective remembrance of habitualized activity, provides a background of stability within which human activity may proceed with efficiency and a minimum of decision making most of the time. Berger and Luckman assert, "this background of habitualized activity opens up a foreground for deliberation and innovation."[6] The bad news is, it is too easy and comfortable to operate in the background. Too frequently, we prefer to relax in the security and self-satisfaction of what we know. We tend to push what we know — our collective memory of what has worked in the past — far out of its realm of competence.

The key words in this principle are "enhance" — to alter and improve — and "efficacy" — in this case, referring to the power of institutional knowledge to produce an effect. The idea of conscious transformation of context, where context is equated with institutional knowledge, is embedded in this principle. This idea provides a direct link with the definition of a Learning Company developed by Pedler, Burgoyne and Boydell. "A Learning Company is an organization that facilitates the learning of all its members and *consciously transforms* itself and *its context*."[7] Our concern in this principle is not with how to sustain institutional knowledge and the status quo; this process is well understood and we tend to be good at it. Rather, our concern is with change and balance. Our enthusiasm for change is related to the potential for institutional knowledge to be used to produce the effects we desire — to seek the assimilation of new knowledge from new sources. With balance, our interest is in building the capacity to hold institutional knowledge both loose and tight — to use it and not be used by it — to maintain openness to new reality but to not "throw the baby out with the bath water."

As previously argued, many culture change and organizational learning interventions tend to center on modifying behavior. They seem to have a "just say no" character to them. There is a logical inconsistency running through some current applications of organizational learning and culture change theories and processes. While phrases like "challenging assumptions" appear with great frequency, the focus turns out to be on behavior and not on assumptions. The focus, in other words, turns out to be on creating "assumption challenging language" and superficial changes in behavior and not on understanding and changing underlying assumptions. For example, no matter how much we talk about creating environments where people treat each other with trust and respect, if our assumptions about each other don't include: "we are worthy of trust and respect" and "it is in our collective best interest to treat each other with trust and respect," our acclaimed trust and respect will be short-lived and mostly fictitious. As individuals and as collections of individuals, we must become aware of and understand the categories, structure and content of our own stocks of institutional knowledge and how they interact. It is self-evident that we can't alter these constructs if we don't know what they are. Given awareness, our challenge operates on three levels:

1. To develop the capacity to assimilate new and relevant knowledge
2. To be able to avoid the tendency to simply replace one set of assumptions with another
3. To maintain the ability to reproduce actions with an economy of effort most of the time

2.4 An Integrative Model for Learning and Change

At the beginning of this chapter, we connected the constraints on learning and change as developed in Chapter 1 with the three principles which have been introduced in this chapter. The model proposed and described in the remainder of this chapter is the model referenced in the outermost ring of the "Leadership Paradigm" in the Introduction to Part One. It seeks to integrate constraints and mitigating principles with application of these principles. The Integrative Model for Learning and Change, shown in Figure 1, represents the interactions of the relevant factors, framed and modulated by a common dynamic theme and points to the organization of the remainder of this book. The model is intended to convey the notion

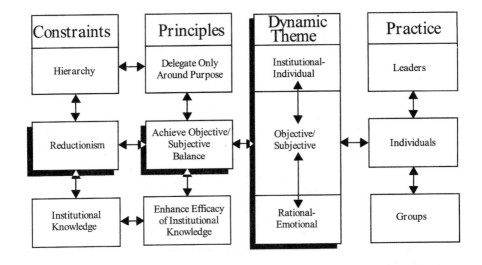

Figure 1   Integrative Model for Learning and Change

of lateral movement, i.e., left and right movement through the center of the schematic and vertical movement within each column, i.e., Constraints, Principles, Dynamic Theme and Practice. The interplay among the Constraints is mirrored in the interaction among the Principles. We have argued that reductionism is the core constraint. With *Achieve an Operative Balance of Objective and Subjective Factors* as the counter-force to reductionism, this principle occupies a similar position in relation to the principles *Delegate Only Around Purpose* and *Enhance the Efficacy of Institutional Knowledge.* This core principle is animated by the Dynamic Theme which gives expression to the relationship of the apparently opposite and conflicting aspects of reality in organizations.

Figure 2 represents the operation of the core principle and the Dynamic Theme. It illustrates the interaction of objective and subjective factors, the interaction of that dialectical relationship with Purpose and Institutional Knowledge and the interaction of Purpose and Institutional Knowledge with each other. As we think about Figures 1 and 2, the interplay among the Principles unfolds:

- Subjective factors either facilitate or inhibit the process of creating clarity and alignment around Objective Purpose and comprehension and enhancement of Institutional Knowledge.
- The creation and articulation of a clear purpose and the development of patterns of purposeful delegation require comprehension

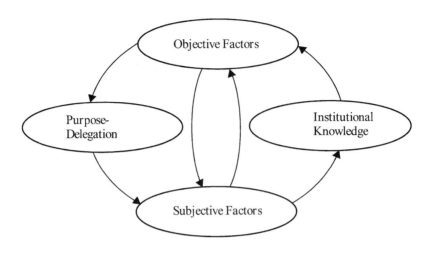

Figure 2   Dynamic Theme

of the content and the interlocking nature of the components of institutional knowledge. Comprehension will bring to light the extent to which institutional knowledge is or is not congruent with objective purpose. The capacity to bring institutional knowledge into alignment with purpose is a collateral requirement leading to modified perceptions of collective success and associated good performance.

■ Subjective issues associated with motivation and perceptions of loss and/or gain intervene in the process of comprehending and enhancing institutional knowledge. Connected with such undertakings, there is a need for a clear motivation — a highly developed sense of collective gain, to justify the effort and potential discomfort. The motivation to engage in these undertakings and to transcend narrow self-interest is likely to emerge only in the presence of an objective, common cause — a clearly articulated purpose coupled with accountability expressed in purposeful delegation.

2.4.1 Dynamic Theme

The Dynamic Theme calls attention to the dynamic relationship between and among factors that inform the meaning of the model in Figure 1. The Dynamic Theme refers specifically to the dual nature of reality in organizations, the relationship between the extremes of these realities and the mechanics of transition between the extremes. The dual reality is first expressed as the differentiation between objective and subjective factors and points to the differentiation of institution and individual, rational and emotional. Additional sets of relational terms further illuminate the concept of the Dynamic Theme. For example, objective is to subjective as social/economic/political is to imagination/belief/aspiration as strategy/execution/measurement is to motivation/perception/cognition.

These aspects of reality exist in a constant state of interpretation, negotiation and reconciliation. The relationship between these pairs of factors is dialectical, a term which represented one of Hegel's favorite ideas, the "productive clash of opposites." Another perspective on this relationship is revealed by the editors of the 1996 book *Organizational Learning and Competitive Advantage.* Their perspective pertains to the need to promote "interdisciplinary thought and research aimed at understanding the role of learning in achieving competitive advantage." This theme is developed further, in a general sense, by pointing to what the editors believe is the unreconciled nature of the relationship between the objectively aligned structuralists and the subjectively-aligned cognitivists.[8]

The concept of the Dynamic Theme is perhaps best expressed by Berger and Luckman as: "Society is a human product. Society is an objective reality. Man is a social product." Restated for our purposes, we could express this circular relationship as: Organizations are created by individuals. Organizations take on the form of objective reality. Individuals are shaped by organizations. Berger and Luckman argue further that habitualized behavior is at the core of institutionalization and "institutionalization is incipient in any social situation continuing in time." The institution appears as objective reality yet this objective world is humanly constructed. The institution and the individual exist in a dialectical relationship, with each informing the nature of the other. Enhanced learning and beneficial change flow from understanding this dynamic relationship and acting within the framework of such understanding.

Figure 3, Stages of Transition relates to the operation of the Dynamic Theme and specifically refers to the stages of transition between the conflicting and apparently dichotomous aspects of reality in organizations. To illustrate the role of the Dynamic Theme in practical terms, our experience with application of the principle, *Delegate only around Purpose,* is arrayed against the stages of transition shown in Figure 3:

> At the Level of Effect — As obvious and fundamental as delegating around purpose seems, it tends not to happen very often in most organizations. Consequently, vertical hierarchies are established and sustained, motivation pertaining to common cause is diluted and individuals take narrow views of their roles. Efforts to alter patterns of delegation are strongly resisted.

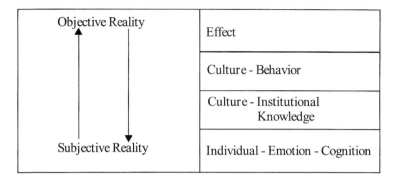

Figure 3   Stages of Transition

At the Level of Culture-Behavior — We observe habitualized/institutionalized patterns of behavior oriented to tasks. As a result, work behavior tends to become sub-optimized and concentrated on functional units and activities and not on purpose.

At the Level of Culture-Institutional Knowledge — Pertaining to the issue of purposeful delegation, we find the following two examples of collective assumptions: 1. Focusing on objective, organization-wide results creates conflict which is to be avoided. 2. While it is useful to talk about results, it is safer to generate high levels of activity and to be held accountable for activity.

At the Level of the Individual — Cognitive and emotional factors are revealed. Issues of perception, belief, attitude and fear are dominant — along with imagination, creativity and motivation.

A constructed objective reality is operating at the level of Effect. This reality seems determined — as if it had a life of its own. It is unyielding with respect to change. Change efforts directed only at the level of Effect will rarely succeed because while effects are seen as objective, when this objective reality is internalized by people, it becomes subjective to them and embedded in their sense-making apparatus. Effect, however, expressed in terms of objective results, such as growth, market share, patient outcomes, etc. is the common cause that drives successful organizations. Change undertakings must, therefore, deal with Effect but the real leverage in change efforts flows from understanding and dealing with the subjective factors as they manifest themselves at the levels of behavior, institutional knowledge and the individual, and as they interact and roll up to create objective reality.

2.4.2 Application of the Principles

Returning to the Integrative model in Figure 1, the principles are connected to Practice by way of the three organizational dimensions of Individuals, Leaders and Groups. Change occurs in organizations one person at a time, therefore, the connection to Practice in the model is through the dimension of Individuals.

- *Individuals*

  A critical mass of change in individuals is a precondition for enhanced learning and effective organizational change. Individuals are at the core of organizations. Their own sense of purpose and meaning adds to or detracts from the collectively understood purpose and meaning of the organization. Unreconciled issues among individuals and between leaders and individuals usually result in unconscious and/or conscious sabotage of achievement. There is a need to understand and address, individually and collectively, issues of motivation, perception, need, defensiveness and ways of thinking to create a critical mass for change.

- *Leaders*

  The leadership component of an organization brings substance and drive to change efforts. Attention to the role and behavior of leaders is essential — otherwise, change efforts will tend to be shallow, unsupported, misunderstood and misguided. As we have argued, facilitating the creation of clarity of purpose is the first duty of leadership at all levels, and purpose must frame all change endeavors. Bearing the individual dimension in mind, however, leaders must be continually aware that what is heard is at least as important as what is said.

- *Groups*

  Most of the work of organizations is accomplished through the efforts of groups. Group effectiveness is therefore a critical ingredient in the achievement of objective results. Groups are, of course, comprised of individuals. Their composite and emergent motivations, perceptions, needs and defenses create dynamics that either support purposeful group behavior and achievement or lend themselves to dysfunction. It is remarkable how aligned and effective groups appear until some individual's territory or prerogatives are challenged. Such circumstances are inevitable, however, if the efficacy of institutional knowledge is to be enhanced and if achievement of objective results related to purpose is to be realized.

In our experience, the three principles applied in all three dimensions comprise the set of gateways to the preconditions and ultimately to enhanced learning and beneficial change. The application of the principles within the context of Individuals, Leaders and Groups provides the structure and the basis for Parts Two, Three and Four of this book.

References

1. Hall, E. T., *The Silent Language,* Doubleday, 1959, 23.
2. Berger, P. L. and Luckman, T., *The Social Construction of Reality: A Treatise in the Sociology of Knowledge,* Penguin, 1966.
3. Douglas, M., *How Institutions Think,* Syracuse University Press, Syracuse, 1986, 92.
4. Douglas, M., *How Institutions Think,* Syracuse University Press, Syracuse, 1986, 92.
5. Woodward, S. N., The Myth of Turbulence, *Futures,* August, 1982.
6. Berger, P. L. and Luckman, T., *The Social Construction of Reality: A Treatise in the Sociology of Knowledge,* Penguin, 1966, 71.
7. Pedler, M., Burgoyne, J. and Boydell, T., *The Learning Company,* 2nd ed., McGraw-Hill, London, 1997.
8. Moingeon, B. and Edmondson, A., When to Learn How and When to Learn Why: Appropriate Organizational Learning Processes as a Source of Competitive Advantage, *Organizational Learning and Competitive Advantage,* Sage Publications, London, 1996.

INDIVIDUALS

Introduction

Application of the principles introduced in the previous chapter is envisioned in three dimensions. The Individual plane in this matrix is the first and leading dimension of practice. We have argued that change is a one person at a time undertaking. Any successful effort to enhance learning and beneficial change in organizations, therefore, begins with individuals. In our experience, it bears little fruit to consider and address issues related to individuals as leaders and individuals as members of teams and groups without first thinking about and dealing with individuals as individuals. Throughout any process of organizational change, concerns associated with intrapersonal dynamics must always be a conscious part of work related to developing leaders and improving group dynamics. The effectiveness of leaders is largely determined by their own state of internal development and coherence. The work of leaders is accomplished by other people; therefore, it matters at least as much what these individuals hear, perceive and make sense of as what leaders say and do. We bring our complete selves to group encounters whether or not we reveal all aspects of ourselves and what we bring to groups plays an important role in the character and dynamics of groups.

The next three chapters pertain to application of the three principles as these principles relate to individuals. How we answer and deal with issues related to the following questions frame these chapters:

How able are individuals to see, comprehend and internalize reality?
What is the potential for individuals to learn beyond a narrow and circumscribed context?

To what extent are individuals able to reconcile personal meaning with the purpose of the organization and to become aligned with purpose and committed to it?

What is the potential for effective, purposeful and non-defensive communication and working relationships among individuals?

From the perspective of individuals, the chapters that follow address perception, motivation, attribution, cognition and emotion.

In Chapter 3, Individuals: *Achieve an Operative Balance of Objective and Subjective Factors*, we will explore how our mental models and the results and process of attribution work together to form our perceptions. We will examine how behavior is influenced by perception and how threats to our views of the world and sense-making become reshaped and actualized as defensive attitudes and behaviors. We will see how our perceptions and defenses alter those of other people and how patterns of flawed perception and defensiveness close down communication and learning and bring about ineffective relationships. What individuals bring to their encounters with other people largely accounts for the quality of their interactions. Improved communication, enhanced relationships and a stage set for learning can be the consequences of altered modes of perceiving and behaving. Communication is the most frequently mentioned concern when we speak to members of organizations about sources of problems and dysfunction. Our sense is that when communication is identified as a problem what people really mean is that information transferred is invalid, irrelevant or masks the truth. Valid information, according to Chris Argyris[1], is the first governing condition associated with a model of organizational life that supports learning and effectiveness. If Argyris' insight is accurate and we believe it to be, it is difficult to overestimate the influence of perception, attribution and defensiveness in either supporting or restraining both the generation and comprehension of valid information, and thus creative discourse and useful communication.

Since the terms "subjective" and "objective" are used in subtly different ways in this chapter, it is important that we try to eliminate any confusion about what we mean by these terms. Simply stated, by subjective we mean that which exists in the mind of the individual and is a part of the substance of the person. Emotion, along with at least the idiosyncratic aspects of perception and sense-making belong within the subjective sphere. By objective we refer to that which exists, at least to some degree, apart from the person. Given this definition of objective, the term may apply to factors that are separated from individual selves in some people and not in other people. These factors can include attitudes, perceptions and behaviors which can move along a continuum representing subjectivity for some people and objectivity for others. At the objective end of the spectrum, the subjective/objective continuum may contain what would appear to be purely objective factors, such as an organization's mission, strategic initiatives and operating results. These factors can exist clearly and fully apart from an individual's perception of self. On the other hand, if individuals internalize these seemingly objective factors and make them part of themselves, they can become relatively more subjective.

The focus of Chapter 4, Individuals: *Delegate Only Around Purpose*, is on those to whom leaders delegate. We are aware that delegation is a term that may strike some readers as a reference to an archaic concept, a concept out of step with organizational dynamics in information age, knowledge-intensive organizations. However, the simple reality is that work continues to be done in organizations by way of delegation whether or not we like the concept. The point in question, then, is not delegation itself but rather the basis of delegation and the nature of the process. The subject matter of this chapter embraces personal meaning, motivation, connection with organizational purpose and the concept of leverage for individuals. These factors take shape around the dynamics of involvement, empowerment and finally delegation. A sense of meaning for individuals brings alive the concepts of personal leverage, empowerment and purposeful delegation. What is meaningful for individuals, while highly variable from person to person, is a powerful force. Viktor Frankl, in his book *Man's Search for Meaning*, dramatically argues for the motivating influence of meaning. His study of holocaust survivors identifies the perception of meaning in one's life as a central factor in survival. "Man's search for meaning is the primary motivation in his life and not a 'secondary rationalization' of instinctual drives. This meaning is unique and specific in that it must and can be fulfilled by him alone; only then does it achieve a significance which will satisfy his own *will* to meaning."[2]

Chapter 5, Individuals: *Enhance the Efficacy of Institutional Knowledge*, addresses aspects of building the capacity to comprehend and alter institutional knowledge to bring about desirable effects. Examining and rethinking assumptions, formulating new and more relevant ones when there is a need to do so and sustaining this practical ability over time defines the essence of a learning oriented culture. Linkage of the principle invoked in this chapter with individuals brings attention to bear on freeing individuals from the grip of institutional knowledge and on the role of individuals in collective learning. As individuals, how we can learn to stand apart from ourselves, observe and catalogue our own deepest assumptions and become participant-observers will be explored. The use of imagination and our own experience to create frames of reference when confronting ambiguity, uncertainty and change will be examined. Choosing to do so is the companion of being able to engage with other individuals in successful learning and change. The chapter closes with this thought: the ability to examine assumptions objectively and escape the grasp of defensiveness and the past are factors that hold equal standing with the motivation to do so.

References

1. Argyris, C. and Schon, D. A., *Theory and Practice: Increasing Professional Effectiveness*, Jossey-Bass, San Francisco, 1974, 86.
2. Frankl, V. E., *Man's Search for Meaning*, Washington Square Press, 1984, 131.

Chapter 3

Individuals: *Achieve an Operative Balance of Objective and Subjective Factors*

Anticipatory Summary

As individuals, we tend to see our own patterns of thinking and perceiving as objective and rational and those of others as rather more subjective and idiosyncratic. However, this is an illusion. The truth is that, within all of us, subjective and objective factors are at work at the same time.

- The essential question underlying our ability as individuals to change is: How able are we to separate ourselves (our subjective being) from our views of the world and other people (aspects of our objective being)?
- The dynamics of change at the level of the individual:
  - constructive-developmental theory describes stages of adult development and the dynamics of transition between stages (a stage is defined as the relationship between what an individual perceives and feels as subject and what is perceived by the individual as object);
  - to the extent that this separation of objects from self cannot be made, change will be very difficult or impossible.

3.1   *Perception — Mental Models*

- These screens and filters represent our attitudes, assumptions, world views, biases, opinions, preconceptions and beliefs.
- Since how we behave is largely driven by what we perceive and feel, our mental models exert a powerful influence over our lives.

3.2   *Attribution*

- Attribution is both an effect and a process. Attribution is the handmaiden of mental models in bringing about the consequences of perception.
- Attribution is the process by which we determine causes for what we see. Attribution begins with perception, progresses through judgment about causes and ends with behavior.
- Attribution Theory is concerned with understanding the logic, processes and knowledge structures associated with attribution.
- The process and result of attribution are deeply embedded in communication. We have adapted four maxims for interpersonal explanation and conversation.
- Our concern with the process and results of perception is on three levels: awareness, accuracy and relevance. Bringing perception into greater congruence with reality is the aim.

3.3   *The Role of Defensiveness in Perception and Cognition*

- Defensive behavior is the result of largely unconscious mental processes and serves to protect the perceiver from threat or to enable the individual to avoid such threat.
- This places the demand upon the individual to discern the authenticity of the perceived threat and to either act to eliminate the threat or to alter his or her response to it.

3.4   *Defensive Responses to the Perceptions and Defenses of Others*

- The behavior of one individual can trigger defensiveness in another which can in turn elicit reciprocal defensiveness creating a downward spiral in the character of the relationship.
- Over time, barriers and misunderstandings may intensify causing relationships to disintegrate.

3.5   Insights into Defensive Behavior

- Individuals have a duty to understand how their ways of perceiving and behaving contribute to patterns of defensiveness and suboptimal learning.

3.6   Communication, Relationships and Preconditions to Learning

- What individuals bring to their encounters with other people largely accounts for the quality of their interactions.
- Improved communication, enhanced relationships and a stage set for learning can be the consequences of altered modes of perceiving and behaving.

3.6.1   Role Negotiation

- Role negotiation is a practical intervention that identifies and seeks to balance and integrate subjective and objective factors pertaining to the various parties.

Individuals: *Achieve an Operative Balance of Objective and Subjective Factors*

In our experience, the most important question in working with individuals within change-seeking organizations is how able are these individuals to learn from their experiences and the experiences of others and change. In other words, how able are they to perceive a new or changing reality, to alter their assumptions about the organization and their relations to it and to reorient themselves to become committed and aligned around a new and more relevant direction. Change occurs one person at a time; a critical mass of individuals having learned and changed, therefore, drives organizational learning and change. Changing people, however, is difficult. Because of this, leaders often settle for changing structures, policies, processes and other purely objective artifacts even though such changes rarely lead to desired changes in individuals. How and whether individuals can learn and change are, therefore, highly pertinent in organizational change efforts and provide the basis and construction of this chapter.

As individuals, we tend to see our own patterns of thinking and perceiving as objective and rational and those of others as rather more subjective and idiosyncratic. However, this is an illusion. The truth is that, within all of us, subjective and objective factors are at work at the same time. These factors are in tension with each other and the relationship between them influences our encounters with other people and our ability to effectively comprehend and deal with reality. The essential question underlying our ability as individuals to change is: How able are we to separate ourselves (our subjective being) from our views of the world (aspects of our objective being)? These views incorporate our assumptions about the world, our place in it and about other people. Are these views or assumptions separate and apart from ourselves or are they inseparable from ourselves? Have we internalized these assumptions so much that we cannot distinguish them from ourselves (how we think and feel)? Essentially, have we become our assumptions? Has our identity become so intertwined with our assumptions that we cannot tell one from the other?

As consultants and managers we have been struck by the apparent inability of many individuals to change. This inability is often present regardless of the strength of the argument for change and irrespective of what these individuals say about change. In this connection, we have been eager to gain a better understanding of the dynamics of change at the level of the individual and to gain insights about how to intervene more effectively. Robert Kegan in his book, *The Evolving Self*,[1] presents a theory of personal meaning-making and social development, that pulls together disparate ideas and integrates them into a consistent theoretical whole. Kegan's synthesis of factors relates to the stages and dynamics of human psychological development. It "attends to the development of the activity of meaning constructing" and is, therefore, termed "constructive-developmental" theory. "Its origins lie in the work of James Mark Baldwin, John Dewey and George Herbert Mead; and its central figure has certainly been Jean Piaget." Kegan's synthesis and insights are intuitively powerful. There is a strong ring of relevance and truth in them and a high degree of congruence with our experience of working with individuals in organizations. His constructive-developmental theory describes stages of adult development and the dynamics of transition between stages. The central argument relates to the defining nature of the relationship between what an individual perceives and feels as *subject* and what is perceived by the individual as *object* at each stage of development.

According to Kegan's perspective, individuals are embedded or stuck in their perceptions when those perceptions cannot be separated from their essential being — their subjective selves. To expect a person who is unaware of the content and structure of their views to change them is like asking an eight year old child to view his family as an abstraction.

Rather than concluding that a person won't change or won't learn, it is more accurate to conclude that the person can't change or learn. The fundamental insight for us in our work with individuals in changing organizations is the role of subject/object differentiation in shifting the perceptions and behaviors of individuals to bring about change. To the extent that an individual is able to separate her self — her subjective being — from her attitudes, beliefs, mental models, patterns of defensiveness and attribution, the individual can examine these objects, evaluate their relevance and usefulness and alter them. To the extent that this separation of objects from self cannot be made, change will be very difficult or impossible.

We have experienced working with individuals who are members of management and other work teams who not only do not change but appear to be profoundly unable to see that the assumptions that drive their behavior are counterproductive and inappropriate. They appear to be clearly stuck in some meaning-making context out of which they are unable to move. They express a sense of certainty and absoluteness about their perceptions with an associated inability to consider other points of view. They don't *have* attitudes and views. They *are* their attitudes and views, i.e., what is a part of their essential being comprises the very attitudes and beliefs that must shift in order for them to change and grow. A circumstance that illustrates the influence of the inability to differentiate subject from object, i.e., self from perception, comes from an individual with whom we worked as a member of a management team. This person was notorious for his demeaning behavior toward peers and subordinates and overall poor interpersonal skills. Despite direct coaching from his boss on numerous occasions, he never recognized that the performance difficulties of his unit were related to his own attitudes and behavior. As a last resort, he was sent to a leadership development program of several months duration at a local university. From all the material presented to him, he appeared to hear only two assertions. One was that "there are four types of people — willing and able, unwilling and able, willing and unable and unwilling and unable" which he internalized as confirming his view that "I'm okay and most of you aren't." The second assertion was that people will become more cooperative if they think their ideas are listened to. Between these two assertions, the change in management approach that this person understood and implemented was to make his subordinates think that his ideas were theirs so that they would be more cooperative. It never occurred to him that their ideas might actually have value on their own and that he didn't have to manipulate them to engage their cooperation.

3.1   Perception — Mental Models

All of us have mental screens and filters through which we see and make sense of what goes on around us and within us. These constructs or models represent our attitudes, assumptions, world views, biases, opinions, preconceptions and beliefs. These structures, or mental models, are based on and nourished by how we are raised as children, how we are socialized and what we experience in life. These mental models express our ideology, and to a significant degree, our identity. Our mental models harden as we experience life. They shape each of us into something like a micro institution — our mental models represent the institution which is us. They are often so close to the core of us that we are not conscious of their presence and their effect as in the "embeddedness" described by Kegan and previously discussed. Since how we behave is largely driven by what we perceive and feel, our mental models exert a powerful influence over our lives.

Whatever we call these constructs, the concept of their existence and operation has been a part of theorizing about perception for a very long time. Plato's parable of the cave describes a powerful image of perception expressed in the relation between the individual thinker and society. "In the *Republic*, Socrates presents men as prisoners in a dark cave, bound and forced to look at a wall against which are projected images that they take to be the beings that are for them the only reality. Freedom for men means escaping the bonds (taken to mean civil society's conventions), leaving the cave and going up to where the sun illuminates the beings and seeing them as they really are. Socrates' presentation is meant to show that we begin from deceptions, or myths, but that it is possible to aspire to a non-conventional world, to nature, by the use of reason."[2]

The term "mental models" was probably first used by Scottish psychologist Kenneth Craik in the 1940s. Peter Senge in his book, *The Fifth Discipline*, defines mental models as "images, assumptions, stories which we carry in our minds of ourselves, other people, institutions and every aspect of the world."[3] Chris Argyris of Harvard has studied and written about the consequences of perception on learning and defensive behavior since the early 1970s. His perspective on mental models sees "human beings as having been taught early in life how to act in ways to be in control, especially when they are dealing with issues that can be embarrassing or threatening. People transform these lessons into theories of action." These theories of action, more specifically, "theories-in-use," contain rules that are used to design and implement actions in every day life. Argyris equates "theories-in-use" to programs in our heads and contrasts them with our "espoused-theories." Our espoused-theories, frequently in conflict with our theories-in-use, represent what we say are our attitudes, beliefs and rules of conduct in life.[4]

There are several reasons why we care about mental models. Based on what we see, we make "leaps of abstraction," i.e., we jump from what we observe to generalization, usually without being aware that we are doing it. Cardinal Bernadin of Chicago was interviewed on National Public Radio regarding the Common Ground Initiative within the American Roman Catholic Church aiming to reconcile the "at odds" segments of the Church. He expressed the view that the greatest challenge in this effort is related to overcoming our tendency to leap to the worst case extension of any opposing point of view thereby skewing our perceptions and closing down dialogue. For example, the non-traditionalists see only the aspects of the traditionalist view that is most at odds with their own while the traditionalists see only the most extreme views of the liberals. The role that our mental models play can create errors in our perception. They can have a significant impact on how and if we learn. They can determine whether or not we can make important changes in our attitudes, assumptions and behavior and ultimately create objective beneficial consequences for ourselves and our organizations.

As an illustration, the description of a failed business partnership sheds additional light on the effect of mental models on perception and behavior. While there were many reasons for the failure of the business in question, the consequences of this partnership between two individuals played a significant and catalytic role. The partnership involved an American and a British citizen. The American, an acknowledged Anglophile, held assumptions about the character of British people that while perhaps true in a general sense, were not true with regard to this individual. The American, whose American sensibilities were well developed, had successfully avoided manipulative and unethical Americans. At the same time, she was patently unable to see and respond to such behavior on the part of her British partner. In spite of observed behavior and the warnings of associates, the American could not see through her strong Anglophile mental models. She simply held assumptions about the nature of the culture, transferred those assumptions to an individual, was blinded to the reality of the character of the individual and consequently acted in ways that were not in the best interests of either individual and ultimately the organization they led.

For further illustration, consider the underlying assumptions or mental models associated with the well-known Theory X and Theory Y styles of management as described by Douglas McGregor.[5] Theory X assumptions include "the average human being has an inherent dislike of work and will avoid it if he can. The average human being prefers to be directed, wishes to avoid responsibility, has relatively little ambition and wants security above all." Theory Y assumptions, on the other hand, include "The expenditure of physical and mental effort in work is as natural as play or rest. Man will exercise self direction and self control in the service of objectives to which he is committed." We have discovered that many individuals wish to believe that Theory X managers are extinct. Expressed in terms used by Argyris, almost all managers espouse Theory Y but Theory X continues to be the "theory-in-use" for many managers despite the disguise of politically correct rhetoric. The truth is that the behavior of human beings varies greatly from consistency with Theory X assumptions to consistency with Theory Y assumptions and all points in between. Our concern is not with the consequences of merely holding negative perceptions of other people but rather with the predisposition to holding unexamined or even unconscious negative perceptions regardless of the nature of the individuals with whom we interact. Since being held by our assumptions implies that we see what we expect to see and that we act in congruence with our perceptions, the consequences of our actions can cause actions in others that are identical to our expectations — like a self-fulfilling prophecy. For example, we could be working with someone with great intellect and capacity but wouldn't know it or benefit from the talents of this person because of our misperceptions. Furthermore, we might even turn him into a marginal performer through our perception driven behavior towards him. All of this is not to suggest that if we just have high expectations of everyone, everyone will be a star performer. The reality is that sometimes we do have marginal performers, and we can't make "silk purses out of sows' ears" just by believing or wishing it to be so and behaving as if we can. We know of a senior executive, hired under a canopy of great expectations and fanfare, who proved to be incompetent. This person was retained and supported for several years, in spite in his poor performance, because of the emotional commitment of the CEO to him. No matter how hard the CEO tried, he could not make an effective manager of him. Even though he was eventually asked to leave, his legacy endures. Throughout his tenure, he hired marginally competent people who would not be a threat to him. The result was an empire of incompetence, a bureaucracy that seems impenetrable even to this day.

Our mental models are our own and they are not inherently good or bad. Regarding any particular subject, they may be accurate or not, i.e., they may or may not be relatively congruent with reality. In many ways, our mental models serve a useful purpose. They help us to quickly make sense of an event or circumstance and to act without undue delay. The downside is that our mental models lock us into preconceived notions and predictable and sometimes counterproductive behavior.

3.1.1 Left-Hand Column

Chris Argyris has described a metaphor and a tool that he calls the "Left-Hand Column."[6] We are invited to imagine a blank sheet of paper upon which we draw a line down the middle. Regarding any situation, we make note of the things we say in the column on the right hand side of the page. In the left hand column, we record the things that we think and feel but don't say. In our group sessions with managers and others, we encourage participants to literally do that. At various points, we ask the group members to update their left-hand column and to speak about this if they wish. The point is to create an explicit awareness of the thoughts and feelings that aren't being expressed and how these differ from what is being said.

An additional application of the left-hand column is associated with the case method.[7] In the case method, we ask program participants to select a non-trivial human problem that they have been unable to solve. Bearing this problem in mind, each person is asked to construct a context for dealing with this problem and then to write a conversation in the right hand column incorporating what they would say and what they think the other person would say in the course of working this problem. In the left hand column of each page, they are asked to record what they are thinking and feeling as this imaginary conversation plays out. The cases are then analyzed in one-on-one sessions to understand:

1. What is not being said in interactions with specific other people
2. How there are consequences of not expressing feelings and concerns
3. How what is thought and felt and not expressed informs the nature of their mental models
4. How those assumptions have an effect on their ability to solve real problems

The left-hand column is useful in helping to bring assumptions to the surface and providing a context for reflecting on the content of our mental models and how they operate. People relate well to this concept and speak about its usefulness as a learning tool. Over the course of a project, however, we frequently hear group members ask each other "what's in your left-hand column?" This question suggests that people are much more eager and comfortable in speculating about what is in someone else's left-hand column rather than what is in their own.

3.2 Attribution

Attribution is both an effect and a process. Attribution is the handmaiden of mental models in bringing about the consequences of perception.

Attribution as a process also brings some of its own dynamics to perception and consequential behavior. If our mental models describe the screens and filters through which we see the world, attribution is the process by which we determine causes for what we see. Attribution is how we explain the actions of ourselves and our fellow human beings; it begins with perception, progresses through judgment about causes and ends with behavior. Faced with ambiguity and limited information, attribution is the process through which we fill in the blanks of the meaning we make of the behavior of other people.

Attribution theory represents several tracks of thinking and work within the field of social psychology and is concerned with understanding the logic, processes and knowledge structures associated with attribution. Miles Hewstone in his book, *Causal Attribution: From Cognitive Processes to Collective Beliefs*, surveys the major threads of development in attribution theory and concludes: "(they) all address the kinds of information that people use to determine causality, the kinds of causes that they distinguish and the rules they use for going from information to inferred cause. Most important, all share a concern with common sense explanations and answers to the question 'why?'"[8]

We can think about attribution as defined across a spectrum between automatic and controlled. On one end of the spectrum, those judgments and explanations occur rapidly, unconsciously and almost in a stimulus-response mode. On the other end, judgments and explanations flow from formal problem solving and time-consuming logical analysis. Controlled attributions, while interesting to consider, are not especially enlightening with respect to our concerns in this section. Errors in perception, behavioral consequences of such perception, the shape of our defensive responses and the triggering of defenses in others, as these occur in everyday life, are the central concerns of this section. According to Hewstone, attributions that can be characterized as automatic, therefore, shed a great deal of light on these concerns. Hewstone defines attributions as automatic to the extent that they fulfill three criteria: "1) they occur without intention; 2) they occur without giving rise to awareness; 3) they occur without interfering with on-going mental activity."[9]

Attribution appears to meet our needs and purposes in several ways. There is some controversy surrounding the functions of attribution and mixed results in studies, but there is general agreement around three main functions, two of which have relevance here:

1. The control function refers to the need and motivation of individuals to sense a degree of control over the physical and social world. "For example, people derogate others who are victims of

negative events in an attempt to maintain the belief that negative events will not happen to them personally."[10] This function is operating when we hear about or observe something negative happening to another person, and our immediate reaction is to begin to rationalize how the other person is different from us. We tend to distance these people from us. One example comes from working with outplaced people where the majority of them seem to be cut off from their former colleagues — both intentionally and unintentionally. The phenomenon of invisibility or untouchability surrounding the outplaced person is a common expression of the control function of attribution. David Noer in his book, *Healing The Wounds,*[11] describes the "contagion anxiety" that exists in interactions between those who were asked to leave an organization and those who will stay: "Survivors are reluctant to engage with these victims. Conversation is stilted or nonexistent, and empathy and concern are often suppressed."

2. The self-esteem function relates to the well established need of human beings to validate and enhance their sense of personal worth. "The attributions people make for performance outcomes do indeed influence their self-esteem after such outcomes."[12] It has been shown that we tend to attribute internal causes, i.e., our skills, attitudes and personal characteristics for our successes and external factors, such as circumstances and actions of other people, for our failures. We know of one executive who long coveted being chosen as the CEO of an organization when the incumbent retired. He believed that he would be chosen despite much competition. He prepared the new organization's strategy, designed the new organization chart and selected his top management team. He even had his press releases ready, acceptance speech written and champagne cooling in the refrigerator. When another candidate was chosen, instead of looking at his own track record (which was put on hold while he campaigned), he blamed every circumstance and every person for his failure from the former CEO for lack of support to the victorious candidate for playing it so cool.

The theme of this chapter is the role that individual members of organizations play in bringing about organizational learning and change. The process of attribution creates consequences that help determine how individuals associate themselves with change which accounts for our interest in it. Hewstone identifies three types of consequences of attribution which are briefly summarized as follows:

1. The first consequence of attribution is what we remember about people and events — our memory. Our memory about people and events seems to be influenced by how clearly we are able to explain and attribute causes to events and the actions of people. There is also evidence that we tend to discount the implications of behavior and events that threaten our beliefs enabling our beliefs to persevere even if they are negative or counterproductive. What may strike us, therefore, as selective memory in others when applied to their explanations of behavior and circumstances is, in fact, just that and the same selectivity operates within ourselves as well as within others. We are going to remember more about an event which we believe we understand fully and which confirms our beliefs. Since attribution pertains to explaining and assigning causes, the judgments and decisions we make about people and events are significantly influenced by the process of attribution. If we think about any conflict between two people and when the conflict is recalled with either person, they never remember it or explain it the same way. Each person's memory of the conflict is selective, i.e., what they remember is what best explains the conflict for their own purposes.

2. A second consequence of attribution is how we feel. There is impressive empirical support for the assertion that how we think about causes and explanations influences how we feel. The role of attribution in emotional reactions to success and failure and in depression has received the greatest attention. "Considering the five key emotions, anger, happiness, pity, pride and love, it has been argued persuasively that the first four can be accounted for from an attributional perspective."[13]

3. A third consequence of attribution is how we behave. It is self-evident that how we behave is in some manner determined by how we explain and judge events and the actions of people and by how we feel about such attributions. The behavioral consequences of attribution in how individuals interact in organizations is the focal point of interest in attribution. Of special interest is the part expectations of others and self-fulfilling prophecies play in the character of interpersonal relations through "behavioral confirmation." Behavioral confirmation is the "idea that one's beliefs about another person (expressed in behavior towards that person) confirm one's prior beliefs."[14] (Comments in parentheses are those of the authors). A classic example is the Helen Keller story. If Helen Keller's teacher and caretaker, Anne Sullivan, made the same attributions everyone else did about her, then Helen Keller's talents and potential would never have been realized.

Furthermore, the care and treatment of physically and mentally challenged people was considerably altered as a consequence of how Anne Sullivan and Helen Keller related to each other.[15]

In pragmatic terms, we can perhaps learn most about the process of attribution by becoming aware of generalized biases in attribution. Attribution processes are subject to error. Specifically, bias refers to systematic distortion whether or not such distortion results in error in an absolute or relative sense. Three of the most central biases in attribution have been identified as the fundamental attribution error, self-other differences and self-serving biases:[16]

1. The fundamental attribution error is defined as the tendency for individuals to underestimate the impact of situational factors (factors pertaining to external circumstances) and to overestimate the role of dispositional factors (factors pertaining to temperament and personal characteristics) in making sense of the behavior of others. To cite Heider, one of the founders of attribution theory, "changes in the environment are almost always caused by acts of persons in combination with other factors. The tendency exists to ascribe the changes entirely to persons."[17] Studies have shown that the tendency to inadequately account for external circumstances in the behavior of others is extremely widespread and is thought to be shared by almost everyone socialized in our Western culture. It is in short "thoroughly woven into the fabric of our culture."[18]

2. Another central bias in attribution is characterized as self-other differences. To cite Heider again, "the person tends to attribute his own reactions to the object world (i.e., circumstances apart from himself) and those of another when they differ from his own, to personal characteristics."[19] (Comments in parentheses are those of the authors.) Stated another way, in conflict between individuals, there is a tendency for individuals to attribute situational causes for their own behavior and causes related to personality and character traits for the behavior of the other person.

3. The third type of bias, self-serving biases, helps satisfy the requirements of the self-esteem function associated with the process of attribution as previously discussed. There appears, in fact, to be two biases. The first, a self-enhancing bias operates to assign internal causes to success. Such causes include hard work, competence, ambition and drive. The second, a self-protecting bias, attributes failure to external causes such as timing, the recession, the competition, etc.

These three types of biases are all driven by the internal-external distinction or the discrimination we make between subject (what pertains to *me*) and object (what pertains to *other*). Illustrations of attributional biases at work are easy to find. We encounter them operating within ourselves on a regular basis as we drive the freeways. When the driver in front of us crosses three lanes of traffic without a signal to make an exit, we have little doubt about this person's lack of intelligence, general level of civility and heredity. When we do the same thing, however, there is also little doubt that we did it because of the meeting we were late for, the scheduled flight departure in 10 minutes or the conspiracy of the other drivers failing to give way to our needs.

Attribution as a process and as an explanation of causes is neutral in a value sense. All of us engage in the process of attribution. Like the effect of mental models, attribution can serve useful purposes. It can help us to make sense of the behavior of other people and to act with an economy of mental effort. The process of attribution is also subject to error and can create consequences which we may not intend. It is especially relevant to consider attribution as it relates to the ability of individuals to associate with each other in productive ways. From a learning standpoint, our patterns of attribution play a significant role in how accurately we perceive, assess and deal with reality.

In a practical sense, our concern with the process and results of attribution is on three levels. The first level relates to awareness. To the extent that we are aware of the functions, consequences and biases associated with attribution, we can consciously alter our behavior. The second level pertains to accuracy. Personal benefit accompanies the ability to make accurate attributions and valid inferences. The practice of testing attributions can enhance our ability to perceive and comprehend reality as it is. The third level of concern has to do with relevance. In organizational life, as expressed in interpersonal and intergroup dynamics, context determines whether or not our attributions matter.

The process and result of attribution are deeply embedded in communication. Four maxims for interpersonal explanation and conversation have been adapted and represent a useful guide for dealing with our attributions.

1. The maxim of quality — speakers (attributors) should say what they know not to be false, and not say something for which they lack adequate evidence;

2. The maxim of quantity — speakers (attributors) should make their contributions as informative as required for the purposes of the exchange but not more informative than necessary;

3. The maxim of relation — speakers (attributors) should be relevant;
4. The maxim of manner — speakers (attributors) should avoid obscurity and ambiguity, they should be brief and orderly.[20]

To conclude this section on attribution, we feel that a caution against over-generalization is indicated. While there is good evidence for the material summarized in this section, these dynamics operate differently in different people and their influence varies by degree.

3.3　*The Role of Defensiveness in Perception and Cognition*

Defensive behavior is the result of largely unconscious mental processes and serves to protect the perceiver from threat or to enable the individual to avoid such threat. In great measure, defensiveness is driven by the emotion of fear or anxiety — fear of loss of control over circumstances, anxiety associated with potential loss of self-esteem or advantage over other people. In generally healthy people, the defensive aspects of our personalities have been defined as our dark or shadow sides while our non-defensive features are equated with our productive and natural strengths. Chris Argyris has studied defensive behavior, its origins and consequences in organizations. He describes an additional dimension of dysfunction associated with patterns of covering up defensive behavior. He refers to these patterns of defensiveness and cover-up, as they become hardened and slip from the awareness of individuals, as "defensive routines."[21] The dynamics of defensive routines exacerbate the problem of creating non-defensive behavioral norms.

A prominent neurosurgeon, a member of a group with whom we were working on the mechanics and effects of defensiveness, reminded us that defensive responses to threat are natural in all living creatures and can serve useful purposes. His assertion is obviously valid and bears remembering. It is also obviously valid that a prolonged defensive posture is detrimental to the effectiveness of the creature whether it is a human being or a fruit fly. This places the demand upon the individual to discern the authenticity of the perceived threat and to either act to eliminate the threat or to alter his or her response to it. Our concern with defensive attitudes and behaviors is with those whose natures are embedded and prolonged and rests on two levels. The first relates to the role of defensiveness in perception and cognition; the second pertains to defensive behavior in individuals in response to the perceptions and defenses of others.

We will quite naturally protect ourselves from a threat in our physical environment and avoid it, such as not going out at night in a dangerous part of town. Likewise, we will seek protection from threat and avoid what we sense as a menace to our comfortable views of the world and to our processes for making sense of what goes on around us. Thinking back to the introduction of this chapter, the greater the degree of embeddedness of an individual's views of the world and sense-making apparatus, the greater the perception of threat to these constructs will be felt and reacted to. As our defenses engage, our potential for generating flawed perceptions increases. The mode of thinking which Argyris calls "defensive reasoning" functions to maintain and strengthen our perceptions whether or not they are accurate. When individuals are reasoning defensively, their assumptions remain unidentified, the processes by which they reach conclusions are unexpressed, and the data they use to conceive their assumptions and conclusions tend to be soft and untested. "Defensive reasoning is self-serving, anti-learning and over protective."[22]

3.4   Defensive Responses to the Perceptions and Defenses of Others

Our perceptions drive our actions. In other words, what we see determines what we do. Our mental models play an important role in how we perceive other people and their circumstances. The more unaware we are of these screens and filters, the more powerfully they affect our perceptions. As we have seen, the functions and the systematic bias of attribution also work together to bring about the potential for flawed perceptions. Quite unintentionally, then, the behavior of one individual can trigger defensive responses in another individual which can, in turn, elicit reciprocal defensive responses creating a downward spiral in the character of the relationship between the two individuals. Defensive reasoning on the part of both individuals caught in such a spiral will ensure that the assumptions and the subjective interpretations of events and circumstances affecting these individuals will remain unexpressed and untested. Over time, great barriers and misunderstandings can build up and cause a relationship to disintegrate. Stephen Covey uses the metaphor of "emotional bank accounts" in relationships.[23] We make deposits and withdrawals in each other's accounts, and the result over time is either generally positive or negative feelings about other individuals. Eventually, these deposits or withdrawals lead a relationship to become either prosperous or bankrupt. When a pair of individuals are working out of emotional overdrafts with respect to each other, the resulting relationship can be nothing but ineffective and broken as defensiveness shapes the relationship.

As counterproductive as full blown bi-lateral defensive communication may be, the consequences of defensiveness do not end there. Perhaps an even greater and more insidious effect of defensiveness is connected with avoidance. There appears to be a widespread tendency for non-confrontational behavior in organizations. To the extent that an emotionally negative response by another person is anticipated and the circumstance thought to trigger such a response is avoided, a pattern of under-the-surface defensiveness will be created. Under these conditions, not only will the consequences of defensiveness exist but the sources will be hidden and the pattern will be hardened.

3.5   *Insights into Defensive Behavior*

"Social Science research has demonstrated a few truths quite convincingly. One of these is that people behave in very diverse ways, so that one can find at least a few instances that match or contradict virtually any assertion about human behavior."[24] Individuals need to gain insights into their own unique behavior, particularly their defensive behavior. There are several good instruments available to help give people feedback in a constructive way. However, we always caution people that the instruments are only tools. We have seen the reductionism constraint creep into the use of virtually all good organizational tools. Again, this can be controlled by the person using the tool and the person to whom it is administered. There is always the risk that individuals will overreact to the feedback and treat it as the absolute truth and not as a potential for insight to be carefully thought about and tested. In the instruments that we have used for purposes of feedback, there are no absolutes. Rather, there are ranges of strengths and weaknesses. For example, we have used the Management Effectiveness Analysis and the Leadership Effectiveness Analysis from the Management Research Group. They list behavioral characteristics on a numerical scale corresponding with designations of low, low-mid, midrange, high-mid and high with accompanying descriptions of potential assets and potential liabilities. As background to the use of their instruments, the Management Research Group also list management role assumptions upon which the instrument is based.[25] Another instrument, The Birkman Method, captures the rich diversity and uniqueness of individuals as expressed in the complexity of their interests, behaviors, needs, ways of thinking and personality styles. As part of our use of The Birkman Method, we have been able to access individuals' propensity towards stress (defensive) behavior and help them identify the particular defensive behaviors that others can expect to see exhibited under stress. Some individuals with whom we work can easily admit to and identify their defensive behavior. Others just as easily blame their defensive behavior on external circumstances — ranging from their bosses to the weather — if they even admit to having other than consistently stellar behavior. The Birkman Method provides a unique perspective on defensive behavior which acknowledges that defensive behaviors exist for every individual and they vary by intensity and form from person to person.

It is important for us to point out the incompleteness of every human being. A key part of using any personality or behavioral assessment instrument is to realize that while we need to identify and build up our strengths, we also need to acknowledge our weaknesses. The Management Research Group has stated that the developmental aim of their Management Effectiveness Analysis "is to help you achieve your goal of increased managerial competency. Your management development is increased through 1) recognizing or being able to diagnose your strengths and weaknesses, and 2) designing strategies to sustain strengths and attack liabilities."[26] Our incompleteness not only predisposes us to defensive behavior but also compels us in our "usual" or "active" behavior (in Birkman terms), when we are feeling confident and assured, to seek out other individuals different from ourselves. Others peoples' styles and strengths complement ours as we complement theirs in the process of becoming more complete. In the words of Roger Birkman in his book, *True Colors:* "Actually, there is great freedom in knowing one's own strengths and weaknesses, for as soon as these are identified, it becomes a much simpler matter to focus on the things you do well and look for help in your weaker areas from someone who is strong in those areas."[27] When we actively include and openly solicit and welcome the ideas and talents of others and acknowledge them, we can be seen as acting out of an "abundance mentality." The opposite is thinking and behaving in a "scarcity mentality" — withholding information, exhibiting turf building and paranoia. As Stephen Covey says: "It's difficult for people with a Scarcity Mentality to be members of a complementary team. They look on differences as signs of insubordination and disloyalty."[28]

3.6   Communication, Relationships and Preconditions to Learning

The essential questions that arise in this chapter are: How able are individuals in organizations to see, hear, comprehend and express reality? What is the potential for individuals to learn beyond a narrow context? What is the potential for individuals in organizations to form and sustain effective, purposeful working relationships? We have explored how our mental models and the results and process of attribution work together to play a substantial role in forming our perceptions. We have seen how behavior is influenced by perception and how threats to our mental models and sense-making become reshaped and actualized as defensive attitudes and behaviors. We have also seen how our perceptions and defenses alter those of other people. Finally, we have examined how patterns of flawed perception and defensiveness close down communication and learning and bring about ineffective relationships. What individuals bring to their encounters with other people largely accounts for the quality of their interactions. Improved communication, enhanced relationships and a stage set for learning can be the consequences of altered modes of perceiving and behaving.

Communication is the most frequently mentioned issue when we speak to members of organizations about sources of problems and dysfunction. "Our problem is a communication problem," "communication is poor in our department," "we have to learn how to communicate better" are examples of assertions that, while ubiquitous, give little clue to what people really mean when they utter them. Most attempts to improve communication focus on form, i.e., more meetings, newsletters, townhall rallies, etc. with little effect. We know of a management group that meets as a group every day for one to two hours and poor communication is their chief complaint. The meaning of poor communication must relate directly to perceptions of poor information quality. Our conclusion is that when communication is identified as a problem what people really mean is that information transferred is invalid, irrelevant or both. To restate Argyris' insight, valid information is the first governing condition associated with a model of organizational life that supports learning and effective-ness.[29] Perception, attribution and defensiveness are influential in either supporting or restraining both the generation and comprehension of valid information and, thus, useful communication.

As a final note regarding communication, Hage and Powers in their book, *Post Industrial Lives*, assert that "symbolic communication consists of two channels: a verbal or cognitive channel and a nonverbal or affective channel."[30] Both channels are necessary for effective communication. The suggestion is that messages comprise both information and feeling and that it is necessary to comprehend the objective and subjective components and how they are linked in any communication. While it is hard to disagree that emotion is an important aspect of communication and that the ability to read nonverbals is a useful skill, our interest and aim is to go beyond mere observation. Rather, our hope and intent is to see individuals in organizations develop the capacity to unambiguously express themselves, fully and appropriately, rather than hoping to be interpreted and understood through their subtleties and their patterns of avoidance or defensiveness. At the same time, individuals need to listen and receive what other people are communicating to them. This type of deep communication is expressed by Carl Rogers in his book, *Freedom to Learn*: "Hearing has consequences. When I do truly hear a person, hearing not simply his words, but him, and when I let him know that I have heard his own private personal meanings, he feels released with a new sense of freedom and becomes more open to the process of change."[31]

3.6.1 Role Negotiation

Role negotiation is a practical intervention that identifies and seeks to balance objective and subjective factors. It connects individuals with other individuals in various kinds of working relationships by making explicit and integrating what is subjective and objective to the various parties negotiating their roles. We have used the process most extensively in accountability relationships, i.e., between and among one or more managers and individuals where accountability for performance, either directly or laterally is the basis of the relationship.

Related to the objective factors, clarity and alignment around expectations and accountability is the intent. Explicit naming of objective outcomes is the aim of this aspect of the role negotiation. Even in instances where a result may not be measurable in usual terms, questions such as "how will we know we were successful" must be asked and answered.

Subjective and objective factors are intertwined in any relationship. The process of establishing the objective basis of a working relationship itself necessitates dealing with subjective issues. Given that there is agreement on objective goals, subjective factors will either facilitate or constrain the achievement of those goals. The point of dealing with subjectivity and working relationships has ultimately to do with objective aims. Our approach along the subjective track is to encourage and facilitate a process of surfacing issues that the individuals are bringing to the relationship. These issues may represent unresolved and avoided sources of conflict, inaccurate perceptions of each other and defensive postures that have in the past determined the character of the relationship in question. Resolving issues of this sort is difficult and tends to be resisted especially by individuals who are accustomed to repressing subjectivity. It is clear to us, however, that failure to successfully deal with issues of emotion and subjectivity will result in constrained objective achievement. Bearing in mind the dynamics of perception and defensiveness as described in this chapter and using tools such as structured interviews and The Birkman Method, a mode of productive reasoning is introduced and maintained to frame the process. Productive reasoning begins by becoming aware of and expressing our own reasoning processes. When individuals are reasoning productively, they express and illustrate the observable data that leads them to inferred meaning, they make all their inferences explicit and they express their conclusions in ways that invite inquiry into them.

As we have reasoned, learning and change is a one-person-at-a-time proposition. Establishing the individual as the focal point of interest in this chapter, therefore, acknowledges that reality and the application of the principle, *Achieve an Operative Balance of Objective and Subjective Factors,* lays the groundwork for subsequent chapters.

References

1. Kegan, R., *The Evolving Self: Problem and Process in Human Development,* Harvard University Press, Boston, 1982.
2. Bloom, A., *The Closing of the American Mind,* Simon & Schuster, New York, 1987, 264.
3. Senge, P. M., *The Fifth Discipline: The Art and Practice of the Learning Organization,* Doubleday, New York, 1990, 174.
4. Argyris, C., *Overcoming Organizational Defenses: Facilitating Organizational Learning,* Allyn & Bacon, Boston, 1990, 12.
5. MacGregor, D., *The Human Side of Enterprise,* McGraw-Hill, New York, 1960.
6. Argyris, C., *Overcoming Organizational Defenses: Facilitating Organizational Learning,* Allyn & Bacon, Boston, 1990, 16.
7. Argyris, C., *Knowledge for Action: A Guide to Overcoming Barriers to Organizational Change,* Jossey-Bass, San Francisco, 1994, 134.
8. Hewstone, M., *Causal Attribution: From Cognitive Processes to Collective Beliefs,* Blackwell Publishers, Oxford, 1989, 29.
9. Hewstone, M., *Causal Attribution: From Cognitive Processes to Collective Beliefs,* Blackwell Publishers, Oxford, 1989, 111.
10. Hewstone, M., *Causal Attribution: From Cognitive Processes to Collective Beliefs,* Blackwell Publishers, Oxford, 1989, 61.
11. Noer, D. M., *Healing the Wounds,* Jossey-Bass, San Francisco, 1993, 50.
12. Hewstone, M., *Causal Attribution: From Cognitive Processes to Collective Beliefs,* Blackwell Publishers, Oxford, 1989, 62.
13. Hewstone, M., *Causal Attribution: From Cognitive Processes to Collective Beliefs,* Blackwell Publishers, Oxford, 1989, 67.
14. Hewstone, M., *Causal Attribution: From Cognitive Processes to Collective Beliefs,* Blackwell Publishers, Oxford, 1989, 66.
15. Peare, C. O., *The Helen Keller Story,* Crowell, New York, 1959.
16. Hewstone, M., *Causal Attribution: From Cognitive Processes to Collective Beliefs,* Blackwell Publishers, Oxford, 1989.

17. Heider, F., Social Perception and Phenomenal Causality, *Psychological Review*, 51, 1944.
18. Nisbett, R. E. and Ross, L., *Human Inference: Strategies and Shortcomings of Social Judgment,* Prentice-Hall, Englewood Cliffs, 1980.
19. Heider, F., *The Psychology of Interpersonal Relations,* Wiley, New York, 1958.
20. Hewstone, M., *Causal Attribution: From Cognitive Processes to Collective Beliefs,* Blackwell Publishers, Oxford, 1989, 116.
21. Argyris, C., *Knowledge for Action: A Guide to Overcoming Barriers to Organizational Change,* Jossey-Bass, San Francisco, 1994, 31.
22. Argyris, C., *Overcoming Organizational Defenses: Facilitating Organizational Learning,* Allyn & Bacon, Boston, 1990, 25.
23. Covey, S. R., *The Seven Habits of Highly Effective People: Restoring the Character Ethic,* Simon & Schuster, New York, 1989, 257.
24. Starbuck, W. H., Acting First and Thinking Later: Theory Versus Reality in Strategic Change, *Organizational Strategy and Change,* Jossey-Bass, 1985.
25. Mahoney, J. and Rand, T., *Management Effectiveness Analysis Personal Feedback Profile,* Portland, Maine, 1985.
26. Mahoney, J. and Rand, T., *Management Effectiveness Analysis Personal Feedback Profile,* Portland, Maine, 1985.
27. Birkman, R., *True Colors,* Thomas Nelson Publishers, Nashville, 1995, 31.
28. Covey, S. R., *The Seven Habits of Highly Effective People: Restoring the Character Ethic,* Simon & Schuster, New York, 1989, 219.
29. Argyris, C. and Schon, D. A., *Theory and Practice: Increasing Professional Effectiveness,* Jossey-Bass, San Francisco, 1974, 86.
30. Hage, G. and Powers, C. H., *Post Industrial Lives: Roles and Relationships in the Twenty First Century,* Sage Publications, 1992, 96.
31. Rogers, C. R., *Freedom to Learn,* Charles E. Merrill Publishing Co., Columbus, 1969.

Chapter 4

Individuals: *Delegate Only Around Purpose*

Anticipatory Summary

Delegation is usually viewed as something leaders do. The focus in this chapter, however, will be on those to whom delegation occurs — those in whom leaders hope to find the motivation to achieve. At least as important as what leaders do and say is what those they hope to lead hear and further, whether what those individuals hear has any meaning for them. What individuals hear and make sense of is a function of perception; whether or not there is any meaning associated with what is heard is a function of connection (or lack of connection) with personal motives.

4.1 Purposeful Delegation and Responses by Individuals

- Function or task is the usual basis of delegation. Purpose driven delegation, on the other hand, refers to delegation based on expectations and accountability for producing results that pertain to purpose.
- Purposeful delegation is a key factor in bringing about purposeful organizational behavior.
- Purposeful delegation is difficult but possible; it tends to be resisted by individuals.

4.2   *Motivation*

■ Delegation around purpose can be powerful when purpose is meaningful for those to whom delegation is occurring; commitment can flow from purposeful delegation.
■ The goal of commitment leads to concern for issues of personal motivation.
■ This chapter explores the dynamics and consequences of a critical mass of commitment among individuals and how such a critical mass can be achieved — one person at a time.

4.2.1 *Threats to Motivation*

■ Paradoxically, current management theory acknowledges the objective benefit of engaging people in organizational mission and direction yet many organizations are fixed in practices which bring about disengagement and alienation of individuals.

4.2.2 *Theories and Themes of Motivation*

■ Theories of motivation and variations on theoretical themes are numerous. None of them generally apply and all of them seem to have some application at some time for some people.
■ Theories of motivation are based on assumptions about human nature. Three such sets of assumptions are rational-economic, social and self-actualization.
■ Variables in motivation also include psychological development and situational factors.
■ Generalization, while seductive, is a trap. People must be met where they are and not at some contrived or hypothetical place where we would like for them to be.

4.3   *Meaning Reconciliation*

■ At the level of the individual, commitment can emerge from a combination of higher order motives and a cause — a purpose that has meaning for the individual.

4.4   *Personal Leverage*

■ If commitment is valuable, meaning made from work is significant; if meaning made from work is significant, clarity of purpose is necessary; if purpose is clear, the consequences of effort are the central concern; if the focus is on consequences or results, the concept of leverage comprehended at the level of the individual is important and warrants our consideration.

4.5   *Empowerment from the Perspective of the Individual*

■ To be empowered is to be commissioned to create positive leverage — to add value.
■ To focus only on the management side of empowerment is to fail to understand the concept.

4.6   *Delegation as Viewed by Individuals*

■ The concept and the principle of delegating by way of purpose, from a leadership perspective, is congruent with being empowered from the viewpoint of individuals.
■ Delegation is a two-way street, empowerment is a bi-lateral transaction.

Individuals: *Delegate Only Around Purpose*

Charles Handy in his book, *The Age of Paradox*, contends that sensible organizational behavior is no more or less complex than "a common cause, the willingness to deny oneself in the interests of that common cause, and trust that others will do the same."[1] Consideration in this chapter will be brought to bear on common cause — particularly, common cause that has meaning for me as an individual working within an organization. In the process of relating the principle, *Delegate Only Around Purpose* to individuals, the terms "common cause" and "purpose" can be seen as interchangeable. We have described purpose as the logical and animating construct around which the energy of individuals may be productively applied. From the perspective of the organization, purpose is defined as the enterprise-wide ends or goals expressed in practical, actionable and broadly understandable terms. Purpose embraces the consequences of effort manifested as results or outcomes. Tasks and activities are modes of organizing work which are necessary to produce consequences. They are not, however, meaningful standing alone without a clear connection to purpose. Erich Fromm in his book, *The Sane Society*, describes how historically craftsmanship represents one of the peaks in the evolution of creative work through a sustained orientation to purpose. He says with craftsmanship "there is no ulterior motive in work other than the product being made and the processes of its creation." He continues, "The details of daily work are meaningful because they are not detached in the worker's mind from the product of the work."[2] A common fallacy in organizations is that the successful execution of tasks and activities — the details of daily work — is an end in itself. When we cross these details off our list, we're finished. Although it is easy to observe that most individuals in organizations are busy, it is far less easy to discern how their busyness is related to producing results that have a bearing on purpose.

4.1   Purposeful Delegation and Responses by Individuals

Delegation is the process of entrusting resources to others and empowering them to act. It is the principle instrument of leadership and it may or may not serve the achievement of objective aims. The usual basis of delegation is by way of function or task. Purpose driven delegation, on the other hand, refers to delegation based on expectations and accountability for producing results that pertain to purpose. We have argued that purposeful delegation is a key factor in bringing about purposeful organizational behavior. While the creation of a clear purpose is in itself a significant and challenging undertaking, it is an obvious prerequisite to purposeful delegation. In our work with organizations, some organizational members invariably express the belief that while it may be possible to give expression to organizational purpose at a high level, driving and translating purpose through the layers and the units to individuals is very difficult if not impossible. The reality is that it is difficult, but it is not impossible and, in fact, it must be done. In the presence of a clear sense of purpose, the matter then returns to purposeful delegation which itself tends to be resisted by individuals, whether senior executives or staff members.

There is an assumption that effective leaders create clarity of purpose, articulate purpose in an inspirational and compelling way and that individuals follow. This assumption is, at best, only half true. At least as important as what leaders do and say is what those they hope to lead hear and further, whether what those individuals hear has any meaning for them. What individuals hear and make sense of is a function of perception; whether or not there is any meaning associated with what is heard is a function of connection or lack of connection with personal motives. Given diversity resulting from patterns of socialization, experience, training, motivation, personality — not to mention gender, ethnicity, etc., transcendence can only occur around the perception of linkage of personal meaning with unambiguous organizational purpose. We have been confounded on many occasions by how leaders, who appear to have done everything right, achieve little response from those they hope to inspire and move to action. In these cases, the leaders understood their organization's strategic imperatives, accurately assessed strengths, weaknesses and market dynamics and spelled out a way forward in logical, urgent and objective terms only to be met with the equivalent of a collective yawn.

Leaders obviously play a central role in matters pertaining to purpose and delegation. Leadership factors associated with purposeful delegation will be specifically addressed in Chapter 7, bearing in mind that leaders are also individuals and subject to the dynamics explored in this chapter. The focus in this chapter, however, will be on those to whom delegation occurs — those to whom leaders delegate and in whom leaders hope to find the motivation to achieve. In this chapter, we will consider issues of meaning, motivation and connection, the concept of personal leverage and the dynamics of involvement, empowerment and delegation — all from the perspective of the individual.

4.2   Motivation

Delegation around purpose can be powerful when the purpose in question is meaningful for those to whom delegation is occurring. Accountability for results that matter and commitment to achievement can flow from purposeful delegation. Commitment means being emotionally impelled to connect with a cause in a deep and profound way; it implies dedication, resolution and zeal. Commitment in an organizational context is defined as the "totality of internalized normative processes to act in a way that meets organizational interest."[3] According to this definition, a committed individual will have decided, in lieu of other alternatives, to make the organization's interests his or her own. Organizational interests are no longer out there and purely objective but are now owned and thus part of the subjective fabric of that individual. Peter Senge draws a dramatic distinction between commitment and compliance. "Commitment wants it. Will make it happen. Creates whatever laws (or structures) are needed." Compliance at best "does what's expected within the letter of the law (existing structure and knowledge base)." "The committed person brings an energy, passion and excitement that cannot be generated if you are only compliant." Further, "A group of people committed to a common vision (cause, purpose) is an awesome force."[4] (Comments in parentheses are those of the authors.)

The matter of commitment brings us overtly to the issues of personal motivation in a practical sense and meaning in a deeper sense. Viktor Frankl, in his practice of Logotherapy, challenges individuals to address both aspects of commitment: "One should not search for an abstract meaning of life. Everyone has his own specific vocation or mission in life to carry out a concrete assignment which demands fulfillment. Therein he cannot be replaced, nor can his life be repeated. Thus, everyone's task is as unique as is his specific opportunity to implement it."[5] Our intent is to consider motivation as it relates to commitment and not compliance although compliance may be all that can be expected in some cases. Commitment engages creativity and learning whereas compliance generates nothing more significant than a cadre of good soldiers. Our aim in this chapter is to explore the dynamics and consequences of a critical mass of commitment among individuals and how such a critical mass can be achieved — one person at a time.

4.2.1   Threats to Motivation

It is paradoxical that most current management theory acknowledges the potential objective benefit of engaging people in organizational mission and direction yet many organizations have been fixed in practices which bring about disengagement and alienation of individuals. Recent research at Templeton College, the University of Oxford concerning the consequences of "downsizing, rightsizing and delayering" reports that "psychic dislocation is occurring." It characterizes employee attitudes as progressively "semi-attached and disaffected."[6] In our experience in organizations, this phenomenon is clearly present and represents a breakdown in the psychological contract between organizations and individuals.

4.2.2   Theories and Themes of Motivation

Theories of motivation and variations on theoretical themes abound. Some of these theories have been around for as long as human beings have thought about their own motives and those of others. Some of them are relatively new. None of them generally apply and all of them seem to have some application at some time for some people. Theories of motivation are based on assumptions about human nature. Individuals select specific actions in lieu of other possible actions based on sets of assumptions about needs, attitudes and pre-existing goals. This dynamic underlies these theories.

Three such sets of assumptions have had a significant influence on thinking about motivation. First, rational-economic assumptions rest on the belief that people act to maximize their self interest. Economic man/woman is assumed to be motivated by economic incentives. Many aspects of the practice of management have been and continue to be greatly influenced by this view of human nature. Feelings are seen as irrational and able to interfere with the rational calculation of self interest and should therefore be avoided or by-passed. It is argued by some that in today's organizational and business climate, the rational-economic response is the most appropriate one for individuals. It would be ironic but somehow symmetrical if this was in fact a consequence of management's infatuation with overly objective, people-insensitive change interventions. It would be ironic, in other words, if the cost of management fads would be the supplanting of higher order motives related to meaning and achieving potential with purely economic ones.

Second, the Social assumptions grew from the now famous Hawthorne Studies and other studies, especially the Tavistock Coal Mining Studies, all of which showed the importance of social motives in organizational life. A new kind of hypothesis emerged from the Hawthorne Studies which occurred during the 1920s and 1930s in Western Electric Company's Hawthorne, Illinois plant. As reported by Edgar Schein[7], "the motivation to work, productivity and quality of work all are related to the nature of the social relations among workers and between workers and their supervisors." "Working extra hard because of the feeling of participating in something new and special has come to be known as the 'Hawthorne Effect.'" The set of social assumptions suggests that acceptance and liking by one's fellow workers is more important than other factors. Social needs are considered to be the foremost motivator and interpersonal relationships are presumed to play a key role in shaping an individual's sense of identity. Perhaps the enduring insight from the social assumptions is that the character of social relationships accounts for work performance to a significant degree.

Third, self-actualization assumptions stress the proposition that all people have innate needs for autonomy, challenge, growth and the opportunity to use their skills and talents. Self-actualization is recognized by most of us as representing the top layer of Maslow's Hierarchy of Needs — the argument being that self-actualization is sought when lower level needs pertaining to physiology, safety, social and affiliation and self-esteem have been satisfied.[8] Self-actualization assumptions are best expressed in MacGregor's Theory Y, an idealistic view of human nature, in contrast to his Theory X, which represents a more pessimistic view. The Theory Y assumptions of human nature, as they relate to work, assert: "the expenditure of physical and mental effort in work is as natural as play or rest; man will exercise self direction and self control in the service of objectives to which he is committed"[9] (when lower level needs have been met). Self-actualization as a motivating force differs from Rational-Economic and Social bases of motivation in that factors intrinsic to individuals, such as satisfaction from accomplishment, overrides extrinsic factors such as pay and a pleasant environment.

Theories of motivation derived from earlier times seem static and overly suggestive of general applicability. If we are certain of anything, it is that human beings and their motives are complex and dynamic. A missing ingredient in theorizing about motivation has been that human beings have complex patterns of psychological development — that their values, attitudes, needs, abilities and motives change with circumstances, age and stage of development. The developmental perspective of Robert Kegan and others build on the work of Jean Piaget and posit that the mechanics of development extend beyond childhood throughout adult life.[10] Therefore, motives clearly vary among individuals according to their developmental stage. The developmental perspective points to the variability of the motives of an individual over time. Taking self-actualization as an example, challenge, satisfaction and perception of accomplishment mean different things to different people and may mean different things to the same person at different times in their life. Edgar Schein in his book, *Organizational Psychology*, asserts that "much of the variation in human motivation can be understood only if we realize the multiplicity of forces which act on every child in the process of growing up and the complexity in each human being of the ego ideal (set of goals and aspirations)." (Comments in parentheses are those of the authors.) This is all seen as the process of working out our self-concept and moving toward such a conception that we value. The ultimate motivator, he argues, can therefore be thought of as the "need to maintain and develop one's self-concept and one's self-esteem."[11]

It is also important to point out that situational factors such as an individual's longevity in a job account for some variability in patterns of motivation. Katz, in a 1978 study,[12] identified the periods of "socialization, innovation and adaptation" as pertaining to an individual's progressing in or through a job. Finally, there is a class of theory referred to as "universal process models of motivation." Expectancy and Path-Goal theories are examples of such process theories and are distinguished by the "hypothesis that the behavior of an individual is in part determined by (a) his expectation that the behavior will lead to various outcomes and (b) his evaluation of those outcomes."[13] In other words, these theories argue, perhaps self-evidently, that higher motivation exists when there is a perceived link between effort, performance and reward. These notional formulations offer no new insights about what motivates people and relate rather to the mechanism or agency of managerially created motivation. Questions such as: What constitutes good performance? What is a meaningful outcome? What is a meaningful reward? are not addressed in these theories.

Given these various perspectives on motivation, some of which are in conflict and others complement each other, what can we take and make use of? The first realization is that personal motivation is complex and that generalization, while seductive, is a trap and is a form of reductionism. We believe that people must be met where they are and not at some contrived or hypothetical place where we would like for them to be. While leaders may be able to meet certain needs and alter certain circumstances, consciously engineering developmental shifts and patterns of higher order motivation in people is usually beyond the capacity of management. It is an interpretive and sometimes difficult task to understand where people are but one which is obviously required if they are to be met there.

4.3 Meaning Reconciliation

In our work with individuals in organizations, we are especially interested in what is meaningful to them and in their capacity to derive meaning from something larger than themselves. We are also interested in the degree to which individuals are motivated by the need to grow and see work as growth producing. We interview individuals and aim to understand them as whole persons placing emphasis on validity, richness and quality of information using an interpretive model of interaction and analysis.[14] We seek to learn about their perceptions of what constitutes success for the organization and what they have "at stake" in that success. We also ask:

What would reaching your potential look like?
What has been most meaningful to you in your life?
Who do you most respect in this organization and why?
If you could be doing anything at all with your life, what would you be doing?

We often ask individuals, as part of a group or as individuals, to write a statement expressing their hoped for legacy to the organization in terms of outcomes or results. The legacy exercise asks them to consider the greatest impact they could have as individuals and to express that impact as how they would hope to be remembered by members of the organization after their tenure. What people say, and whether or not they say anything meaningful, coupled with other observations, helps to form perspectives of individual patterns of motivation. The legacy exercise also reinforces the notion that meaningful, results-oriented contribution is highly valued. We have often used The Birkman Method, a personality assessment tool, in identifying the interests of individuals in a general sense and the expression of potential motivational work interests and goals in a more specific sense. Underlying needs are also presented which, if not met, may result in behaviors that inhibit higher order patterns of motivation.

The interpretive interview often allows us to enter into an individual's subjective space — a special relationship and place where individuals feel free to give voice to and clarify their concerns, give expression to what underlies their fears and frees them to focus on what they find as meaningful in their work. This process has become in itself a powerful intervention. We design this process to be mutually beneficial. It provides us with information and insights into people and organizations. For the person listened to, it is an opportunity to "think out loud," often gaining self-awareness in the process. Thomas Moore in his book, *Care of the Soul*, suggests that "Listening to another and caring for their welfare can be such a comforting experience …".[15] Carl Rogers suggests that a possible outcome through what he calls "the experience of exploration" can even involve the beginning of a change of attitude in an individual.[16]

Having developed a reasonable sense about where people are, i.e., what is meaningful and motivating to them, we can begin to think about potential connections with organizational purpose. This is, in fact, the meaning of meeting people where they are. The challenge is to discover where and on what basis connections between what is meaningful to individuals and what has meaning for the organization can be made. The greatest leverage or potency in this process of meaning reconciliation will occur where there is a sense of common cause — where the purpose of the organization is intrinsically valued by individuals and congruent with their own sense of purpose. This is what Peter Senge calls "shared vision," "collective aspiration and shared commitment."[17] If the greatest leverage in reconciling meaning between individuals and organizations is found in a sense of common cause, the greatest leverage in individual meaning-making flows from personal motives of a higher order than those that are purely economic, affiliative or self confirming. Such higher order motives will be driven by an ability to relate to a purpose beyond one's self, or in Herzberg's terms, by job challenge and accomplishment[18] or in Maslow's terms, by self-actualization.[19]

Chris Argyris and others have argued that in an increasingly complex and competitive world, to settle for lower levels of motivation is a waste of human resources. It is also not at all clear that all people expect their work to provide significant meaning in their lives. Our experience validates both assertions. We hasten to add, however, that while we do not believe that all people are or can be moved to be motivated at higher levels, organizations, which would benefit greatly by such patterns of motivation, often act to close motivation down. MacGregor hypothesizes "that workers have learned not to expect challenge and meaning in their work and have therefore adapted to these lowered expectations." Shein argues that the failure of individuals to seek challenge or self-actualization at work may not be because lower level needs have not been fulfilled but rather because "the organization has trained workers not to expect meaning in their work as part of the psychological contract."[20]

Organizations also tend to undermine motivation when they are in the midst of change. Sue Dopson and Jean Neumann conducted a research project in connection with Templeton College, Oxford and used the concept of psychological contract to frame how change affected a group of middle managers and their jobs. Organization change for these managers was conceived as a resocialization process, driven by a shift in the psychological contract, and aimed towards creating behavioral change. In our practice, we have observed how purposeful, productive people can lose motivation and leave organizations when they experience devaluation through change processes managed by depersonalized communication programs. One of the propositions of the Dopson and Neumann study confirmed our understanding of this dynamic by pointing to the need for organizations, in the midst of change, to address their members with sensitivity, intelligence and respect. They wrote, "… organisational responses to negative reactions from middle managers need to differentiate by degree of negativity: uncertainty, contrariness, and the double-bind (a situation in which no matter what a person does, he or she cannot win) indicate the need for responses tailored to the particular elements of the (new) psychological contract which is most problematic."[21] (Parenthetical comments are those of the authors.)

At the level of the individual, commitment can emerge from a combination of higher order motives and a cause, a purpose that has meaning for the individual. When there is no comprehensible and stimulating purpose, when purpose becomes obscured through layers of functions and an orientation to tasks and activities, when the difficult work of translating and delegating around purpose is avoided, the value of higher order motives in the individual is lost. It is the duty of leaders to access commitment, one person at a time, and with skill and persistence to create a critical mass of commitment. These topics will be addressed in the chapters pertaining to leaders.

4.4   *Personal Leverage*

If commitment is valuable, meaning made from work is significant and worthy of pursuit. If meaning made from work is significant, clarity of purpose is necessary. If purpose is clear, the consequences or the output of effort is the central concern. If the focus is on output or results, the concept of leverage comprehended at the level of the individual is important and warrants our consideration. Archimedes said about leverage, "give me but one firm spot on which to stand and I will move the earth." By leverage we mean creating the greatest good per unit of invested resource. Without a definition of good, leverage makes no sense. Therefore, without a clear sense of purpose and relevant output equated to good, leverage is a meaningless concept. Leverage relates to output per activity and can be thought of as a multiplier where relatively small investments of time, energy and capital can yield large results. The seeking of leverage compels us to sustain an intimacy with purpose or goal or destination and with the consequences of effort, i.e., the output of work expressed and achieved in terms that will bring about the goal or enable arrival at the destination. Leverage is a neutral concept. Low, high, zero, even negative leverage can be created. Leverage can be created around activities and tasks but if these don't produce output related to purpose, they represent poor uses of resources and ultimately drain us and our organizations. Stephen Covey tells the story of an expedition making great progress through a jungle with the use of manpower and tools only to discover that they were in the wrong jungle.[22] We have observed busy members of organizations using tools — computers, meeting and communication skills, time management — to complete tasks that have little or no bearing on producing results consistent with organizational purpose.

As individuals, the single most important resource and perhaps the only resource we truly possess is our time. It is the one absolutely finite resource we are granted. Given the motivation to achieve, individuals can maximize their investment of time and their contribution through the creation of positive leverage. Stated another way, individuals can maximize their personal effectiveness and the work-related meaning in their lives through leverage. We encourage individuals to carefully analyze their activities and the output associated with each activity. If there is no output connected with an activity, that activity generates negative leverage, i.e., there is an opportunity cost associated with it and the doing of it should be questioned. The allocation of time to those activities that produce the greatest output should be enlarged. The key is in the understanding of purpose and in the expression of purpose in terms of results or relevant output. The analysis of tasks and activities thus becomes an iterative process of defining and weighing consequences and making choices about what can be done that will have the greatest impact on purpose. A physician with whom we worked had a significant load of clinical, teaching and research outcomes to produce within tight deadlines. The clinic in which she worked was a major source of distress for her because she felt that the time wasted through inefficiency was hampering not only her productivity but that of others. More importantly, patients were inconvenienced and kept waiting. She tried to address the clinic problem, but the general sense was that her other goals were more important and more pressing. She, therefore, repeatedly tried to ignore this nagging problem and to adapt to getting on with the outcomes others perceived as more obviously connected to purpose. The clinic situation, however, continued to get in her way of producing results and was emotionally draining. She eventually became quite aware that her sense of purpose included the successful and smooth operation of the clinic. Furthermore, she realized that the successful operation of the clinic was the point of greatest leverage for her in producing all of her other outcomes. Finally, her boss agreed to let her take on this problem. In addition, she was empowered with the authority and support she needed to be successful. This ultimate success started with this physician's strong sense of personal leverage and then being empowered to act on her good instincts and motivation.

4.5   Empowerment from the Perspective of the Individual

Empowerment, when viewed from the perspective of the individual, connotes the state of being entrusted or enfranchised to use resources to produce results. To be empowered is to be commissioned to create positive leverage — to add value. Empowerment is a word which has a noble and elevating ring to it and finds its way into vision and mission statements with some regularity. Unfortunately, while empowerment is an important concept in modern organizations, it seems to be somewhat misunderstood and the word itself is overused.

Empowerment as a management technique tends to be seen in uni-directional terms and used in only a task-assigning sense. In other words, empowerment is seen as flowing from leaders to followers and related to performing tasks and not necessarily creating results. Empowerment must be comprehended as a multi-lateral or at least a bi-lateral concept. To focus only on the management side of empowerment is to fail to understand the concept. There is an essential quid pro quo in any empowerment transaction. At the simplest level, the person being empowered must be willing to take risks, and the person doing the empowering must be willing to allow the empowered individuals to fail. One of the characteristics of a "learning company" discussed in the book by the same title is "a learning climate." The authors describe one of the "hallmarks" as "What happens when a mistake is made? The non-learning reaction is to cover up, not to admit fault, to try and 'pass the buck'. While not actually encouraged, mistakes in Learning Companies are more in the way of being experiments that didn't produce the right results. Why not? And how can we do better next time? How mistakes are handled is an instructive marker of the overall learning climate of the company."[23]

The individual being empowered must be empowerable, i.e., able to accept empowerment, willing to be held accountable for results and able to learn from mistakes and successes. A strong sense of internalized personal purpose and motivation coupled with a healthy level of self-esteem are essential for an individual to risk failure in the knowledge that successful outcomes more than compensate for the risk. Charles Handy, in his book, *The Age of Unreason*,[24] argues for a reasonable selfishness or a "proper selfishness" among individuals aiming to make significant contributions in organizations. These individuals "(a) take responsibility for themselves and their futures; (b) have a clear view of what they want their future to be; (c) want to make sure they can get it; and (d) believe that they can." While it is certain that when there is no clear purpose in an organization, there is little to which individuals can anchor their own sense of purpose and meaning. It is equally certain, that when work either holds little meaning for an individual or the meaning is incongruent with an organization's purpose, there is little in the individual to which organizational purpose can attach. A successful empowerment transaction can thus be seen as something like a multi-factor equation where both the empowering and the empowered sides of the equation must be satisfied. On the empowering side, leaders must ensure that clarity and relevance of purpose exists, that those to be empowered are aligned with that purpose, and that those empowered be allowed to fail and given the opportunity to learn from failure. On the side of the empowered individuals, they must have a sense of personal purpose that is reconciled with organizational purpose, have a willingness to take risks to create a high degree of leverage and be willing to be held accountable for results.

The lead in an article we wrote in 1993 stated: "Without alignment, empowerment is folly; without risk, empowerment is an empty concept; without a due sense of interdependence, empowerment is open to narrow interests; without the ability to collectively learn, empowerment is a route to mediocrity."[25] It is imperative that the motives of individuals to be empowered be understood and connected in some way with the common cause. We have experienced and observed the process of empowerment where motives of individuals and their organizations were incongruent and the consequences can be seen as clear acts of folly! Without risk, empowerment is hollow but if those empowered are not allowed to make mistakes and fail, they will quickly learn to take no risks. We know of one junior level executive who was publicly humiliated in a board meeting for taking a risk. He almost left this organization and seriously questioned why he chose this field of endeavor. He stayed but was never quite the same. This event occurred three years ago and the behavioral residue is that he works extremely cautiously now and avoids conflict and threats. In working with him, we could see the potential of his high natural energy and motivation, but as much as he makes great starts and has periodic sputters with the promise of great results, he withdraws when things get risky. It is almost as if he is driving a car with his feet on both the accelerator and the brake. The new appearance of a tic in his eye may be a physical manifestation of the conflict going on inside of himself.

The purpose that underlies an effective basis of empowerment, as we have previously argued, must relate to enterprise-wide aims in some unambiguous way and not to narrow interests. Without the ability of individuals to learn from both their mistakes and their successes, the process of empowerment will ensure that the same errors will be made over and over again.

4.6   Delegation as Viewed by Individuals

As viewed by individuals in organizations, delegation is seen as a continuum of entrusting transactions. At one end of the spectrum, delegation is accomplished based on the simple assignment of tasks and at the other end, delegation is based on empowerment to produce results. Leaders can delegate tasks to individuals with little freedom of action or empower them with considerable personal latitude for making decisions and acting. The concept and the principle of delegating by way of purpose, from a leadership perspective, is congruent with being empowered from the viewpoint of individuals. Purposeful delegation means that individuals become accountable for results — for the consequences of work — for relevant output and not for completion of tasks and engagement in activities. Purposeful delegation implies that individuals are relatively free and expected to create leverage within their spheres of accountability. Similarly, delegation based on purpose provides an important avenue for leverage creation by leaders. Simply stated, delegation around purpose gives meaning and substance to the concept of empowerment.

A useful framework for enacting the principle, *Delegate Only Around Purpose*, is role negotiation. Role negotiation in this context clarifies, formalizes and establishes agreement between leaders and individuals for the results or outcomes for which the individuals will be held accountable. In our experience, shifting orientation from one associated with tasks and activities to one which is anchored on results or output tends to be resisted. The initial level of resistance is often associated with the fact that it requires a great deal of thought and work to define roles based on potential contribution to the output of the unit or to the overall organization. Resistance also becomes a consequence of challenging cherished tasks to discover whether or not they have a bearing on purpose and output. Further, there is often considerable perceived threat and therefore defensiveness associated with moving toward purposeful delegation. Defensive behavior appears to arise from the perceived loss of control of the factors which individuals feel make them "look good" — capable, competent, hardworking — or whatever constitutes "looking good" to the organization. Finally, there are structural and cultural factors, such as how performance is measured and what good performance means that will create resistance and which, in fact, must be addressed to enable the successful enactment of a new basis of delegation.

In this chapter, we have addressed issues of motivation, meaning, alignment, personal effectiveness and leverage creation and the dynamics of delegation and empowerment all from the perspective of individual members of organizations. Pertaining to these issues only a portion of the story has been told. Delegation is a two-way street, empowerment is a bi-lateral transaction, structure and culture change require the intervention of leaders and group action. We have attempted to deal only with the interests of individuals and the conditions under which individuals can make significant contributions and drive organizational effectiveness. This chapter, therefore, must be read and interpreted along with subsequent chapters focused on leaders and groups.

References

1. Handy, C., *The Age of Paradox*, Harvard Business School Press, Boston, 1994, 120.
2. Fromm, E., *The Sane Society*, Holt, Rinehart & Winston, New York, 1955, 159.
3. Wiener, Y., Commitment in Organizations: A Normative View, *Academy of Management Review*, 7, No. 3, 418, 1982.
4. Senge, P. M., *The Fifth Discipline: The Art and Practice of the Learning Organization*, Doubleday, New York, 1990, 221.
5. Frankl, V. E., *Man's Search for Meaning*, Washington Square Press, 1984, 131.
6. Undy, R. and Kessler, I., The Big Issue: Insecurity in the Work-place, *Management Studies at Oxford*, Winter, 1995/96.
7. Schein, E. H., *Organizational Psychology*, 3rd ed., Prentice-Hall, Englewood Cliffs, 1988, 57.
8. Maslow, A., *Motivation and Personality*, Harper, New York, 1954.
9. MacGregor, D., *The Human Side of Enterprise*, McGraw-Hill, New York, 1960.
10. Kegan, R., *The Evolving Self: Problem and Process in Human Development*, Harvard University Press, Boston, 1982.
11. Schein, E. H., *Organizational Psychology*, 3rd ed., Prentice-Hall, Englewood Cliffs, 1988, 77.
12. Katz, R., Job Longevity as a Situational Factor in Job Satisfaction, *Administrative Science Quarterly*, 23, 1978.
13. Pheffer, J., *Organizations and Organization Theory*, Pittman Publishing, Boston, 1982.
14. Burrell, G. and Morgan, G., *Sociological Paradigms and Organisational Analysis: Elements of the Sociology of Corporate Life*, Heinemann Educational Books, London, 1979, 227.
15. Moore, T., *Care of the Soul: A Guide for Cultivating Depth and Sacredness in Everyday Life*, Harper Collins, New York, 1992, 90.
16. Rogers, C. R., *Client-Centered Therapy: Its Current Practice, Implications and Theory*, Houghton Mifflin, Boston, 1951, 72.
17. Senge, P. M., *The Fifth Discipline: The Art and Practice of the Learning Organization*, Doubleday, New York, 1990, 205.
18. Hertzberg, F., *Work and the Nature of Man*, World Publishing Company, Cleveland, 1966.
19. Maslow, A., *Motivation and Personality*, Harper, New York, 1954.
20. Schein, E. H., *Organizational Psychology*, 3rd ed., Prentice-Hall, Englewood Cliffs, 1988, 71.
21. Dopson, S. and Neumann. J., Uncertainty, Contrariness and the Double-Bind: Middle Managers' Reactions to their Changing Contracts, *Management Research Papers*, Templeton College, Oxford, April 1994, 17.

22. Covey, S. R., *The Seven Habits of Highly Effective People: Restoring the Character Ethic*, Simon & Schuster, New York, 1989.
23. Pedler, M., Burgoyne, J. and Boydell, T., *The Learning Company*, 2nd ed., McGraw-Hill Companies, London, 1997, 150.
24. Handy, C., *The Age of Unreason*, Harvard Business School Press, Boston, 1989, 64.
25. Douglas, N. and Wykowski, T., Empowerment: The Promise and the Reality, *AFSM International, The Professional Journal*, August 1993.

Chapter 5

Individuals: *Enhance the Efficacy of Institutional Knowledge*

Anticipatory Summary

Individuals create organizations and the perceptions, beliefs, fears and aspirations of individuals shape the cultures of these organizations. These created cultures then take on the character of objective reality, transcending individuals. Through the process of internalizing culture by individuals, culture becomes their subjective reality thus closing the loop. At the level of the individual, this process of internalizing culture defines the heart of the difficulty in altering assumptions and bringing about organizational learning and change.

- Institutional knowledge embodies assumptions that have become crystallized and taken for granted. Since challenges to our hardened assumptions threaten the certainty we believe they represent, individuals tend to defend them.
- If assumptions drive behavior, it follows that behavior illuminates underlying assumptions. What individuals in organizations *do* is the source of illumination, not what they *say*.

- When circumstances change, at least some of the basic assumptions embedded in an organization's culture become no longer valid; the inability to assimilate new knowledge which is incongruent with the stock of existing embedded assumptions is seen as a primary barrier to change.
- The principle, *Enhance the Efficacy of Institutional Knowledge*, refers to building the capacity to comprehend and alter institutional knowledge to bring about a desired effect. The challenge for individuals operates on three levels:
  - to develop the capacity to assimilate new knowledge,
  - to be able to avoid the temptation to simply replace one set of assumptions with another,
  - to maintain the ability to reproduce actions (within the context of existing assumptions) with an economy of effort when appropriate.

5.1   Freeing Individuals from the Grip of Institutional Knowledge

- The preparation or positioning of individuals to engage with other individuals in the process of enhancing the efficacy of institutional knowledge is a matter of choice and ability; it is also a fundamental step in priming an organization for learning.

5.2   The Role of Individuals in Collective Learning

- Examining and rethinking assumptions, formulating new and more relevant ones when appropriate, and sustaining the capacity for such enhancement of institutional knowledge is the essence of organizational learning.
- The mental attitude required of individuals is one of on-going readiness for interpretation — one that seeks to understand, unscramble and explain the meaning of circumstances and events.
- Individuals are required to balance modes of interaction and learning and to apply imagination, frames of reference and colleagueship.
- The interpretive stance of individuals will make participant-observers of them; a critical mass of these participant-observers will prime the organization or the group in question for learning and effective action.

Individuals: *Enhance the Efficacy of Institutional Knowledge*

We have described institutional knowledge as that aspect of organizational culture which embodies underlying assumptions. These assumptions frame collective perceptions in organizations and ultimately influence behavior. The assumptions in question represent attitudes, values, beliefs and myths. There are assumptions about the world in general, the nature of human beings, what constitutes security and insures long-term employment, what good performance means and what is important to customers. Collective experience is encapsulated in institutional knowledge. Sense can be made of such experience in a variety of ways; it can be passed down by word of mouth and storytelling and in formal documents. Whether or not these experience-driven assumptions are valid, they provide a useful function — they answer questions and mitigate uncertainty. These assumptions may or may not be fully comprehended and espoused but they are operative, i.e., in Chris Argyris' terms, these are "theories-in-use." Edgar Schein in his book *Organizational Culture and Leadership* asks, "If a group's culture is that group's accumulated learning, how do we describe and catalog the content of that learning?" He goes on to state "the deeper levels of learning that get us to the essence of culture must be thought of as ... shared basic assumptions."[1] Shared basic assumptions come together to establish the content of institutional knowledge at the most fundamental level.

The meaning associated with the actions of individuals in organizations can be thought of as forming the stocks of institutional knowledge pertaining to those organizations. It follows then that if assumptions drive behavior, behavior illuminates underlying assumptions. What individuals in organizations *do* is the source of illumination, not what they *say*. For example, when individuals in organizations say that "people are our greatest assets," yet treat people as if they had little value, the underlying assumption is that people do not matter. If members of an organization talk about how important customer satisfaction is but behave in ways that place their own interests ahead of those of their customers, the operative assumption is that the needs of customers are not as important as their own needs. If an organization says that it values open communication and yet punishes those who speak out about important issues, the underlying assumption is that conforming behavior is what the organization values. Our interpretation of the actions of individuals in organizations then takes on meaning and these explicit meanings form what can be thought of as stocks of institutional knowledge.

Institutional knowledge tends to be stable, durable and highly resistant to change. Institutional knowledge embodies sets of assumptions that have taken on a life of their own — assumptions that have become crystallized, most often taken for granted and operate outside of awareness. Since challenges to our hardened assumptions threaten the certainty we believe they represent, individuals are not prone to examination of them, favoring instead to deny the challenges and defend their assumptions. Members of organizations often appear to be blindfolded with their hands over their ears when confronted with challenges to their institutional knowledge. As we argued in Chapter 1, institutional knowledge can become a constraint on learning and effective change, and at a deeper level, on purposeful behavior. The inability to assimilate new knowledge, knowledge that is incongruent with the stock of existing embedded assumptions, is seen as a primary barrier to beneficial change.

Institutional knowledge is not single-dimensional. In differentiated organizations, i.e., those with numerous functions and occupational and professional groupings, multiple stocks of knowledge are typically at work and interacting in unpredictable and often unintended ways. As a result of training and professional socialization, members of such groupings as engineering, geology, manufacturing, sales, software development, surgery, internal medicine and administration operate out of sets of defining assumptions. As individuals with a common orientation come together in units within an organization, other sets of assumptions can be expected to emerge reflecting the context of the units within the organization. The inter-working of different sets of assumptions heightens the challenge of comprehending the dimensions and content of institutional knowledge associated with larger organizations.

All circumstances and environments — markets, economies and internal organizational dynamics — are subject to change and when they change, at least some of the basic assumptions embedded in an organization's culture become no longer valid. The ability to build institutional self-awareness, to learn and adapt must become an aspect of culture for organizations seeking long-term success. The principle, *Enhance the Efficacy of Institutional Knowledge*, refers to building the capacity to comprehend and alter institutional knowledge to bring about a desired effect. Cultural analysis has been defined as the discovery and explanation of basic assumptions. This principle then relates in a direct way to the dynamic process of culture creation and management. The aim is to enhance the relevance and accuracy of the assumptions that drive behavior — to provide, in other words, a necessary precondition for learning and therefore effective change. The challenge for individuals operates on three levels:

1. To develop the capacity to assimilate new knowledge
2. To be able to avoid on a continuing basis the seduction of simply replacing one set of assumptions with another
3. Bearing in mind the beneficial dimension of institutional knowledge, to maintain the ability to reproduce actions with an economy of effort when appropriate

Institutional knowledge represents objective reality. It has an existence apart from the individual members of the organization around or within which such knowledge is present. Yet, as we saw in the explanation of the Integrative Model for Learning and Change in Chapter 2, objective reality exists in a continual state of mutual influence with respect to the subjective nature of the individuals that make up the organization. This relationship was expressed as a circular one: individuals create organizations; organizations take on the form of objective reality; individuals are shaped by organizations. ("Organization" above refers to culture as culture becomes hardened and institutionalized and embraces both behavior and knowledge or basic assumptions.)

The enterprise defined by thought, learning and creativity is essentially a collective matter. The actual process of enhancing the efficacy of institutional knowledge occurs in the crucible of group settings. Individuals, however, form groups and what they bring to groups in the shape of personal embeddedness in one or more manifestations of institutional knowledge plays a major role in the ultimate effectiveness of groups. Returning to the expression of circular relationship between individuals and organizations, individuals create organizations and the perceptions, beliefs, fears and aspirations of individuals shape the cultures of these organizations. These created cultures then take on the character of objective reality, transcending individuals. Through the process of internalizing culture by individuals working in organizations, the culture becomes their subjective reality thus closing the loop. At the level of the individual, this process of internalizing culture defines the essence of the difficulty of altering assumptions and bringing about organizational learning and change.

Recalling constructive-developmental theory as discussed in Chapter 3, the extent to which individual group members are able to detach themselves from their hardened perceptions is highly variable from person to person. In other words, the degree to which individuals are able to avoid the tendency for the organization's objective reality to become their own subjective reality largely determines their learning potential. This capacity on the part of the individuals that make up the group will regulate whether or not the group will be able to decipher institutional knowledge, examine and rethink assumptions and construct new and more relevant ones. Building on the concepts and arguments developed in the previous chapters focused on individuals, this chapter explores the role individuals play in enhancing the efficacy of institutional knowledge, how individuals can become better positioned to fuel organizational learning and change and how individuals can help their organizations escape the grip of hardened and often obsolete assumptions.

5.1   Freeing Individuals from the Grip of Institutional Knowledge

The preparation or positioning of individuals to engage with other individuals in the process of enhancing the efficacy of institutional knowledge is a fundamental step in priming an organization for learning. A group process of this sort is concerned with deciphering and comprehending institutional knowledge, examining and rethinking basic assumptions, constructing new and more relevant ones when appropriate and sustaining the means to do all of this on an on-going basis. As a starting point, individuals must come to terms with the mechanics of perception as it relates to them personally. The ability to discover and understand the character and power of one's own mental models and patterns of attribution and defensiveness is a prerequisite to useful, collective work at any level. We have seen how our mental models and the results and process of attribution work together to form our perceptions and how perceived threat to our assumptions and sense-making plays out as defensive attitudes and behaviors.

All of us have the ability, albeit varying widely, to stand outside ourselves and reflect on what makes us tick, what makes us who we are. To engage with others in a process of understanding and challenging the nature and shape of circumstances affecting the group demands, first of all, a capacity and skill for self reflection. In our work with individuals in various settings, from individual interviews to analysis of cases to preparation for role negotiation, using virtually any legal and ethical methods we can devise, we challenge, encourage and help individuals to reflect on themselves — to access the constructs that drive their perceptions. Our focus is always on perceptions related to the organizational roles of the individuals in question. An approach that frequently bears fruit is to explore the consequences of effort and work backwards to assumptions. We ask individuals to identify, in objective and observable terms, the consequences or results of their efforts in their assigned roles. Working backwards, we explore the actions that would produce such consequences. Working backwards from actions, we try to bring to the surface and make conscious the assumptions that would give rise to their actions. Consider the following simple but meaningful example. A product marketing vice president could assert that the major consequence of her functioning as chief of product marketing would be an improved share of the market for her company's primary product line. The actions she might specify as those most important in achieving her outcome goal could include helping to define a new profile for salespeople, supporting the recruitment of a largely new sales staff and developing a training program for the new people. The assumption underlying these actions would turn out to be something like: "our salespeople are the reason why our market share has not improved." A little further inquiry could bring to the surface some additional factors underpinning her basic assumption. These might include 1) a defensive reaction to the vice president of sales' assertion that the company's products are not competitive and 2) an attribution that poor sales performance is due to the belief that most salespeople are opportunistic, superficial and unwilling to spend the effort to become knowledgeable. These underlying factors define the mental models and patterns of attribution and defensiveness of this person in this situation in interaction with a significant peer (the vice president of sales).

The basic assumption related to poor performance in the marketplace and the mental models and attributions of the marketing vice president may or may not be accurate. Poor market performance could be due to any number of circumstances including those identified by the product marketing chief and/or the perceptions of the head of sales. The point here is not related to accuracy but rather with the role of assumptions, of our personal mechanics of perception, in the actions we take. As individuals, the ability to stand apart from ourselves and catalogue and observe our deepest assumptions translates directly into an ability to do the same at the level of the group or the organization. The analysis by individuals of how their own assumptions and those of the group or the organization as a whole overlap and are or are not congruent further positions individuals to be able to engage in group learning and creativity, to escape the grip of institutional knowledge.

5.2   The Role of Individuals in Collective Learning

Examining and rethinking assumptions, formulating new and more relevant ones when appropriate, and sustaining the capacity for such enhancement of institutional knowledge is the essence of organizational learning. The environment for such work is necessarily groups and the essential mode of interaction within groups is a blend or a balance of dialogue and advocacy. By dialogue, we mean collective discussion and reasoning as a method of intellectual investigation. Dialogue is how we go beyond one person's understanding and develop richer perspectives. Advocacy, in contrast, is the necessary counterpart to dialogue. In advocacy, points of view are argued, decisions are made and courses of action are agreed upon. As previously introduced, Chris Argyris has described two modes of learning that pertain to both organizations and individuals.[2] Single-loop learning implies that assumptions or "governing values" are held constant and that thought and action vary only within the set of existing assumptions. Single-loop learning is appropriate most of the time. It makes no sense to constantly question the assumptions regarding much of the routine of organizational life. Double-loop learning, on the other hand, holds fundamental assumptions up for evaluation and reformulation. Most organizations excel in single-loop learning, a circumstance which subtly works against developing the capacity for double-loop learning, for reshaping organizations when threat or opportunity loom.

These modes of interaction and learning will be fully explored in subsequent chapters pertaining to groups. With our focus now on individuals, however, it must be stated that achieving the proper balance in both modes of interaction and learning is very difficult. The context, the guiding framework and the motivation for individuals to engage in such work can only come from purpose and its common understanding. Purpose is a collaborative notion that transcends individuals without diminishing them. For individuals, a sustained orientation to the actual and potential consequences of action related to purpose can provide both the motivation and the context for stepping outside themselves in the interest of the common cause.

The ability of individuals to suspend or temporarily hold in abeyance their assumptions enables them to hear and comprehend the ideas and perspectives of other people. Making sense and discerning the relevance and merit of other perspectives, both individually and in group processes, requires imagination, frames of reference and colleagueship. As consultants, we seek to be instrumental in preparing individuals for effective group involvement by calling upon the use of imagination in generating a prospective orientation. Thinking about and answering forward looking questions help engage the imagination. Examples of such questions include:

> What does success for your unit look like, i.e., how would you know in three, four or five years that your unit was successful in objective terms?
> What are the observable features of a desired new culture?

How would you know, if you went away for a year and returned, that a new culture was in place?

If you had a magic wand and could change only one thing about life in this organization, what would you change?

What would be the consequences of such a change?

What is the most important result you could achieve to promote the purpose of your department specifically and your organization as a whole?

According to Ray Anthony, an author and specialist in organizational innovation, "imaginative people use 'kaleidoscopic thinking': taking data, situations, phenomena, and assumptions, and then mixing, twisting, shaking, or otherwise manipulating them to see new patterns. They give unpredictable, unexpected answers or interpretations to questions or situations." Anthony has coined the term "assumption bandwidth" which defines the range of assumptions and extent of options a person possesses. The goal is to stretch and ultimately broaden the bandwidth using imagination to not only test but to reconfigure assumptions.[3] We're reminded of an iconoclastic vice president in an international energy company who was out of the norm in terms of style and way of being. He challenged everything; he was also bright and creative. He made great contributions and the company was, without question, better off because of his approach and his accomplishments. There is an imperative for creative and imaginative individuals to challenge assumptions and become catalysts for learning. There is a corresponding imperative for everyone else to allow the out of the norm people to be imaginative and to challenge cherished assumptions in the interest of producing results. The development of such a basis of relating to each other can embolden and help activate the imaginations of everyone else, enhancing the creative capacity of any group. There is an essential test for individuals seeking to engage their imaginations and participate in dialogue and group learning. F. Scott Fitzgerald believed the test of a first class mind to be the ability to hold two opposing ideas in the mind at the same time and still retain the ability to function.

Our personal experiences, as synthesized and collected in our unconscious mental and defensive models, can represent a potential downside for us by constraining learning. However, if we are aware of them, they may also provide a benefit by helping us to understand and relate to new information — to a description of reality that is closer to the truth. Our experiences provide frames of reference without which we are likely to misinterpret, or not interpret at all, events and circumstances that are important to us. Stories of this phenomenon are plentiful. Charles Handy tells the story of the Peruvian Indians who "seeing the sails of their Spanish invaders on the horizon, put it all down to a freak of the weather and went on about their business having no concept of sailing ships in their limited experience."[4] No example of frame of reference is as powerful as that embodied in the history and growth of the early Church especially as related to the institution of the Mass. "It (the Mass) was a conception long sanctified by time; the pagan mind needed no schooling to receive it; by embodying in it the 'mystery of the Mass', Christianity became the last and greatest of the mystery religions. It was a custom lowly in origin and beautiful in development. Its adoption was part of the profound wisdom with which the Church adapted itself to the symbols of the age and the needs of the people; no other ceremony could have so heartened the essential solitary soul or so strengthened it to face a hostile world."[5] Without a frame of reference, Handy's Peruvians made no sense of the sailing ships. In contrast, accessing frames of reference through a process of linking new expressions of worship with previously established models (consciously or otherwise), the Church instituted and has sustained for 2000 years the centrality of the Eucharist.

The process of priming an organization for learning and change requires individuals who are primed for learning and change. As individuals, we need to use every means possible to create an internal atmosphere that will enhance our capacity to learn and grow. A personal tool for priming is to evaluate our experiences and create our own frames of reference. Our experiences in any role in the present or the past can provide a frame of reference for assessing and relating to ideas and perceptions that differ from our own in the immediate context. We can prompt ourselves with questions such as: What does my experience tell me about this? If I consciously scrutinize my experience in other settings and times, does what I am hearing now make any more sense? In large measure, the power of concepts in language and logic such as the metaphor, the paradox, the allegory and the parable lies in the frame of reference they provide. These constructs can provide a linkage between new ideas and our common experience. In *Reframing Organizations*, Lee Bolman and Terrence Deal recommend the use of metaphors, humor and play to "illustrate the important 'as if' quality of symbols. They are indirect ways to grapple with issues that are too complex, mysterious, or threatening to approach head-on. Metaphors make the strange familiar and the familiar strange. They help us capture subtle themes that normal language can overlook."[6] We observed the use of a metaphor in a chemical plant in the Midwest to unleash the creative, problem-solving abilities of several chemical engineers. The team had been groping for weeks to find the source of a leakage problem. They could not find where the flow process was breaking down. Finally, the facilitator jumped up and said, "all right, we are all in a prisoner of war camp and we've all got to get out fast. How can we escape?" The problem was solved within a couple of hours by engaging everyone in the process of transferring the technical leakage problem to the terms and dynamics of the metaphor, i.e., of escaping from a prisoner of war camp. Finding a way out of the prisoner of war camp was like finding the soft spots in the system responsible for the leakage.

Finally, collective learning requires that we hold each other and our often differing points of views with regard and respect. Colleagueship, in other words, is essential for accessing and making sense of the best that individuals bring to groups. Colleagueship suggests the presence of positive assumptions about the motives and goals of others. Colleagueship implies that trust exists; it enables diverse opinions to exist without threatening the cohesiveness of the group. As individuals, we cannot determine whether others will treat us and each other as colleagues. It is only within our power to control our own attitudes and behavior. Since colleagueship begets colleagueship, the imperative for individuals is first to grant colleagueship to others. As the words of the old hymn suggest, "Let there be peace on earth, and let it begin with me." If we find the granting of colleagueship across the board to be too difficult, we can begin by granting colleagueship as the context demands, i.e., granting colleagueship within the immediate setting where everyone in the group has a stake in learning and change.

Sustaining the capacity for examining assumptions and formulating new and more relevant ones when change is indicated is without a doubt a formidable challenge for individuals. When environments change and organizations go through the rigorous and difficult work of adapting (assuming they are able to adapt in time), a great and seductive force emerges which entices organization members to the point of hardening the new assumptions and returning to business as usual. Such a pattern over time looks like a repeated cycle of: learning and nonlearning, learning and nonlearning — with the long-term effect of institutional Russian roulette (maybe the organization will survive through the current dislocation or maybe it won't). Individuals tend to be comfortable with the perception of certainty associated with working and living surrounded by hardened assumptions. However, it is a perception only and a dangerous one in the world of modern organizations and markets. Learning must become a state of being for organizations and for the individuals who inhabit them and not a conception of response to crisis or extreme threat. The mental attitude required of individuals is one of on-going readiness for interpretation — one that seeks to understand, unscramble and explain the meaning of circumstances and events. Shapiro and Carr in their book, *Lost in Familiar Places*, introduce the term "interpretive stance" to assign a name to this way of looking at things. An interpretive stance acknowledges the ambiguities and uncertainties of life. It is speculative and imaginative; "it allows the possibility of proceeding from one hypothesis to another hypothesis rather than from uncertainty to certainly." Building, changing, evolving organizational culture, or more specifically, institutional knowledge, can be described as creating a shared or collaborative interpretation. "Any shared interpretation must bring together individuals, context (purpose) and connections (relationships)."[7] (Words in parentheses are those of the authors.) The interpretive stance of individuals will make participant-observers of them. Participant-observers are able to experience and think at the same time. They stand both inside and outside themselves and both inside and outside their organizations. They employ knowledge about themselves and about possibilities and keep organizational purpose as their guidepost for thought, learning and actions.

Individuals who are committed to learning and striving to see reality more clearly bring value to organizations that transcends their functional expertise. A critical mass of these participant-observers will prime the organization or the group in question for learning and effective action. Leaders have the duty to insure that purpose is clear and that an environment exists which is safe for individuals to reflect and challenge deeply embedded assumptions. An especially challenging task for leaders is to bring about a climate that minimally threatens the identity and perceived integrity of individuals less naturally inclined to interpretations of their surroundings. All of this said, however, for individuals to become learners in the most fundamental sense, i.e., out of a narrow subject matter context, is a matter of choice and ability. No amount of exhortation or incentive will bring individuals to this point. The ability to examine assumptions objectively and escape from the grasp of defensiveness are factors that hold equal standing with the motivation to do so.

References

1. Schein, E. H., *Organizational Culture and Leadership,* 2nd ed., Jossey-Bass, San Francisco, 1992, 11.
2. Argyris, C., *Overcoming Organizational Defenses: Facilitating Organizational Learning,* Allyn & Bacon, Boston, 1990, 92.
3. Anthony, R., 10 Traits of Creative People, *Executive Excellence*, August, 1991.
4. Handy, C., *The Age of Unreason,* Harvard Business School Press, Boston, 1989, 9.

5. Durant, W., *The Story of Civilization: Caesar and Christ,* MJF Books, New York, 1944, 600.
6. Bolman, L. G. and Deal, T. E., *Reframing Organizations: Artistry, Choice, and Leadership,* 2nd ed., Jossey-Bass Publishers, San Francisco, 1997.
7. Shapiro, E. R. and Carr, A. W., *Lost in Familiar Places: Creating New Connections Between the Individual and Society,* Yale University Press, New Haven, 1991, 75.

LEADERS

Introduction

To a greater extent than with individuals and groups, the three principles become integrated around the dimension of leadership. As a consequence, discussion of the meaning and application of these principles in the chapters focused on leaders will be less oriented to the principles as discrete entities and more to how they interrelate. As an additional introductory comment, while it is in fashion to differentiate the meanings of management and leadership, our aim is to not enter this semantic exercise. To describe managers as functionaries and leaders as visionaries does little to advance the understanding and practice of applying resources to achieve useful ends. Such practice can be accurately defined as either leading or managing according to the *Oxford Concise Dictionary*. Terms derived from both manage and lead are therefore used interchangeably with no implied difference in meaning.

This book at its core is about leadership. However, it is about leadership in the broadest sense where the term *leader* may be applied to the committed and the empowered engineer, accountant, physician, nurse, teacher, designer, administrator, staff manager, general manager or chief executive. The difference across this spectrum of roles lies not in the fundamental meaning of leadership but rather in the proportion of time and energy the individual allocates to producing results through other people. The movement across this spectrum from left to right should bring about increasing levels of humility based on the proposition that less and less real work is personally accomplished by the leader. More specifically then, this book is about accessing purposeful behavior to bring about achievement of organizational potential. It is about effective intervention to engender learning and useful and enduring change. It is perhaps not an exaggeration to suggest that the existence of change is why leaders are needed. If a state of changelessness could persist, we could all quite happily go about our static lives without the bother of leading or being led.

Perfection as a standard is irrelevant for human beings and anything we undertake. Therefore, there are no perfect leaders and no perfect models for leadership — highly celebrated successes and exalted leaders notwithstanding. There is no binary state of leadership quality — good or bad. We have to be satisfied with notions of "relatively effective" and "relatively ineffective" as applied to leaders where the essential criterion is results or consequences of leadership intervention. The more relevant standard for leaders is whether or not value is added. There is an argument that leadership is highly situational, that effectiveness as a leader is a function of style or characteristics meeting the requirements of time and place. Our experience suggests that this argument is valid more often than not but that there are exceptions or outliers. Some individuals in leadership positions seem to never add value regardless of time and place, and others seem to be able to create results irrespective of the setting.

The characteristic that seems to be always present in effective leaders is a clear sense of purpose and the ability to engage people and hold them accountable for results related to purpose. Consistently good leadership performance over time embraces the additional characteristic of comprehension of how subjective factors, those residing in the minds and emotions of those being led, will either facilitate or constrain objective achievement. These characteristics, taken with the ability to sustain an environment where basic assumptions are continually in a state of interpretation and enhancement, form the set of characteristics that appear to be present in leaders that succeed over time in various settings. The convergence of the principles *Delegate Only Around Purpose, Achieve an Operative Balance of Objective and Subjective Factors,* and *Enhance the Efficacy of Institutional Knowledge* frames, as clearly as we can, a *leader for all seasons.*

Late 20th century organizations, aiming to become well positioned for the 21st Century, have a profound need for their members to come to a state of thinking and acting like leaders. Individuals growing through the principles articulated and applied in the previous chapters will have become leaders in the most basic sense whether formally appointed as leaders or not. Formal leaders will have moved closer to proceeding and behaving consistently with the vital meaning of leadership. Applied at any level, we believe the essential role of leaders embraces the following: creating clarity of purpose and relevant outcomes; building and contributing to a spirit of collaboration and colleagueship; fostering and participating in interdependent behavior around results; and providing a context for learning. Speaking pragmatically, the consequence of effective performance in this role — the bottom line or the cash value, in other words — is creating leverage. To review, by leverage we mean creating a multiplier effect on the product of time and energy, i.e., adding value to the production of results that exceeds one's direct input.

It is self-evident that leaders who produce outcomes by way of the work of others do not personally produce anything. They don't engineer and build products, they don't sell products and services, and they don't take care of patients, cook meals and clean floors in hospitals. The leader's role is to facilitate the output of those who produce; there is no other reason for the existence of managers at this level. If production is enhanced in terms of quality, quantity or relevance as a consequence of the presence and action of leaders, positive leverage or value is created. If such enhancement does not occur, negative leverage is created, or at best, there is a neutral effect of leadership. This leads us to believe that there should be a Hippocratic-like oath for managers: first, do no harm!

The hubris associated with high management positions often brings about an illusion of control in the minds of some leaders. This illusion is especially strong in leaders who produce limited or marginal results. The practice of killing the messenger, while serving to protect the illusion, is the greatest known method for ensuring that subordinates will lie to leaders and withhold crucial information. Leaders' patterns of defensiveness resulting from failing to deal with important subjective issues will also obscure the truth. If organizational purpose is ambiguous and bureaucracy evolves based on tasks and functions, some purpose will exist in the minds of people but it probably won't be the same purpose as that which exists in the minds of the leaders. This disconnectedness and lack of motivating purpose allows basic assumptions about the organization, its members, its markets and its environment to go unchallenged and remain in place. The organization will be controlled by these assumptions to a far greater extent than by its leaders. Sincere and careful listening to people will tend to dispel this myth of control and free leaders from this illusion. Effective leaders are more secure, less afraid of the truth and uncertainty, more humble and less inclined to believe that they have to be in control in order for results to be produced.

It is the leader's duty and responsibility to create a learning environment — a culture which brings about purposeful behavior and enhanced results. The culture must be one where purpose is not only grasped and internalized by organizational members, but one where purpose itself has been defined and translated as broadly as possible. The culture must be one in which defensive attitudes and erroneous perceptions are readily surfaced and the resolution of conflict and the mitigation of defensive behavior are common features of everyday life in the organization. Relevant opinions must be welcomed and challenging basic assumptions or institutional knowledge must not only be tolerated but encouraged. Learning in such a context must be highly valued and rewarded. The indispensable task, then, for leaders is to design and sustain a framework for individuals, both as individuals and in groups, to be their best — to create a critical mass of people being and doing their best thereby effecting momentum in bringing about useful change and achieving potential.

Discernment and courage are indispensable traits in leaders. Good judgment, a sense of perspective, the willingness to face difficult circumstances and take unpopular and controversial positions flow out of these traits. Nowhere are these as important as in the arena of recruiting, selecting, developing and retaining people. We believe in developing people and that the capacity exists in most individuals to become committed, aligned, empowered and effective. We are not, however, adherents of the "never give up on people" school of thought. Leaders must, therefore, act to sanction or even remove individuals when it becomes clear that the ability or the will to change doesn't exist. Too much damage can accrue from not acting and even delaying action; there is too little time and the cost is too great.

Our final introductory comment to these chapters focused on leaders concerns the notion that leaders represent a practice dimension in the same manner as do individuals and groups. Often, perhaps usually, leaders believe that interventions and developmental work applies only to the others, i.e., the followers, the team. In our experience and much to the surprise of leaders, change is required of them as much if not more as it is required of others. Our most successful work has been when leaders themselves have been open, willing and able to change. In almost all of our projects, we reach a point of asking ourselves, when do we hold the mirror up to the leader? Timing is critical because all too often when a leader is given bad news or when perceptions about his or her effectiveness as a leader are not congruent with their perceptions of themselves, there is always the possibility that the results of the project could be compromised or the project ended abruptly. We have witnessed radical turns in consequences when leaders courageously face up to the implications of their behavior in the success or failure of a project. This is the time when the leader stands alone and makes a private decision to learn and change, laying the foundation for learning and change for his or her group.

Chapter 6

Leaders: *Achieve an Operative Balance of Objective and Subjective Factors*

Anticipatory Summary

Objective factors such as the processes and outputs of production or financial and market performance provide the setting for applying the efforts, skills, creativity and motivation of people. Subjective factors such as imagination, positive feelings and personal commitment can drive objective achievement; negative emotions, erroneous perceptions and defensiveness can constrain achievement. Comprehending the relationship between objective and subjective factors, where each is cause and effect with respect to the other, and acting within such comprehension can be a source of great leadership leverage.

6.1   *The Fine Balance — Equilibrium for Leaders*

■ Operative balance refers to an effective equilibrium — an equilibrium that brings about and sustains a desired state of organizational existence.

■ The pendulum in organizational change efforts swings back and forth between objective focus and subjective focus. The excesses that define the extremes of swings in one direction seem to be the consequences of acting within the extremes of the other.

■ To consider one aspect of reality without paying attention to the other is to misperceive the true nature of the whole of an organization and life within it.

■ The challenge for leaders is to understand this reality themselves and then to communicate their understanding in such a way as to bring about an enriching and broadening of such understanding.

6.2   *The Leader as Creator of Equilibrium*

■ The essential functions of leadership include:
  ■ creating clarity of purpose and relevant output;
  ■ building and sustaining a spirit of collaboration and colleagueship;
  ■ fostering interdependent behavior centered on results;
  ■ providing a context for learning.

■ These aspects of leadership blend objective and subjective factors. For leaders then, the central task is to create an environment wherein an operative balance of objective and subjective factors can be achieved.

■ Perhaps the most significant result of such a balance is an environment that is hospitable to the truth — an environment that frames and supports the seeking and the finding of valid information.

■ Leaders either act to create environments within which valid information is valued and pursued or their attitudes and behaviors bring about environments where the truth seldom emerges.

■ Integrity and success in leadership are vitally linked. Congruent speaking and acting brings forth positive results while incongruence undermines the best intentions.

■ As leverage naturally attaches to leadership, a negative multiplier attaches to the defensive behavior of leaders fueling the creation of defensive norms that take on a life of their own.

6.3   Self-Awareness for Leaders

■ Comprehensive instruments that help to clarify underlying personal needs and potential stress or defensive behaviors are useful in enhancing self-awareness of leaders.

■ Armed with self knowledge, leaders can sustain their own internal equilibrium; they can maximize their strengths and compensate for their weaknesses.

Leaders: *Achieve an Operative Balance of Objective and Subjective Factors*

Results matter and people matter. While results represent an organization's objective reason to exist, people reflect an organization's subjective reality. The relationship between results and people is the central relationship around which organizational success turns, which accounts for the relevance of this principle for leaders. To quote Peter Drucker, "The main purpose and function of the enterprise is the production of goods not the governance of men."[1] But organizations are abstractions — *people* produce goods and services. Factors that are generally understood to be objective, such as the processes and outputs of production or financial performance or market performance, provide the arena for applying the efforts, skills, creativity and motivation of people. Subjective factors, such as imagination, good feelings and personal commitment can drive objective achievement, while negative emotions, erroneous perceptions and defensiveness can constrain achievement. Comprehending the relationship between objective and subjective factors, where each is cause and effect with respect to the other and acting within it, therefore, can be a source of great leadership leverage.

As organizational behavior consultants, we are typically asked to work with organizations on projects where human dynamics issues are thought to be constraining achievement. Often, our involvement is in projects with a purely objective focus that are failing to deliver expected results. Such projects include quality management, re-engineering and work redesign initiatives. More frequently than not, the process being studied and its new design are relatively simple and straightforward — "not quantum mechanics," as one of our clients is fond of saying. Given that new designs of this sort tend to represent no great intellectual achievement, we always ask "why hasn't this been done before?" Our experience suggests that unless that question can be answered, the reasons why problems existed in the first place will be the same reasons why new processes will not be successfully implemented. These kinds of reasons tend to point to subjective factors such as patterns of defensiveness related to territory and status, attribution and individualistic perception.

6.1   The Fine Balance — Equilibrium for Leaders

We have argued that it is a fundamental responsibility of leaders to understand, achieve and maintain a proper and operative balance between the apparent opposites of objective and subjective realities. "Operative balance" refers to some effective equilibrium — an equilibrium that brings about a desired effect. As previously asserted, this desired effect should relate directly to objective results. While there is no formula for how the proper balance should be expressed, it is clear that imbalance means too much of an orientation to objective factors and too little to subjective ones or vice versa. In any given situation, the perception of proper balance comes down to the leader's judgment — based on perspective, wisdom, experience and courage.

A consistent theme throughout this book is that the nature of organizations and the character of life within them is a coexistence of two realities — an objective reality and a subjective reality. To consider one aspect of reality without paying attention to the other is to misperceive the true nature of the whole of an organization and life within it. Thinking about "wholes" with regard to organizations embraces thought about material reality, i.e., physical assets, earnings and markets, along with the less tangible human dynamics affected by thoughts, feelings and perceptions of individuals and the effects of one reality upon the other. Accurately seeing the whole extends across time: the well-being in the present, the fundamentals that drive potential for the future and the effects of the past on both the present and the future. Thinking about wholes leads further to an awareness of the distortions coming from either too much of an orientation to subjective factors or too much of the same related to objective ones. If leaders hope to add value through their efforts, they must understand the whole of their organization's reality and act within that understanding.

We have argued in earlier chapters that the pendulum in organizational change efforts seems to swing back and forth between objective focus and subjective focus. The excesses that define the extremes of swings in one direction seem to be the consequences of acting within the extremes of the other. For example, we have seen organizations that, by any objective standard, have too many employees and where work expands to meet available man-hours. In such organizations, there tends to be a burden of marginal and poor performers that managers appear to be powerless to do anything about. This situation which is or at least has been, a fairly common one, can be traced to a variety of factors not the least of which are the policies that focus too much on the subjective needs of people, policies that overly protect people. These kinds of policies make it so difficult to effectively sanction poor performance that leaders give up and either add people to get the work done or settle for less than adequate performance for their units. In environments such as these, providing a secure, protected and comfortable work climate, for whatever reason, takes precedence over producing objective results.

There are many examples in our experience of how too much of a subjectively good thing creates disastrous objective consequences. An instance that clearly illustrates this circumstance relates to the operation of a key department of a large organization. A unit of the department existed to organize supplies, maintain instruments and provide both instruments and supplies to meet the requirements of specialized procedures. The purpose of the larger department was to organize and support the completion of these procedures. The performance of the unit in question was so poor and had been poor for so long that users of the department's services had reached a state of complete frustration and many were taking their business elsewhere. The horror stories regarding this unit were legendary. The employees of the unit were relatively low skill-level people. All indications were that the solution to this long standing and significant problem required a transition to employees with higher levels of skill and motivation. The leaders of the department and the unit, however, failed to set objective standards, hold employees accountable for those standards, upgrade skill levels and begin to replace employees. Instead, they continued to counsel and work with existing employees in the apparent belief that if these people felt supported and felt good enough about themselves, they would improve. The leaders were also careful to follow human resources policies and fearful of potential grievances and even union action. All the while, "Rome was burning!" In over two years, the problem was never solved. The objective needs of the department seemed to be held hostage to a subjectively-driven view of the needs of a small number of low-level employees. The consequences in terms of lost business for the department and the organization, the reputation of the organization and its competitive position vastly overshadowed any potential downside associated with acting to solve this problem.

At the other end of the swing of the pendulum, we find organizations that are focused on objective results measured and comprehended in the relatively short term to the exclusion of consideration of subjective factors.

The cycle of re-engineering, restructuring, cost cutting and downsizing has been a near-addiction with Pavlovian-like responses in the financial markets. Past excesses and structural upheaval in some industries notwithstanding, there is little evidence that this addiction is producing generally healthier organizations. An article published in *The Economist* entitled, "The Anorexic Corporation,"[2] reported that "managers have treated slimming as an end in itself, rather than as a means to corporate renewal." "And, they have failed to recognize that slimming brings costs as well as benefits." Restructuring must be linked with a strategy for recovery and growth. Otherwise, it is merely a reductionist response considering that the consequences on employee morale and, more importantly, on the capacity to build commitment and motivation to achieve results over the longer term suffers. No matter how great the need for restructuring, the failure to create a perception of linkage between cost cutting and downsizing in the near term and strategies for future success in the minds of organization members is a failure of leadership in the present environment. Even in organizations with strong histories of growth and excellence, reserves of committed, motivated and creative people are being depleted in number and in spirit. This is precisely the reservoir of human capital which will create or not create a desirable future for organizations. Charles Handy uses the metaphor of getting caught up in the process of cutting fat so much that we don't know when to stop — resulting in cutting muscle. In organizations, Handy's metaphor points to the overreaction of cutting into the "core employees" when in a frenzy to cut costs across the board.[3]

The two-sided reality of objectivity and subjectivity operating in organizations is a complex one. The challenge for leaders is both to begin to understand this reality themselves and then to communicate their understanding in such a way as to bring about an enriching and broadening of such understanding by everyone involved. We have used systems thinking concepts and certain related constructs to help develop understanding and to provide a basis for communication. The comprehension we have sought is related to the interconnectedness of objective and subjective factors and the "wholeness" this interconnectedness defines. Peter Senge's popular book, *The Fifth Discipline*[4] and *Managing with Systems Thinking* by Michael Balle[5] provide relatively complete descriptions of systems thinking and the tool of system structures or archetypes. Our application of systems thinking and system structures has been somewhat different from that described in either of these books, but the focus on "wholes" and the underlying concepts remain the same. With no intent to duplicate the material on systems thinking, we will offer a brief description of the concepts, one of the structures and an example to illuminate the principle addressed in this chapter.

A system is a set of interconnected elements. Systems thinking is a way of thinking about the interdependence of elements potentially leading to an enhanced perception of the whole. Systems thinking is a logical framework encompassing descriptive images and clear language for analyzing and communicating the dynamics of organizational life. It acknowledges that the interaction of factors in organizations is dynamically complex and that linear approaches are often inadequate for useful analysis and comprehension. Systems thinking is a relatively informal methodology originating with biology and cybernetics and adapted for organizational analysis. The essential tools for systems thinking are generic structures, called archetypes by Senge, which define dynamic circumstances within organizations. The basic building blocks of these structures are feedback processes, graphically represented as sets of factors or elements connected in a circular fashion. The concept of feedback or the reciprocal flow of influence among and between factors is central to understanding these processes. It follows then that each factor so represented is both cause and effect with respect to the other factors. We have argued that in organizations, objective reality and subjective reality exist in just such a state of mutual influence which accounts for the relevance of this brief excursion into systems thinking.

There are two types of feedback processes: reinforcing and balancing. "Reinforcing (or amplifying) feedback processes are the engines of growth (or decline)." In reinforcing processes, small changes build on themselves. "A small action snowballs with more and more and still more of the same, resembling compounding interest." Some reinforcing processes are "vicious cycles" in which things start off badly and grow worse. Other reinforcing processes are "virtuous cycles" bringing about desired direction and results.[6] For example, growth in product or service market share can be expressed as a reinforcing process where satisfied customers produce positive word of mouth, producing sales, more satisfied customers and so on (Figure 1).

Balancing processes modulate or moderate reinforcing processes. Balancing processes may be explicit, i.e., the factors that make them up and the interaction among the factors may be the result of conscious action — as in setting a goal to produce stability. Or, they may be implicit and largely unconscious reflecting natural forces, perhaps best explained by inertia (indisposition to change) on the one hand or entropy (the progressive degradation of a system) on the other hand.

The discipline of systems thinking argues that organizational dynamics can be expressed and understood through system structures. These structures are comprised of reinforcing and balancing processes combined and interacting with each other in various ways. About 12 such structures have been

Figure 1   Reinforcing Process (Source: P. M. Senge, *The Fifth Discipline: The Art and Practice of the Learning Organization*, Doubleday, NY, 1990, 81.)

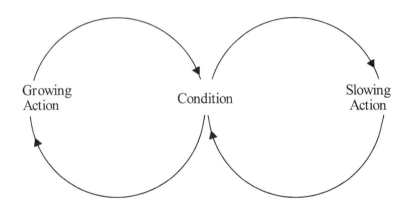

Figure 2   Limits to Growth (Source: P. M. Senge, *The Fifth Discipline: The Art and Practice of the Learning Organization*, Doubleday, NY, 1990, 97.)

identified by researchers. Each structure points to a management principle and suggests the points of greatest leverage in bringing about change.

We have found one of the structures, the Limits to Growth structure, to be especially useful in providing a framework for understanding how objective and subjective factors interact and influence each other. The Limits to Growth structure is a simple one, comprising single reinforcing and balancing processes (Figure 2). When we introduce this structure, we ask leaders to think about it simply as one that expresses growth factors on the left (associated with the Reinforcing Process) and limiting factors

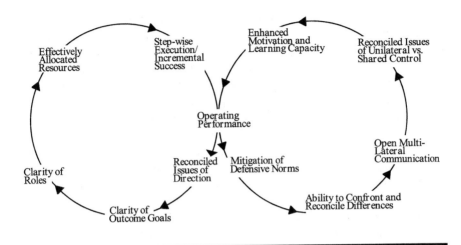

Figure 3   Limits to Growth

on the right (associated with the Balancing Process). Holding the image of this structure in mind, we then ask them to define such a structure pertaining to their own organization. The discrete factors (defined on the left), taken together, fuel each other and drive growth or recovery and well-being. Those factors (defined on the right), similarly taken together and interacting, will either facilitate or constrain growth. In virtually all cases, we find objective factors having been defined on the left in the Reinforcing Process and relatively more subjective ones defined on the right. As an illustration, Figure 3 was developed by a group of leaders with whom we worked in a large medical center.

The Limits to Growth structure and, more importantly, the leader's sense of its meaning, can illuminate how objective factors frame the common perception of purpose, yet subjective ones play the crucial role of governing or regulating achievement. Although most people seem to react to limits to growth situations by pushing harder on the objective factors, the greatest leverage in change lies in addressing the factors on the right. "Leverage lies in the balancing loop — not the reinforcing loop. To change the behavior of the system, you must identify and change the limiting factors."[7]

6.2   The Leader as Creator of Equilibrium

To reiterate, the essential function of leadership encompasses the following aspects: creating clarity of purpose and relevant output; building and contributing to a spirit of collaboration and colleagueship; fostering and participating in interdependent behavior centered on results; and providing a context for learning. These aspects of leadership blend objective and subjective factors; for leaders then, the central task is to create an environment wherein an operative balance of objective and subjective factors can be achieved. Systems thinking, specifically the Limits to Growth structure just described, tells us that the highest leverage in change efforts is achieved through altering the balancing process factors. As we have seen, those factors tend to be relatively subjective in nature when compared with the reinforcing process factors. The objective factors, however, are why we care about the subjective ones. A high order concern, therefore, in creating the necessary environment is to create clarity of objective purpose. By objective purpose we do not necessarily mean a purpose that can be expressed in purely quantitative or measurable terms. The forces underlying reductionism move us in the direction of elevating activities and tasks to the level of purpose just because they can be counted or measured, i.e., procedures performed, customers surveyed, etc. Often those meaningful activities and tasks that add real and transcendent value but cannot be easily measured or counted are excluded, e.g., customer satisfaction, patient outcomes, etc.

While objective purpose can often be expressed, at least in part, in strictly quantitative terms, such as market share or earnings, an illustration of purpose that is apparently more oriented to intangible factors comes from our work with a unit of a large healthcare facility. What came to be seen as the framing of objective purpose for this unit was a result of a broadly based answer to the question "what do we truly want to be?" Their statement is quoted below:

> Patients not only receive the best medical and technical care but feel that they have received the best and most sensitive care; patients are welcomed enthusiastically; smooth interconnections and information flow exists among functional areas with the focus on the patient; participants in planning and the provision of treatment are able to define the processes that create the best results; allied health and nursing personnel are fully trained and able to take care of day to day treatment and a partnership exists between them and the medical staff that provides an opportunity for participation in planning and delivery of patient treatment; issues are faced squarely and resolved within the appropriate context (as opposed to shifting responsibility and dealing with symptoms).

Most of the elements of this statement seem not to lend themselves to quantification or even clarity. The statement, however, did become the objective aim for members of the department. Specific outcome goals were identified and pursued by answering such questions as: what does "best medical and technical care" look like? How will we know that patients "feel that they have received the best and most sensitive care?" What are the objective consequences of "partnership and participation to define the processes that create the best results?"

Clarity of objective purpose is both a consequence of an effective and operative balance of objective and subjective factors and a motivating agent for creating such a balance. Perhaps the most significant result of such a balance is an environment that is hospitable to the truth — an environment that frames and supports the seeking and the finding of valid information. Such an operating context is truly and fundamentally a precondition to organizational learning.

In an earlier reference to Chris Argyris' model for organizational learning and effectiveness, valid information was identified as the most basic governing value. The full impact of this assertion is not immediately obvious. It sounds self-evident, axiomatic and perhaps even trite. Would invalid information ever be a governing value? Would members of organizations ever aim to produce false perceptions of reality? Clearly, leaders and members of organizations do not aim for such dysfunction but a state of such dysfunction may be the norm rather than the exception. In our experience, failing to grasp and address important human dynamics, i.e., subjective factors, is endemic and tends to be responsible for not only erroneous perceptions but an organizational climate that systematically masks the truth. (It strikes us as ludicrous to refer to current times as the "information age" bearing in mind that information theory determines the information quality of data by the validity of its content. To have achieved a "valid information age" would be truly noteworthy, otherwise, the term seems at best naive and misleading.)

Having become sensitive to the role of valid information in organizational effectiveness and the fact that organizational settings are not necessarily conducive to it, examples are easy to find. At the level of individuals relating to organizations and vice versa, performance reviews and disciplinary actions are illustrative. It is a common occurrence to find a supervisor unable to terminate an employee for poor performance or disruptive behavior because the employee has a record of good, if not outstanding, performance reviews sometimes over a period of twenty to thirty years, often accompanied by promotions. In most cases, the employee has never been told the truth about his or her shortcomings.

Therefore, the employee never learned, improved or adapted. It typically falls to some manager at some time to take action when performance is no longer tolerable. At this point, everybody gets hurt. This circumstance can be multiplied by factors in the hundreds or thousands in many organizations. We tend to be socialized to avoid emotional situations, those that will upset other people and cause us to be upset as a result. Frequently, managers are required to review the performance of employees who have become their friends which can trigger the manager's emotional blindside and generally exacerbate the problem. In a very real and direct way, we can say that circumstances of this sort are the result of failing to deal effectively with subjective factors. In many organizations, this circumstance is an aspect of culture; outstanding evaluations are the norm along with a high degree of angst when poor performance has to be dealt with.

Our closely and subjectively held perceptions of other people determine what we hear them say, governing if we can even *hear* valid information when it comes our way. It has been said about certain individuals that if they knew and tried to speak about the secrets of the universe, it wouldn't matter because they wouldn't be heard. Our views of the world, which tend to be constructed so as to not threaten us, also filter the messages of others. The unhappy fate of prophets of any age is to deliver messages — valid information — that no one is either prepared for or wants to hear. Often, these messages are counter-cultural and further complicate how they are heard. Walter Brueggemann, in his book, *The Prophetic Imagination*, equates prophecy with social action. The hypothesis that he explores is: "The task of prophetic ministry is to nurture, nourish, and evoke a consciousness and perception alternative to the consciousness and perception of the dominant culture around us."[8] We will address the issues of dominant culture for leaders in the next chapter.

On the other hand, *how* arguments are presented can cause them to be heard and enhanced or can shut down expression by others and generate defensiveness. We recently observed a meeting of senior managers in which one of the participants said with great emphasis, "the problem is that Department X has been treated so favorably that all the other departments are demanding some equal treatment!" There was no response. Whether the assertion was valid or not, it wasn't challenged because challenge would have created conflict, and a strong norm existed which dictated that "we avoid conflict at all costs." Consequently, in the absence of valid information, there was no learning, perceptions hardened and defensiveness was reinforced — especially on the part of the head of Department X.

Leaders either act to create environments within which valid information is valued and pursued, or their attitudes and behaviors bring about environments where the truth seldom emerges. An example on a grand scale illustrates this point. We are acquainted with an organization which was highly regarded within its industry in spite of what many of its members described as "no leadership at the top." The chief executive officer of this organization, whether consciously or not, had not created a climate where leadership potential would emerge and be nurtured. One member of the senior leadership group described the climate as one where the spotlight would be shined on one person long enough for that person to feel secure and favored and then the attention would be switched to another person and the process would begin again. Consequently, each individual felt off base and distracted. It could be argued that this Darwinian approach would be effective if strong leaders emerged as a result of it. Rather than strong leaders, however, what emerged was a leadership culture that has been characterized as highly defensive and territorial. Lack of trust, individual agendas and the collective need to look good were factors that conspired to keep the senior management group from addressing real and substantive issues. In other words, individual perceptions and patterns of defensiveness and attribution served to isolate the group from reality. The few messengers who sought to deliver valid, if less than welcome, information were summarily shot — in true Homeric fashion! The leadership group generally came to be seen as out of touch and ineffective.

Many leaders see the need and intend to create a learning environment among the units they lead and the individuals who report to them. Their words include "we need to create a spirit of inquiry," "I want our people to confront each other — to take each other on," "the sort of atmosphere I want to create is one where, if I appeared unannounced, the group would be engaged in problem solving, challenging each other and producing ideas and I wouldn't be able to tell whose functional areas owned the problem in question." What these leaders are saying is that they want their people to learn from each other, to produce better solutions to problems, to collectively perceive reality more accurately, to vigorously pursue valid information. No amount of wishing or declaring it so, however, will make it happen. The environment so constructed must be seen as safe for the truth; it must be made favorable for interacting within the framework and standard of valid information.

If "the truth will set us free," it is also a fact that the truth can make us very uncomfortable and frightened. As leaders, the truth can point to those occasions when we are exposed, when we are wearing no clothes, so to speak, and doing ourselves and our organizations little good. The truth can introduce uncertainty to which we will naturally recoil and seek to eliminate. Yet, perceiving in ways that move us closer to reality and acting with consistency to that reality yields profound objective results. The instigation of processes by leaders to create environments based on the standard of valid information, therefore, requires a clear vision of the good that can follow coupled with a substantial amount of courage. The great barriers to individuals operating within the standard of valid information are related to the nature of the relationships among them and the information content of their communication. Given commitment and having articulated intent, the leader's greatest leverage in achieving the desired environment is to personally demonstrate the attitudes and behaviors that are necessary to bring it about.

Integrity and success in leadership are vitally linked. Congruent speaking and acting brings forth positive results while incongruence undermines the best intentions. Modeling the behavior leaders want to see and expect in others, therefore, requires that leaders practice what they preach. To the extent that a leader's mental models and attributions screen and skew interpretation of reality, the leader must comprehend these constructs and make them open to challenge and move them to higher levels of accuracy. Defensiveness, activated by leaders or anyone else, functions to prevent the experience of threat, embarrassment or conflict. Patterns of defensiveness among individuals within organizations literally close down efforts to invoke the standard of valid information. In contrast to defensive reasoning, the task for leaders is to demonstrate what Argyris calls "productive reasoning."[9] When individuals are reasoning productively, they tend to base their patterns of thinking on what they know (directly observed) rather than what they infer, or worse, what someone else infers. When they deduce or make inferences, they make such inferences public and explicit; when they attribute meaning to the actions of other people, they test the validity of their attributions. When they reach conclusions, they are careful to not shut down expression of other opinions by articulating their conclusions in ways that invite inquiry into them.

If productive reasoning and nondefensive behavior creates leverage for leaders in bringing about environments friendly to learning, defensive attitudes and behaviors on the part of leaders create ripple effects throughout the organizations they lead and close down learning. As leverage naturally attaches to leadership, a negative multiplier attaches to the defensive behavior of leaders fueling the creation of defensive norms that take on a life of their own.

Demonstration of behavior that leaders seek to promote creates an implicit awareness of valued behavior on the part of those they seek to influence. Explicitly, leaders can encourage and reward individuals whose behavior is consistent with the standard of valid information. Productive reasoning can be compensated in one form or another; conversely, defensive reasoning, closed mindedness and hyperbole can be punished. If punished is too severe a word, the absence of reward will suffice to make the point. A leadership group with whom we worked created a set of behavioral norms to which they aspired and agreed to be held accountable. Some of the group's behavioral aims are listed below:

> I will speak face to face with you before 'going public' or before I speak to anyone else about any conflict we are having; if the past is getting in the way of solving a problem, I will put those issues and experiences out on the table with the person(s) involved; I will be specific and approach problems in real time; I will test attributions with the person(s) of whom I am making the attributions; I will challenge attributions pertaining to others stated to me by others; I will express my individual needs which impact how I do my job and how I relate to my fellow team members; I will deal with issues that pertain to the group with the group and not with individuals or subsets of the group.

As a description of productive patterns of behavior, these norms are well conceived. We would like to be able to say that these desired norms became reality and that the group became better positioned to deal with its most significant objective issues. However, these norms did not become reality, and the group did not deal with its long-standing operational problems in spite of extreme pressure to do so. When threatening and emotionally charged issues were identified and placed in front of the group, it lost its cohesiveness and its espoused new way of being. It became fragmented, it closed down dialogue, it returned to business as usual and failed to produce results.

The reasons for this disappointing performance are instructive. First, it is clear that even though certain members of the group expressed commitment to the new ways of behaving, their underlying attitudes and assumptions about relating to other people did not change. When pressure was applied, they returned to their habitualized patterns of behavior. Perhaps a more fundamental causal factor was that the leader of this group did not behave in a manner consistent with the new norms. This leader's behavior sent a clear message that valid information was, in fact, not valued and that the new behavioral environment was not safe.

There is a special challenge for leaders in maintaining the proper balance between objectivity and subjectivity as the proper balance relates to themselves. All of us have feet of clay; we have our own unique blindspots, our Achilles' heels; it is no more or less than an aspect of human nature. Leaders have weaknesses, which are no different from any of the rest of us, except that the consequences can be greater. There is a multiplier associated with the blindspots of leaders. Leaders often have greater than usual difficulty accepting the notion that there are circumstances and people around which their own behavior is irrational. We have never worked with a leader who did not have blindspots including ourselves. The objectivity of leaders can be compromised by subjectively held fancies pertaining to ideas, projects, products or people. The emotional attachments of leaders, whether related to favorite ideas, pet projects, products or personalities, whatever the underlying causes, tend not to be good for the leaders or their organizations. Although we are not necessarily addressing romantic relationships that exist in organizations, there are similarities if the blindspot is related to a person or to people. Emotion is involved and there tends to be blindness to the potential and actual negative consequences, and when observed, appears as if the parties are "in love."

6.3   Self-Awareness for Leaders

As discussed previously in the section on individuals, we have found the Leadership Effectiveness Analysis, the Management Effectiveness Analysis and The Birkman Method to be effective in creating awareness about an individual's perceptual characteristics, personality and behavior. The focus now will be on how we use these instruments with leaders. The Management Research Group uses their Leadership Effectiveness Analysis and Management Effectiveness Analysis as developmental tools. In using these instruments with leaders, they can become aware of their leadership and management styles and can gain insights into how they behave in certain leadership and management functions. Furthermore, they can become aware of both the assets and liabilities of the characteristics they manifest in their relationships with others. For example, under the "evaluation function," there are three sets of characteristics (conservative, innovative and technical) for which there are scores. Leaders can see both the assets and the liabilities of their scores. In addition, leaders and managers can then engage in what the Management Research Group terms, "action planning" for "sustaining assets" and "addressing liabilities" with concrete "developmental action steps." With The Birkman Method, we are able to hold up a mirror to leaders about their interests, behavior (both under ideal circumstances and under stress), their intellectual styles and their leadership behavior. The benefit is twofold: self-awareness and to let them know how they are seen by other people including the ones they lead. These types of feedback can be quite powerful, and we have been surprised many times at just how *new* this information can be to leaders.

One leader, the head of a major research group, told us that feedback on his interests and behavior was the single most important intervention for him at this particular time in his life because it made him aware of just how much he was behaving *out of obligation* rather than *out of passion* in both his work and his family life. This was causing him great stress and his behavior regularly reflected his psychic pain and unmet needs. This defensive behavior tended to spill over on to the people he led and to his interactions with his boss. His objective outcomes were affected by these subjective issues. We looked carefully at his interests, and these were not expressed in any part of his work. He was like a fish out of water — surviving but losing credibility because he was simply miserable by trying to be someone he was not and his defensive behavior further exacerbated the negative effect he had on those he led. We also administered a Birkman to his boss and discovered that his boss had a high degree of empathy and was able and willing to engage in a conversation dealing with these subjective issues. We were then able to coach and work with both people in improving their communication with one another. This leader needed to have his boss listen to him first of all, understand why he was being defensive and then get to a place where he could negotiate the expression of his interests and needs in his work, and at the same time, be accountable for the department he led. Their meetings together shifted from rubbing each other the wrong way and creating mutual stress which played out in defensive patterns which hardened over time, to productive discussions and collaborative outcomes with some hearty and healthy laughter about their former interactions. They can now catch themselves and each other when they start to go into defensive behavior.

Preceding this successful outcome, plenty of front end work had to be done by the leader's boss addressing multi-generational issues since relationships do not play out in a vacuum. Part of the result of holding up the mirror to both this leader and his boss was that they each felt empowered to change their own behavior rather than trying to change each other. Bill Ferguson in his book, *How to Heal A Painful Relationship*, refers to the ever failing but tenacious attempt to always change someone else.[10] In our own experience in organizations we have observed how people will expend enormous amounts of energy trying to change other people and this simply does not work. The potential of fully comprehending the scores of instruments such as those discussed in this section and then acting upon them by taking responsibility for exercising positive behaviors and mitigating defensive behavior is probably one of the main reasons leaders will find value in feedback instruments. Beyond the relationship with his boss, this leader of his research team had to then look at a new way of delegating, again giving himself an opportunity to focus on meeting his interests and his needs.

Subjective issues can frustrate and perplex leaders. One day we walked into a leader's office and found him alone literally banging his head on his desk out of deep frustration from not getting his section leaders to cooperate first and then collaborate. We gave him some tough feedback in a very straightforward manner. (We knew about his courage when he surmised the feedback would be negative and still chose to have both his new associate director and financial manager present.) The process using The Birkman as a tool for insight helped him to understand more fully his needs that drove his behavior and his natural leadership style. This prompted him to then recognize the diversity of leadership interests, needs and behaviors of his entire team. Furthermore, he gained a sensitivity to others and a knowledge about their personalities that led him to interact with them as unique individuals — each person with a set of talents and corresponding interests and needs that, when met, helped them to reach their potential and keep their stress behaviors in check. Because he became less defensive, so did they. He started using The Birkman as a mentoring tool. By focusing on the strengths of people, leaders can select assignments for them that bring out the best in people and give expression to their interests and their passions.

Using a highly synthesized version of The Birkman Method called a leadership style grid, we can access the diversity of leadership styles and obtain composite grids with multiple scores. The grid is expressed as four quadrants with the colors of blue, green, yellow and red representing the interests, behaviors (usual behavior and stress behavior) and needs of a leader. In highly summarized terms, blue leaders tend to be seen and act as thinkers and planners. Yellow leaders are called guardians, creating and keeping track of systems, procedures and processes. A motto for a red leader might be, like the Nike slogan, "just do it!" since reds tend to be action oriented and decisive. Greens are termed communicators enjoying being on the stage, and you can find these leaders holding townhall meetings, giving motivational speeches and sales presentations and sparking involvement and collaboration from seemingly unconnected colleagues. Irrespective of a leader's Birkman scores, a leader can on any given day do whatever needs to be done — planning, selling, acting decisively, establishing systems. The leadership grid, however, does indicate the most comfortable and natural style and orientation for the leader indicating a tendency to revert back to this style most of the time.

There are 11 behavioral components that are used in The Birkman Method. Out of these, the behavior and need scores on Authority, Esteem, Challenge, Structure, Empathy and Decision-making can be significant for determining a leader's style and, depending on other people's styles and needs, their responses to this leader. A leader's expression of authority, whether it is assertive or suggestive, is received quite differently by employees depending on their needs for authority. The same holds true for the structure score. We know of one highly structured leader who demands that people adhere to his strong sense of structure by always being on time and leaving on time for meetings. Towards the end of a meeting, his eyes gaze at the wall clock, and he actually begins to return chairs to their original position before anyone leaves the room, sometimes while someone is getting out of their chair if they don't do it quickly enough. The challenge score determines the expectations that leaders hold for themselves and others. We know one leader with the highest possible challenge score who drives herself and all the people who work with her to overcome seemingly impossible odds to be successful. Once she accepts a project, she will meet all the deadlines and work any problems and never give up. At the same time, she will usually blame herself if anything goes wrong even if it is beyond her control. Differences in authority scores, even if understood, cause leaders much angst. For example, one leader who has a democratic, participatory style selected a person with a highly autocratic, assertive style of expressing authority to be his second-in-command person. They were in conflict on so many occasions that eventually the leader had to demote his subordinate because the subordinate never could acknowledge the leadership position of his boss. These differences seriously restrained their collaboration to produce the results they both were in agreement with.

Another leader used The Birkman Method to substantially cut his learning curve about his new team when he accepted an assignment in another country. Fortunately, he was able to bring each new person in to work with him during this transitionary period, and a Birkman was administered. Before long, a very insightful profile appeared and patterns were discerned as personalities emerged. The most striking was the preponderance of similar leadership scores for the executives under stress. Most of the leaders openly admitted that they would become dogmatic, not open to change and over-controlling. They saw this stress behavior as a definite disadvantage as a leadership team and set up a system to openly give each other feedback when they observed each other and the team engaging in their defensive behaviors. Also, in openly discussing the similarities and differences between the new leader and his new team members, issues got put on the table and resolved before he moved into his new job and new country.

Contrary to what was more popular a decade ago, cookie cutter leadership styles simply do not work. It was in vogue to have effective leaders profiled, studied and in the spotlight with their trailing portfolios of dramatic organizational turnarounds and successes. Emerging leaders were schooled using these models with accompanying techniques, leadership styles and blueprints for success. As more and more successful entrepreneurs emerged with their own patents for successfully building an organization, heroes took on different sizes, shapes and styles. We have seen consistent evidence across differences in leadership styles that the application by leaders of the principle, *Achieve an Operative Balance of Objective and Subjective Factors*, works. To ignore the human, subjective factors is fatal to organizations. Without objective aims, there is no substance for leaders to lead. The very delicate balance is the challenge for leaders in any organization.

References

1. Drucker, P., *The New Society*, Heinemann, London, 1951.
2. The Anorexic Corporation, *The Economist*, Sept. 3rd, 1994.
3. Handy, C., *The Age of Unreason*, Harvard Business School Press, Boston, 1989.
4. Senge, P. M., *The Fifth Discipline: The Art and Practice of the Learning Organization*, Doubleday, New York, 1990.
5. Balle, M., *Managing with Systems Thinking: Making Dynamics Work for You in Business Decision Making*, McCall-Hill, London, 1994.
6. Senge, P. M., *The Fifth Discipline: The Art and Practice of the Learning Organization*, Doubleday, New York, 1990, 101.
7. Senge, P. M., *The Fifth Discipline: The Art and Practice of the Learning Organization*, Doubleday, New York, 1990, 101.
8. Bruggemann, W., *The Prophetic Imagination*, Fortress Press, 1978, 13.
9. Argyris, C., *Overcoming Organizational Defenses: Facilitating Organizational Learning*, Allyn & Bacon, Boston, 1990, 105.
10. Ferguson, B., *How to Heal a Painful Relationship*, Return to the Heart, Houston, 1990.

Chapter 7

Leaders: *Delegate Only Around Purpose*

Anticipatory Summary

Organizations, as social systems, are purposeful by definition. While the human dynamics may look the same in organizations and other social systems such as communities and families, communities and families exist to *be*; organizations exist to *do*. What organizations *do* is their purpose. The challenge for leaders is to see through tasks, functions and activities, as necessary as these may be, to consequences — to outcomes connected with purpose in a real and discernible way.

7.1   The First Requirement of Leaders

- Leaders cannot delegate the responsibility to create, or otherwise bring into being, a clear purpose and to achieve the engagement and alignment of people around that purpose. All of the interventions of leaders at any level revolve around this first and primary requirement.
- The leader's task is to engage people in the process of translating organization-wide purpose into an expression that has meaning and relevance for the people in the units they lead.

- A clear mission and vision can sustain coherence and enable an organization to produce meaningful results.
- Statements of vision and mission are aspects of purpose; standing alone, however, they are incomplete. Vision and mission are made operative by a "statement of direction" which embodies unambiguous, objective, outcome aims over some relevant period of time.
- Direction setting cascades through several levels of analysis and discrimination.
- There is a paradox surrounding the convergence of current management theory and current management practice. While we talk about trust, values and commitment, we act as if these factors were meaningless.
- Clarity of purpose and congruent patterns of delegation define a natural and renewing path to dealing with this paradox.

7.2   Output and Leverage

- Sustaining an orientation to consequences, to outcomes or results is the only way to achieve clarity, consensus and alignment around direction.
- Without a clear sense of purpose, output makes little sense and leverage even less. Consequences of effort, effects of work, outcomes and results are all ways of speaking about output.
- From the standpoint of leadership, leverage refers to adding value, to creating the greatest good per unit of resource invested.
- A special circumstance exists when purpose is intangible and output is not measurable in a conventional sense; results or output associated with purpose, if not measurable, must at least be recognizable and unambiguous.
- The challenge for leaders is to keep themselves and their people connected with what matters, to lead the expression and production of output to that which has a bearing on purpose.

7.3   Delegate ONLY Around Purpose

- To delegate and not empower makes little sense.
- To empower without motivational alignment is at least naive and probably foolhardy.

- Common motives and expectations, expressed across organizational levels and interests, are achieved through purpose and perception of relevant output.
- Purposeful delegation must become an organizational norm if purposeful and coordinated action is the goal.
- The achievement of purposeful delegation will inevitably flatten organizational structures and mitigate the negative effects of hierarchy.

7.4 Machiavellians

- Machiavellians say all the right things about common cause and teamwork and act in their own self interest.
- The only way to successfully deal with Machiavellian behavior is to unwaveringly maintain a focus on purpose and delegate and maintain accountability relationships *only* around purpose.

Leaders: *Delegate Only Around Purpose*

The late spring of 1942 was the lowest point in the War for the Allies. Winston Churchill in Volume 4 of *The Second World War* wrote "I have called this volume the *Hinge of Fate* because in it we turn from almost uninterrupted disaster to almost unbroken success. For the first six months of this story, all went ill; for the last six months, everything went well." The campaign in North Africa was part of the turning from disaster to success. The forces of the British Empire had seen the German Afrika Corps under Field-Marshall Rommel roll up victory after victory in this strategically vital region. The "disasters in the Western desert" produced frustration and anxiety for the Prime Minister and the War Cabinet in London. Based on their perceptions of leadership vacillation and timidity resulting in lost opportunities for the British forces, the decision was made to replace the highest-ranking members of the Command for North Africa. The Prime Minister gave the new Commander, General Alexander, the following directive:

> "Your prime and main duty will be to take and destroy at the earliest opportunity the German-Italian Army commanded by Field-Marshall Rommel, together with all its supplies and establishments in Egypt and Libya."

Defeat Rommel! Purpose and outcome could not be more clear. Rommel was defeated at El Alamein in a great victory by Generals Alexander and Montgomery. "It marked in fact the turning of the 'Hinge of Fate'. It may almost be said 'before Alamein we never had a victory. After Alamein we never had a defeat'."[1]

In 1982, Eastside High School in Patterson, New Jersey, was also a battle zone although one of a different sort. The students ruled and their standard was brutality and intimidation. The educational mission of the school was, at best, marginalized. Less than 30 percent of the students were able to pass the Minimum Basic Skills Test. The motion picture, "Lean on Me"[2], relates the story of Eastside High School and the arrival, efforts and success of the new Principal, Joe Clark. Mr. Clark's assignment was simple and clear: raise the passing performance of the students on the Minimum Basic Skills Test from 30 percent to 75 percent in one year. His assignment was not to restore order, increase attendance, clean up the physical facility, although all these things happened, but rather, to produce an outcome consistent with an educational purpose.

These are dramatic stories, and we in no manner wish to imply that the principle, *Delegate Only Around Purpose,* applies only to circumstances of high drama. We also do not mean to suggest that these very complex sets of conditions can be reduced to simple explanations. These stories, however, illustrate this principle in an unambiguous way. While delegation based on accountability for producing results related to purpose may seem to be a practice of obvious merit, in our experience, it is not a practice that is widely adopted. Delegation based on function or activity is much more typical and apparently less threatening both to leaders and to the people to whom these activities are delegated. It is sometimes argued that daily operational life in modern multi-functional, multi-layered, multi-dimensional organizations does not lend itself to purposeful delegation. While we agree that purposeful delegation is difficult to achieve, we do not agree that it can be avoided if leaders aim to bring about purposeful behavior. The challenge for leaders is to see through tasks and functions and activities, as necessary as these may be, to consequences — to outcomes connected with purpose in a real and discernible way.

In Chapter 4, which pertains to the principle of purposeful delegation from the standpoint of individuals, we argued that relationships concerned with the consequences of effort and associated accountability for results is, at a minimum, a bi-lateral proposition. There always are at least two actors, the person being delegated to and the person doing the delegating. This chapter closes the loop on this relationship of bi-lateral cause and effect. In this chapter, we will explore issues of meaning, motivation and objective outcomes, the dynamics of involvement, empowerment, leverage, delegation and accountability — all from the perspective of leaders.

7.1 The First Requirement of Leaders

Effective leaders bring about a collective striving to accomplish something that matters. The something that matters is the driving force; its power comes from a common perception of its validity, merit and relevance and the collective striving is the consequence of its common perception. Purpose is the something that matters. Purpose, even though its expression may change, is the foundation around which organizations are successfully led through periods of great change and dislocation. The common perception of purpose equates to common cause, and common cause is that factor that has meaning for both leaders and other members of organizations, as individuals, and the organization as a social system and an economic unit.

In an academic medical institution, we worked with a physician administrator of a surgical department who had built a pre-eminent service from a mediocre one within five years. He recruited outstanding people and developed vastly improved volumes of services. The department is financially profitable, runs well and is highly regarded both inside and outside of the institution. It was clear that this leader remained absolutely focused on the common cause not only for the department, but for the department's involvement in a multidisciplinary center. He was very steadfast and persistent and overcame any problem that threatened purpose. Moreover, his analysis and insights have led him to carefully triage the resources of time, talent and money to achieve the greatest benefit to purpose.

He has not tolerated mediocre performance on the part of faculty members, administrators, nurses or secretaries. This lack of tolerance pertains to both his leadership function and his performance as a surgeon. He is passionate about his purpose and that of the people he leads and expects the same passion for excellence from all with whom he works. He has very high standards and he acts based on those standards.

While other types of social systems may exist for various reasons, organizations are by definition purposeful. Human dynamics may look the same for organizations, societies, communities and families; however, societies, communities, and families exist to *be*; organizations exist to *do*. What organizations do is their purpose. We have defined what we mean by purpose. To briefly revisit that definition, purpose is the logical and animating construct around which the talents and energies of people is applied. Purpose represents the overarching result or outcome goals of the organization expressed in practical and widely understood terms. Purpose embraces the consequences of effort and not the effort itself.

Peter Drucker describes universities, hospitals, businesses and labor unions as all belonging to the same species: "They are all organizations — the man-made environment, the 'social ecology' of post capitalist society." He goes on to say that: "Because the organization is composed of specialists, each with his or her own narrow knowledge area, its mission must be crystal clear. The organization must be single-minded, otherwise its members become confused. They will follow their specialty rather than applying it to the common task. They will each define 'results' in terms of that specialty, imposing their own values on the organization. Only a clear, focused and common mission can hold the organization together and enable it to produce results."[3] The double-edged sword of specialization, as Drucker describes above, is a significant barrier to purposeful organizational behavior. On the one hand, narrowly based and focused expertise is required to deal with highly developed technologies and disciplines. On the other hand, specialization and its associated institutional knowledge can obscure or replace larger purpose and become subject to its own standards and aims. We can only expect this dilemma to grow worse and the need for clarity of purpose and congruent alignment to strengthen as specialization and the shape of organizations continue to evolve.

What leaders cannot delegate is the responsibility to create, or otherwise bring into being, a clear purpose and the engagement and alignment of people around that purpose. All of the interventions of leaders at any level revolve around this first and primary requirement. If organizational purpose is clear, the leader's task is to engage people in the process of translating organization-wide purpose into an expression that has meaning and relevance for the people in the units they lead. It is this process of dynamic interpretation coupled with accountability for outcomes related to higher purpose that drives global purpose throughout an organization and makes it real for the people that will make it happen. The lack of clarity of organization-wide purpose, however, does not relieve leaders at any level from the requirement to bring about some clarity of local purpose to their units. To fail to meet this requirement for any reason is to fail to lead. In many organizations, we have been confronted with the argument that "if senior management can't be clear about 'where we're going' as an organization, how then can we bring about any clarity of purpose for our people?" The fairly prevalent asking of this question notwithstanding, we have never worked with a group that could not develop a sense of meaningful and viable purpose on its own. Regardless of how far down the hierarchy the unit existed or how little clarity of purpose existed at the top of the hierarchy, our experience has been the same. In one organization in which we worked, senior management could not articulate a clear direction for the organization despite several strategic planning initiatives. Instead, infighting and political upheaval preoccupied these leaders. They were perceived throughout the organization as pursuing their own individual agendas and being ineffective as a group. In spite of the malaise at the top, leaders of certain departments strove to create clarity of purpose for their departments and succeeded in bringing about purposeful behavior. Significant achievements, emanating from lower levels in an organization, can also be ultimately beneficial for the larger organization in an inadvertent way. They can bring about involvement of individuals throughout the organization and, while usually unintended, can help to add clarity to purpose at the highest level. As leaders of entities at the bottom and in the middle forge ahead with defining purpose for their own units, this process will have the cumulative effect of forcing senior management to come to grips with organization-wide purpose — if only by default.

Statements of vision and mission are the necessary, if usually lofty, expressions of an organization's reason to be. They may exist at the level of the organization as a whole or at the level of the units that make up an organization. These statements are typically expressions at a very high level and, while they should inspire people, they tend to be crafted in such a way as to cover all the bases and minimize controversy. Statements of vision and mission are aspects of what we call purpose, but standing alone, they are incomplete. They do little to inform decision making about allocation of scarce resources at any level or to frame perceptions of leverage-producing undertakings and accountability. They do not provide the basis for deciding to pursue one option in lieu of another or to rationally assess the performance of units or the organization as a whole. Something more is needed. That something is what we have called a dynamic "statement of direction." This aspect of purpose embodies unambiguous, objective, outcome aims over some relevant period of time. The term, "dynamic," is used to suggest that such an expression should exist in a constant state of evaluation and interpretation and should be an energizing force for individuals. We have argued that the time and effort devoted to strategy by organizations would be far more productively applied to the level of analysis required to develop and maintain a statement of direction than to the development of strategic plans. Such plans tend to be the result of burdensome processes and reflect little discrimination in defining how resources would be most productively applied. Since organizational aims related to the results or consequences of effort are usually not in place, the application of resources tends to be based on political factors or on the demands of the most vocal and strident people with the result that strategic execution is perceived as less than satisfactory. In most organizations today, vision and mission statements are in place. Usually, members of organizations are not at odds with these expressions. What achievement *looks like* with respect to vision and mission, however, is usually not made explicit. The development of this later aspect of purpose provides leaders with a basis for accessing the higher order motives of individuals and ultimately commitment as described in Chapter 4. A key determinant in bringing about alignment and engagement around purpose is the degree to which individuals are able to make the organization's purpose their own — the degree to which achievement of outcome aims has personal meaning for those so engaged. The crucial first step in determining how connected or how close individuals may become to organizational purpose is the extent to which they are involved in setting direction. We have had the privilege of working with leaders committed to creating clarity of purpose and to the process of engaging their people and seeking their commitment. The development of purpose, specifically the development of a clear sense of direction, is a difficult process in both objective or purely rational terms and in organizational behavior terms. It is perhaps one of the clearest examples of how an equilibrium or an effective balance of objective and subjective factors must be achieved to produce mutually rewarding results. Subjective issues of territoriality, self-interest, perception and defensiveness along with objective differences of opinion must be brought to the surface and resolved in order for the result to be achieved. Regardless of the difficulty, however, effective leaders have little choice but to undertake this process. In our experience, with skill and persistence, it can be accomplished and it will form the platform for purposeful delegation and commitment to achievement.

Our approach in working with leaders and their people in defining direction is essentially pragmatic. We are clear in our conviction that steadfastly sustaining an orientation to effects — to consequences, to outcomes, to results — is the only way to achieve any clarity, consensus and alignment around direction. Our use of the term "pragmatism" is adapted from the works, *Pragmatism* and *The Meaning of Truth,* by the American psychologist and philosopher, William James. James defined pragmatism as "first a method and secondly, a theory of truth." He says, "To attain perfect clearness in our thoughts of an object ..., we need only consider what conceivable effects of a practical kind the object may involve."[4] The practical "cash value" of an idea or an object is the principal determinant of its relative merit in truth.

From the point of view of method, we have found it useful to address the task of setting direction in a cascading sort of way. In other words, each level of analysis leads to a subsequent one and ultimately to where we want to be. Given mission, the process begins by deconstructing the various aspects of mission and defining what each means in terms that make sense to those involved in the process. Having made operational sense of mission, then the question, "what does success look like?" must be answered. This visualization of success begins to make perceptions of objective achievement more concrete, tangible and understandable. Maintaining a focus on the image of success, attention is brought to bear on the intermediate results or outcomes that will drive success, and then on the undertakings required to bring about the outcomes, and finally, on which outcomes will create the greatest leverage in bringing about success. The last stage of the process, the yield of which is the definition of direction, is obviously the difficult and tenuous aspect of the process. Up to this point, the process will probably have proceeded smoothly. It is at this point, however, when issues of turf and protection of position will play out. Under ideal conditions, the participants will have moved through the process and the key aspects of direction will have emerged as unassailable — transcending individual self interests. When the ideal doesn't happen, the leader and the group will at least be armed with an objective perception of the organization's best interests and any conflict can be resolved within that framework.

In an earlier chapter, we spoke of the paradox surrounding current management theory and current management practice. While we talk about trust, values and commitment, we act as if these factors were meaningless. We are speaking from both sides of our mouths. To speak of engaging people, accessing their creativity and building shared vision while behaving as if the only circumstances that matter are lowest cost, highest rate of revenue per person and next quarter's earnings, is an oxymoron. Still worse, it is the pinnacle of hypocrisy. It violates the most basic principles of those who would lead — integrity and credibility. A company we know about decided to close its regional customer service offices and centralize customer service in its headquarters. This change would result in layoffs of the regional people and the hiring of a smaller number of headquarters people. The plan for this change called for maintaining secrecy around the change until days before the layoffs would occur. While this is not an uncommon approach towards implementing this kind of change, the ethics are, at best, dubious. The planners' intent was to avoid trouble from the people who were to be laid off, opting instead to spring the news on them and have them depart with no opportunity for disruption. One leader in this company pointed out how this approach was thoroughly inconsistent with the espoused values of the company and argued for informing the employees and working with them to outplace themselves over the period of the transition. This leader influenced the planners to announce their plans and work with the employees to be laid off to meet their needs while meeting the company's needs during this transition. The change was implemented successfully and the approach that was taken created an enormous amount of goodwill between the managers of the company and their employees — with values and integrity on both sides intact.

All of this is not to suggest that many organizations have not been or are not at present in need of restructuring — usually meaning downsizing, flattening, slimming or whatever term is currently in vogue. It is a fact that many functions within organizations have become bloated and irrelevant. Layers of hierarchy have become thick with bureaucratic invention. It is our perspective, however, that the current state of affairs in many organizations has come about as a result of losing sight of purpose and relevant output. The focus, instead, has been on functions whose narrow interests have been allowed to control and allocate resources and obscure the larger purpose. It is one of the great economic injustices of our times that the senior managers who presided over and engineered all of this non-purposeful behavior and reductionism and who currently preside over the reengineering and sometimes the overreaction, tend to get rewarded and escape with their prestige and economic well-being in tact. Lower level employees tend to lose their jobs.

Short-term earnings, lowest operating cost and share price, as important as these measures are, simply cannot be the rationale for existence. "While the bottom line is one tool for assessing (organizational) health, its very strength is its limitation." "Like any tool, the bottom line is only as effective as the person who uses it. As Abraham Maslow stated, 'if you only have a hammer, you treat everything like a nail'. We hear a lot of hammering going on, reiterating the message that the bottom line is the focus of the organization."[5] Taken to their logical extreme, orientations only to the short term and to cost represent a route to nonexistence. This assertion notwithstanding, we are fully aware of the structural changes in the employment market place and the disquiet and perception of loss associated with them. We are also aware and led to believe that those mourning the loss of lifetime employment and blind company loyalty to its people are mourning the loss of something that never existed in reality. Organizations are and have always been economic and purposeful entities (regardless of how clouded the latter may have become) and have always acted to sustain their economic viability. If it ever looked otherwise, it was a faulty perception.

It is probable that organizations will continue to seek to maintain relatively low levels of employment by using contract people as needed and adopting flexible employment practices. This is all rather rational. It also continues to be true that *people* discover opportunity, produce innovation and create growth. It is our fervent belief that clarity of purpose and patterns of delegation and accountability for results consistent with purpose is a natural and renewing path to dealing with the current paradox. Regardless of the employment status of people, organizations need people who are clear about "what we're doing here" and accountable for doing it. Perhaps it is not too fanciful to suggest that this is the model of the post industrial or "valid'" information age organization person — and not a terribly new model after all.

7.2   Output and Leverage

It is self-evident, that without a clear sense of purpose, output makes little sense and leverage even less. We have made numerous references to consequences of effort, effects of work, outcomes and results. These are all ways of speaking about output. The fundamental distinction that is being drawn is that output is not effort or activity. It is not busyness or a tightly booked calendar. Output is the result of effort, the consequences of activity, and one would hope, the outcomes associated with a manager's busy schedule. It is common for a manager's output to be seen as decisions made, presentations given, reports written and meetings attended. These are not outputs; they are things leaders do but they don't constitute output. Andy Grove, the Chairman of Intel, has defined a manager's output to be "the output of his organization plus the output of the neighboring organizations under his influence." He goes on to say that "at Intel, if a manager is in charge of a wafer fabrication plant, his output consists of completed, high quality, fully processed silicon wafers. If he supervises a design group, output consists of completed designs that work correctly and are ready to go into manufacturing. If a manager is the principal of a high school, his output will be trained students. If a manager is a surgeon, his output is fully recovered patients."[6]

In interviews, we frequently ask managers — "for what output are you accountable?" The answers are interesting and sometimes creative; they rarely describe output. In group sessions with leaders, we ask — "what output are you collectively engaged in producing?" In response, we tend to get puzzled looks and questions from group members approximating — "what are you really driving at?" It is clear to us, at least within the context of our experience, that most leaders are not oriented to results and outcomes. They are not in touch with relevant output. Not only are these leaders apparently not oriented to output, their responses and actions suggest that, to them, it is a foreign and not a very pleasant concept.

Sometimes leaders behave as if the concept of output is just too esoteric. Given that it could hardly be the case of too much complexity, our speculation turns to two possible explanations. It could be that organizational purpose has become so muddled that output doesn't make much sense. Or, perhaps in connection with a muddled sense of purpose, there is a perception of too much risk associated with being clear about output. After all, if output expectations are clear, one could be held accountable for producing this output. It is our practice in groups or with individuals to work through an analysis of output. It is an iterative process framing a number of redundant-sounding questions. Why does your unit exist? How would the larger organization miss you if you weren't here? Why do you do this thing? So what if you accomplish that thing? What are the consequences of performing that task? As a result of this process, there is an opportunity for people to become connected or reconnected to purpose. The process can also be quite informative to both leaders and those being led when there is reluctance to answer the questions. Unclear purpose is often what lies behind this reluctance to define and act with regard to output. Even when purpose is clear, however, such reluctance can be the result of fear of being held accountable. When accountabilities are air-tight, there is little room for activities which do not produce output. This is terrifying to people who previously existed in a cocoon of largely irrelevant and muddled performance standards.

A special and more challenging circumstance exists when purpose is comparatively intangible and output is not measurable in a conventional sense. However, the requirement to be clear about purpose and output, if different in these cases, is an even stronger necessity. Service organizations, especially those where the services provided are of a personal nature are examples of organizations with an intangible purpose. Some organizations of this type, such as healthcare and educational institutions, provide services of the most vital sort. The output of a healthcare services organization, for example, is difficult to measure and often intangible. However such organizations exist to eliminate or mitigate the effects of disease and injury and to reduce the occurrence of premature death and their output is equivalent to patient outcomes. While there are many important operational and financial functions in these organizations, they exist only to support and facilitate the production of outcomes related to fundamental purpose. We have argued that the results or output associated with purpose, if not measurable, must at least be unambiguous. There must be a common perception of how purposeful achievement, of how output, in other words, is recognizable. The key terms are "common perception", that view of achievement which members of the organization collectively hold, and "recognizable" which refers to the observable effects or consequences of effort. The temptation to substitute factors that can be measured for meaningful output just because those factors can be measured should be strenuously avoided. Management by Objectives, now largely forgotten, was an idea that was good in theory and bad in practice. The technique failed and fell into discredit in many organizations because the emphasis came to be based on that which could be counted and not on that which mattered. The challenge for leaders is to keep themselves and their people connected with what matters — to lead the expression and production of output to that which has a bearing on purpose.

The term "leverage" has been introduced in this narrative in various contexts. From the standpoint of leadership, leverage refers to adding value — to creating the greatest good per unit of resource invested — to increasing or otherwise improving the output of the units led or influenced. Stated another way, if the output of an organization is not influenced in a positive way by the presence of a leader, there is no justification for the leader. Returning to Andy Grove's perspective on output and leverage, he says, "The art of management lies in the capacity to select from the many activities of seemingly comparable significance the one or two or three that provide leverage well beyond the others and concentrate on them."[7]

Among high leverage producing activities for leaders, developing and articulating a clear sense of purpose and output are primary. In the presence and awareness of purpose and relevant output, thoughts of leverage turn to the actions that will bring about achievement. Figure 1 illustrates an integrative model for framing change efforts where the aim is innovative and coordinated action. The model defines four non-linear stages of effort for achieving a high degree of leverage in an organization's change undertakings.[8] A few years ago we were asked to become involved with a group of leaders in a large energy company in connection with their Continuous Quality Improvement program (CQI). The members of the group had been trained in the technical aspects of the CQI program and the methodology appeared to be well founded. Assuming that organizational purpose and the purpose of the CQI program were well understood, our attention was brought to bear on issues related to group effectiveness (the "accessing collective intelligence and diversity" aspect of our model). There appeared to be some general frustration in the group, which moved to hostility on the part of some members, until the question operating in their minds was given voice: "Does the company want us to do our jobs or do CQI?" CQI, in other words, did not represent real work to members of this group. There was no perception of potential output enhancement and therefore leverage associated with CQI. Organizational purpose was not clear, the purpose of CQI was not clear and

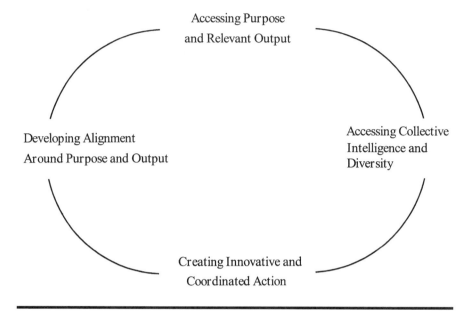

Figure 1   High Leverage Change Model

notions of relevant output varied from person to person. Only after the development of a common perspective of underlying purpose and output was the group able to relate to CQI as a leverage producing activity, achieve some alignment and make progress. Until then, there was no basis for focusing on group effectiveness and learning.

7.3   *Delegate ONLY Around Purpose*

Delegation is the process of entrusting resources to others and empowering them to act. We have expressed the belief that delegation is the principle instrument of leadership. Further, that delegation around purpose is delegation based on expectations and accountability for producing results that pertain to purpose. Leaders often express to us the opinion that while delegating around purpose sounds good and could work for some high level operating managers, it just couldn't apply across the board, i.e., to support and staff functions and to non-managers. Their suggestion is that, although delegate *only* around purpose is a nice ideal, it is perhaps impractical and unachievable. We disagree with these assertions. Our argument unfolds something like this: To delegate and not empower makes little sense. No leverage flows from such a transaction and the leader might just as well do the work himself or herself. To empower another person without the motivational alignment of that person is at least naive and probably foolhardy. Virtually every failed working relationship we have ever encountered has been the result of incongruent motives and expectations. The only way we know that a common perception of motives and expectations can be expressed across organizational levels and interests is through purpose and relevant output. We conclude, therefore, that purposeful delegation must become an organizational norm if purposeful and coordinated action is the goal. We argue, in fact, that if some relevant purpose doesn't frame any act of delegation, the function and/or the person in question are probably not needed.

Delegation expressed in hierarchy, the manifestation of what Gowler and Legge call, "management-as-hierarchy" (vs. "management-as-achievement"), constrains the efforts of leaders even though it is intended to do the opposite. The achievement of purposeful delegation will inevitably flatten organizational structures and mitigate the negative effects of hierarchy. Oppressive bureaucracy and irrelevant functions simply cannot survive the discipline and rigor of delegation based on purpose. Issues of protection of turf, narrow self-interest and out-of-control specialties will be minimized and interdependent behaviors will be nourished.

It is not our intent to describe this principle as a panacea, although it may come about as close to a universal remedy as anything we are likely to find. To achieve it requires a great deal of effort, embracing much of what this book is about in its entirety. As in the case of individuals' responses to defining output, it will be resisted by many for many of the same reasons. A good place to start is to begin to redesign the meaning of good performance — the standard for this redefinition will be outcomes or output related to purpose.

A striking illustration of the failure to delegate *only* around purpose can be found in the history of the application of information technology in large organizations. Throughout the years, there has been an assumption, a kind of faith, that investment in information technology would produce results that would in some way benefit the larger organization. Precisely what results or how such benefit would be achieved has remained something of a enigma in many organizations even at the current state of technological development. Therefore patterns of delegation and empowerment for managing the information technology resource has been unrelated to outcomes. It has been focused instead on the function itself and based largely on the notion that everybody is doing it and we have to keep up. As a consequence of all this, we know of very few senior managers and CEO's, even today, who don't question the merit of information technology and, in private, gnash their teeth over the level of their investment in it. Bensaou and Earl, of INSEAD and the London Business

School respectively, continue in their advocacy for organizations to apply information technology in the service of organizational aims rather than exalting IT and fearing it. In a recent *Harvard Business Review* article, they compare the management of IT in the West and Japan. They observe that in spite of attempts in recent years to bring about alignment between organizational strategy and information technology, organizations in the West continue to treat the IT function as if it had a life of its own. On the other hand, the 20 leading Japanese organizations which were studied treated IT as a "competitive lever," in the same category as quality, customer service or new product development.[9]

One of us was at one time a Vice President of Information Systems in a large organization. My perception of success as a Chief Information Officer was comprised of having a water-cooled machine, a small army of systems programmers and looks of amazement and awe from my peers over the esoteric things we were doing. Having achieved these trappings of success, a new CEO came to our organization and announced that he didn't care much about water-cooled machines and esoteric applications. When he discovered the economic threats to the organization and the medieval quality of our financial control systems, he made something like the following declaration: "Your purpose here is to produce accurate statements of financial performance for our operating managers within five working days of the end of each month and to reduce the number of days of revenue in accounts receivable from 120 to 45, all to be achieved within one year!" We cried, "But we don't control all the variables to make these things happen," secretly lamenting the interruption to our high profile and attention-getting work. His response was, "Fine, I'll hold you *and* the Chief Financial Officer jointly accountable for these outcomes. If you achieve them, you'll both succeed; if you don't, neither of you will succeed." We did succeed; we were able to keep our jobs and the economic well-being of our organization improved significantly. We were even able to return to work on more interesting applications of information technology, but not without a clear sense of why we were doing it.

A case in our experience exemplifies the principle, *Delegate Only Around Purpose*, and how in practice, this principle becomes connected with the principles related to objective/subjective balance and institutional knowledge. It also illustrates how the process of purposeful delegation has multiple facets and requires conscious and sustained effort. The senior leader featured in this case is a Professor and Director of a multidisciplinary service of a large academic medical center. The service, considered to be clinically advanced with unique research opportunities, was well positioned for growth and contribution to the state of knowledge and practice. The Physician-Leader of this service, let us call him, Dr. Lang, had followed the progress of a similar service in another institution. He had become aware of how that organization had essentially lost its way and failed to achieve its potential. This other organization's failure was seen by its Chief to be the result of "multiple competing agendas — no perception of common cause." Dr. Lang's organization was growing rapidly, but he was beginning to observe patterns of fragmentation and working at cross purposes not unlike those reported by his colleague in the other institution. Eager to avoid a similar fate, we were asked to intervene to help bring about clarity of purpose, alignment around direction and achievement of potential.

Dr. Lang's sense of vision and mission was strong. He was recruited to build an excellent program. However, his vision based on his perception of the opportunity, was to build the "premier service of its kind in the world — to be the best and to be seen as the best." "We're going for the gold" was his way of expressing his intent for the direction of the service. There was general support and enthusiasm for the mission and vision of the service both among the members of the service and in the larger organization. Many members of the service team had been recruited within the context of Dr. Lang's vision and his obvious level of commitment and passion for the mission. The precise meaning of the vision and mission, however, was not clear to team members and most of them reported that they were uncertain about the direction of the service. Since they were not clear about how their individual efforts played a part in becoming "the premier service in the world," the vision was less than completely real for them.

A task of fundamental importance for leaders is to engage people in the interpretation of vision and mission and to bring about a sense of meaning and relevance and in the process, to access higher levels of motivation and commitment. Consistent with this notion of engagement and interpretation, a series of sessions with Dr. Lang and individual team members was organized and completed. In each session, individuals were challenged to identify how their own objective success would further the vision and mission of the section. In other words, what would be the objective consequences of effort that would signal achievement and success. Individuals were then asked to reconcile such achievement with their own personal interests and goals. A complicating factor in this process was that the mission of the service encompassed clinical, research and teaching functions. There was an especially close connection between the clinical and research components that had to be comprehended by each individual. While the aims of research were to generally improve understanding and knowledge, measures of improved clinical outcomes for patients treated by the service were significantly dependent upon the results of research. Through this process, a collective perception of the meaning of the vision and mission in concrete terms began to take shape and emerge and the groundwork was laid for higher levels of personal motivation.

Concurrently and interweaved with the emergence of a clear sense of direction, additional individual sessions were conducted within the framework of role negotiation. Role negotiation has been defined as an intervention designed to enhance accountability relationships by reconciling subjective issues within the framework of objective achievement. Dr. Lang and individual team members were the parties to role negotiation sessions. Bearing in mind that the service represented multiple disciplines and departments, some role negotiations involved department heads from the disciplines associated with those members of the service team. For example, a surgeon was a member of the team yet he was also a member of the Surgery Department. The Chairman of Surgery was, therefore, brought into the role negotiation session for the surgeon, and the chairman actively participated in it.

Within the context of each role negotiation, individuals were asked to identify the specific outcomes related to the overall success of the service that they would pursue and for which they would agree to be held accountable. The question to be answered was: "how will we know in three or four or five years, in end result terms, based on measurement or direct observation, that your efforts alone and in collaboration with others have been successful?" This process was, in most cases, an iterative one and while it was resisted by some team members, individuals were led from defining tasks and activities to defining outcomes in a general sense then to defining outcomes in a very specific sense. Examples included: improved outcomes for certain types of patients; funding and grants received for specific research ideas; publication of a certain number of peer reviewed papers pertaining to designated research efforts; development and implementation of clinical protocols with recruitment of a target segment of the patient population.

Having established patterns of accountability and the objective basis of the relationships between Dr. Lang and individual team members, attention in each role negotiation turned to subjective factors. Issues of emotion, perception and attribution were addressed. The meaning individuals made of certain situations was tested for validity and frequently modified. Misunderstandings were made public and either cleared up or identified for on-going attention. Unexpressed feelings associated with past events were surfaced and the effects of existing or potential defensiveness were mitigated. This is not to say that this process was without much angst. There were tears and there was rage along with acknowledgments and new understandings. As we have contended throughout this book, the point of dealing with subjective factors is not to create warm feelings and a conflict-free environment. The point rather is to communicate and behave in ways that reduce the negative effects of subjectivity on objective performance, and at the same time, access the positive effects to elevate motivation to drive achievement. The process of role negotiation does not always proceed from objective factors to subjective ones. Sometimes, objective issues cannot be reasonably addressed until certain issues of a more subjective nature are dealt with. As is always the case in thinking about the objective and subjective aspects of organizational life, each must be seen as existing in a state of mutual influence with respect to the other.

Immense inroads were made in creating a team that has gone on to accomplish outstanding outcomes in the areas of patient care, research and education. However, each individual did not "live happily ever after." Some expectations were not met, some losses occurred and some painful changes in fundamental attitude and behavior were brought about. As the tough times were occurring, Dr. Lang had to persevere in maintaining pragmatic and utilitarian perspectives, focusing first and foremost on outcomes or consequences of effort and finally on what would produce the greatest good for the greatest number of people.

Certain organization-wide assumptions surfaced as key determinants in establishing new perceptions of accountability and performance. These aspects of institutional knowledge pertained to culturally embedded answers to questions such as: "What is the meaning of good performance and achievement?" and "How do traditional organizational structures relate to lateral or multidisciplinary ones?" The role of leaders in changing culture and evolving institutional knowledge will be the subject of the next chapter. For now, let it be sufficient to say that work was undertaken to shift these assumptions both in role negotiation sessions and in subsequent group sessions.

In a group setting, team members presented their outcome aims, how they planned to achieve them and what they needed from others and from the organization to be successful. In this manner, the aggregate results or consequences of effort for the entire service were identified and made public. It was a straightforward and non-controversial step for the group to then synthesize the major components of an overall statement of direction for the service. Among the individual plans, some areas of overlap were identified and new possibilities for collaboration became known. As expected, some conflict over access to resources arose. By remaining focused on outcomes as they were then understood, however, each area of contention was evaluated for potential contribution and the conflict was at least provisionally resolved. As a result of the group sessions, the team members became absolutely certain about the direction of the service and the roles that each of them would play as individuals and as members of the team in achieving their potential. Some modification of individual goals and perceptions of accountability was also a result of the group sessions.

Whether or not this service realizes its ambitious vision will be determined in the course of time. Purpose is now clear; the team is aligned around purpose and the foundation is laid for committed and purposeful behavior. The work that has been undertaken and completed, however, is only a beginning, and this beginning must become a way of being. Outcomes themselves must continue to evolve and remain the basis for delegation and empowerment. The commitment to deal with subjectivity, both its upside and its downside, must endure and become a fabric of the team's culture. Perhaps most importantly, as a matter of routine practice, individuals must be held accountable for achievement of outcome goals.

7.4   Machiavellians

In about the year 1500, Niccolo Machiavelli wrote "it can be observed that men use various methods in pursuing their own personal objectives, such as glory and riches. And so, he should have a flexible disposition, varying as fortune and circumstances dictate... he should not deviate from what is good if that is possible but he should know how to do evil if that is necessary."[10] Machiavellians, now taken to be exemplars of behavior advocated by Machiavelli, are defined as deceitful and cunning — amoral, double dealing and unscrupulous — yet astute, shrewd and wily. Machiavellians say all the right things about common cause and teamwork and act in their own self-interest. After all the work to create clarity of purpose, gain alignment and commitment and bring about purposeful behavior, the question remains: "what can be done about Machiavellians?" Some profoundly self-interested people are able to espouse commitment and appear to be aligned yet behave in ways that will set people against each other and undermine achievement.

The perception of individual leaders, as refined as it may be, can never be good enough to consistently discern Machiavellian behavior. A favorite strategy of those whose aim is manipulation for personal gain, is to endear themselves to leaders. Such emotionally-laden attachments can further blind leaders to unexpressed and incongruent motives. Our intent here is not to propose methods to identify and weed out suspected "Machiavellians" — as in an inquisition or a witch hunt. Not only is it virtually impossible and almost always doomed to failure, but it would almost certainly create a paranoiac and defensive environment. Machiavellian behavior, however, is a significant problem in almost all organizations. In our experience, the only way to consistently and reliably deal with Machiavellian behavior or the inclination to behave this way is to unwaveringly maintain the focus on purpose and delegate and maintain accountability relationships only around purpose. As a final thought on purpose itself, if a Machiavellian is able to successfully influence how purpose is defined and articulated and if that expression of purpose is at odds with the organization's rationale for existence — its mission, then delegating around this flawed direction would be consistent with the principle but would create undesirable consequences.

References

1. Churchill, W. S., *The Hinge of Fate,* Houghton Mifflin, Boston, 1950, 471.
2. *Lean on Me,* Warner Brothers, Norman Twain Productions, written by Michael Schiffer.
3. Drucker, P., *The Post Capitalist Society,* Harper Collins, New York, 1993, 52.
4. James, W., *Pragmatism,* Harvard University Press, Boston, 1975.
5. Douglas, N. and Wykowski, T., Beyond the Bottom Line, *Executive Excellence,* August, 1992.
6. Grove, A. S., *High Output Management,* Random House, New York, 1983, 40.
7. Grove, A. S., *High Output Management,* Random House, New York, 1983, 58.
8. Douglas, N. and Wykowski, T., High Leverage Change, *Executive Excellence,* October, 1991.
9. Bensaou, M. and Earl, M., The Right Mind-set for Managing Information Technology, *Harvard Business Review,* September-October, 1998.
10. Machiavelli, N., *The Prince,* Penguin Books, Harmonds Worth, Middlesex, 1961, 101, 131.

Chapter 8

Leaders: *Enhance the Efficacy of Institutional Knowledge*

Anticipatory Summary

Leaders play an important role in the creation, preservation and change of the basic and tacit assumptions that drive collective behavior in organizations. We have described these institutionalized or hardened assumptions as institutional knowledge. The ability to comprehend the nature and dynamics of culture, specifically institutional knowledge, will lead to a breaking down of patterns of circumscribed or determined behavior providing an opportunity for the intervention of leaders.

8.1 Perspectives on the Nature of Institutional Knowledge

- When basic assumptions about an organization are tacit, unexamined and unchallenged, the actions of the organization will be controlled to a far greater extent by its culture than by its leaders.
- There is an illusion that basic assumptions drive values (espoused) and that values activate behavior.

- Speaking about values, unfortunately, usually turns out to be meaningless; if there is a relationship between basic assumptions, espoused values and behavior, it appears to be a very loose and unreliable one.
- The implications of the dichotomy between basic assumptions and "values" are important for leaders, especially concerning the degree of symmetry between what leaders say and what they do.

8.2 Dimensions of Institutional Knowledge

- There is a requirement for a working classification or taxonomy of the scope and potential contents of basic assumptions related to culture.
  - Assumptions pertain to external environments and managing internal integration.
  - More fundamental assumptions relate to questions such as the meaning of truth, time, space, human nature and human relationships.
- Institutional knowledge is not single dimensional. In most organizations, multiple stocks of such knowledge exist and interact with each other.
  - These subcultures can be congruent and mutually supportive; or at odds with each other when reconciliation among them around a common cause or purpose does not occur.

8.3 Freeing Leaders from the Grip and Consequences of Institutional Knowledge

- The freeing process is a one person at a time proposition; it begins with leaders.
- Institutional knowledge has consequences for leaders. Leaders tend to assume that there is a direct cause and effect relationship between what they *say* and what people *do*; what people hear and make sense of, however, is often more related to institutional knowledge than to what leaders say.
- If purposeful behavior is the aim, a fundamental duty of leadership must be to enhance the relevance and accuracy of institutional knowledge.

8.4 *Discovering and Changing Institutional Knowledge*

- Any purposeful and intentional change or movement from the status quo requires a compelling reason.
- The task for leaders is to build a motivational framework based on a state of anticipated change in the status quo in contrast to current or imminent threat or opportunity.
- An environment that supports a posture of virtually continuous examination of assumptions would be likely to produce unsustainable anxiety and associated defensiveness.
- Paradoxically, such an environment is required for organizational learning and the absence of defensiveness is a precondition to creation of such an environment.
- In any change effort, there is a requirement to maintain grounding in something to sustain a sense of identity and integrity.
- Given that institutional knowledge usually operates outside of consciousness, the first requirement is to bring institutional knowledge into individual and collective awareness.
- Becoming aware of existing assumptions and identifying new and more relevant ones, however, does not automatically turn the new expressions into assumptions-in-fact.
- The process of these assumptions becoming operative is identical to the process that embedded the old assumptions.

8.5 *Creating and Maintaining a Balanced Learning Capacity*

- An environment is required where individuals are comfortable with one hypothesis pointing to another rather than uncertainty pointing to certainty.
- The balance is essentially one of a state of equilibrium between modes of learning; the maintenance of this balance is a function of leadership.

Leaders: *Enhance the Efficacy of Institutional Knowledge*

Leaders play an important role, arguably the most important role, in the creation, preservation and change of the basic and tacit assumptions that drive collective behavior in organizations. We have described these institutionalized or hardened assumptions as institutional knowledge. The leader's role in enhancing the quality of such knowledge to bring about useful and desirable behavioral effects is the focal point of this chapter. The focus of this chapter, in other words, is the leader's role in culture change. Briefly reviewing culture and our meaning of institutional knowledge: Culture exists on two planes or in two dimensions — behavior and the knowledge that sets behavior in motion. Behavior is the aspect of culture that we see. Behavior is what people do and is represented in the symbolic and physical manifestations of deeply held assumptions. Knowledge refers to these assumptions which tend to be highly resistive to change and usually unconscious. Institutional knowledge is the collective equivalent of the mental models of individuals and is especially influenced by those of leaders. In culture change efforts, behavior change is the aim yet changes in behavior without changes in the assumptions, i.e., the underlying institutional knowledge, will be superficial and short-lived.

Culture has a potent capacity to influence purposeful behavior and achievement of organizational potential. As we argued earlier, the influence of culture may produce desirable or undesirable effects. To the extent that culture is not understood, i.e., when basic assumptions about the organization, its markets, its members, its environment are tacit, unexamined and unchallenged, the actions of the organization will be controlled to a far greater extent by its culture than by its leaders. It is likely that this aspect of control fueled by culture was created by the actions, beliefs and attitudes of leaders, but it would have subsequently assumed a life of its own. In other words, control would have moved from the conscious and intentional actions of leaders to the indirect and largely unconscious control of tacit assumptions. John Hassard, in *Sociology and Organization Theory*, refers to Robert Merton's analysis of the effects of leadership culture by describing "how the rules of the organization can become over internalized by organizational members." "Although rules are designed to achieve the organization's goals, they can often develop into phenomena which are prized independently of this objective. Merton talks of 'goal displacement' and suggests that when rules take on an instrumental value of their own we encounter undesirable and unanticipated social consequences." From the standpoint of leaders, culture can produce unanticipated and unintended consequences often in spite of the best efforts of leaders.[1]

As we stated in the introduction to these chapters, the principles become integrated around the dimension of leadership. Clarity of objective purpose and accountability for purposeful behavior will provide the motivation to first understand and then change culture. The ability to effectively deal with subjectivity, i.e., issues of perception, ways of thinking and defensiveness, within the framework of objective purpose, will make change possible. The capacity to enhance the validity of information communicated around change will make change relevant and beneficial. The ability to comprehend the nature and dynamics of culture, specifically institutional knowledge, will break up patterns of circumscribed or determined behavior providing an opportunity for the intervention of leaders.

8.1   Perspectives on the Nature of Institutional Knowledge

Edgar Schein argues that culture can be analyzed at several different levels where the term "level" refers to the degree to which cultural phenomena may be observed.[2] The surface level, which we have described as behavior, is described by Schein as the "level of artifacts." This level includes both the visible behavior of the group and the consequences of such behavior. When a stranger, for instance, enters a new and unfamiliar group, that person will encounter the artifacts. These artifacts will determine what the stranger sees, hears and feels.

According to Schein's analysis, basic assumptions operate at the deepest or lowest level. "Basic assumptions ... have become so taken for granted that one finds little variation within a cultural unit." As referenced earlier, basic assumptions, in this sense, are similar to what Argyris has identified as "theories-in-use," the implicit assumptions that actually guide behavior, that tell group members how to perceive, think about and feel about things. Schein also defines an intermediate level between artifacts and basic assumptions which he calls espoused values. Schematically, he proposes a direct and linear relationship among the levels associated with artifacts, espoused values and basic assumptions.[3] This relationship suggests that assumptions drive espoused values and espoused values drive behavior, and further, that sometimes the influence flows the other way.

In our experience, espoused values do *not* drive behavior, and if there is a relationship between basic assumptions, espoused values and behavior, it appears to be a very loose one. Speaking about values, unfortunately, usually turns out to be an exercise in empty and meaningless expression. In most cases, it *is* a matter of *espoused* values, and there is little, if any, connection between these expressions and either the assumptions that drive behavior or the behavior itself. Argyris uses the terms "espoused theories" and "theories-in-use" to contrast what people espouse as values with the assumptions that truly drive behavior. He finds incongruence between these theories to be widespread, a circumstance that is clearly borne out in our own experience.[4] A recent illustration pertains to an international energy company that received a great deal of publicity over the alleged attitudes and actions of senior leaders resulting in apparently blatant racial discrimination. The alleged attitudes reflect negative racial stereotyping and the resultant actions include the use of crude and cruel language and discriminatory practices in hiring, promotion and compensation. The espoused values of equal opportunity and the merits of diversity in this company had been widely communicated through diversity training programs and corporate rhetoric. From the point of view of leaders, the degree of symmetry between what is said and what is done has important consequences. When there is congruence, leaders will be seen as well grounded and trustworthy; when there is little congruence, they will be seen as not credible and ineffective. Ken Sheldon in his book *Beyond Counterfeit Leadership*, attributes connecting what is espoused and what is practiced with leaders possessing integrity. Sheldon asserts, "Integrity means your mission, motives and means are aligned; you walk your talk; you practice what you preach; your beliefs and behaviors are congruent." "An organization is an ecosystem, a total environment, and the achievement and the maintenance of quality in products and services are intertwined with the integrity of the people from the top down."[5]

Karen Legge, in *Human Resource Management: Rhetoric and Realities*, comprehensively addresses the issues for human resource management in her critical analysis of the rhetoric and the realism of organizational behavior. In her usual thorough style, Legge takes into account the socio-political-economic context under which organizations operate. In one of her conclusions, Legge states, "It is important to emphasize the likely gap between espoused and operational policy, as much of the discussion about the nature of human resource management, with some honourable exceptions, ... still rests on statements of 'espoused' policy rather than rigorous examination of enacted practices."[6]

Gordon Bethune is credited with galvanizing his employees and turning Continental Airlines around. He speaks quite strongly about their policy and practice of communication, making sure the gap between what is espoused and what is done is kept closed. "... nearly everybody's worked in a place where there was a new, flavor-of-the-month management strategy coming down all the time, manifested in posters about leadership, a bunch of new catchphrases, and lists of new rules to memorize and phrases to parrot when the big bosses were around — and it all leads to nothing. What makes the Go Forward Plan different is that we mean it. All the things we talk about, we do. And all the things we do, everybody knows about. The lines of communication here are open from the customer straight up to me. Everybody knows what the goals are; everybody knows what the deal is."[7]

We described various perspectives on institutional knowledge in Chapter 1. These perspectives spring from social psychology in Schein's "basic assumptions", from Argyris's "theories-in-use" in Organizational Behavior and Berger's and Luckman's insights regarding institutionalization as sociologists. Mary Douglas, an Anthropologist, has written about Fleck's conception of the "thought style" and the "thought collective." Additional perspectives include: Kuhn's notion of "paradigm" developed within the context of the philosophy of science, the "tacit infrastructure" as expressed by the physicist David Bohm, the "formative context" of political scientist, Roberto Unger, and the psychologically based "institution-in-the-mind" of Shapiro and Carr. All of these perspectives refer to institutional knowledge as seen through different lenses and understood in different frameworks.

8.2   Dimensions of Institutional Knowledge

Turning our attention back to organizations and leaders, there is a need for some frame of reference for what is meant by institutional knowledge in this context. In other words, there is a requirement for some classification or taxonomy of the potential contents of basic assumptions related to culture. Edgar Schein has drawn on the models developed by sociology, particularly group dynamics, to define a very useful pattern for cataloging and thinking about institutional knowledge. He asks, "If culture is shared basic assumptions, we need to specify — assumptions about what?" Schein has articulated the categories of assumptions that pertain to all organizations. These assumptions deal with external environments and managing internal integration — with both underpinned by assumptions about more fundamental questions such as the meaning of truth, time, space, human nature and human relationships.[8] Assumptions associated with the external environment relate to matters of survival, adaptation and growth. Examples of these include assumptions about markets, products, competitors and success. Issues pertaining to language and relevant concepts, boundaries, distribution of power and status and the meaning of good performance are examples of assumptions related to internal integration. An analysis of institutional knowledge within the framework and intent of potential change and enhancement will be shallow and incomplete if the shared assumptions associated with more fundamental questions are not asked. Examples of those questions include:

What is the nature of reality and truth?
Is truth given or discovered?
Whose perception of truth matters?

Is human nature good, evil, neither, both?
What is the meaning of human activity?
What is the nature of relationships?
Is life cooperative or competitive, individualistic or collaborative?

Our experience in a high technology products and services company illustrates the dimensions and power of institutional knowledge. At the time of our initial involvement, the company, which we will call ABX, was about 15 years old having been founded by an engineer who continued to be involved in the company along with his co-founder, as non-executive chairman and vice chairman. The company had been successful in a niche market and held a dominant position in a highly demanding segment of that market. A new president and chief executive officer was recruited at about this time, and the founder and former CEO formally stepped aside to the role of chairman. The assumptions about the business held by the former CEO and most of his long term associates, based on the past and their strong beliefs, were that the company was well positioned for the future. Linear projections were provided for the new CEO which suggested that the proper course for the future was to do the same, only more of it. The new president, having known the company and the founders for a number of years, accepted their highly optimistic assessment of the company's prospects with little question.

As the new leader assumed his post, however, and became engaged in the operation of the company, the assumptions that were so clear in the mind of the chairman (and seemed to be driving behavior in the organization) looked less and less like reality. At the level of observable behavior, the organization was profoundly inward looking. Many members of the organization seemed smug, self-satisfied and antagonistic to criticism of any sort. Customers, while loyal and continuing to value the company's products, viewed the organization as generally arrogant, and uninterested in their opinions. At the level of performance, while the company was profitable, all the important indicators pertaining to future performance, were headed in the wrong direction. Product margins were falling, the level of earnings was declining, strong new competitors were emerging and market share was being lost in the segment where it had been dominant. These factors, to the extent they were recognized at all, were attributed to the sales force which was seen as unmotivated and unskilled. The attachment of blame for bad news to the sales department notwithstanding, the new CEO concluded fairly quickly that the past did not necessarily represent the most effective way forward and began the process of thinking about and introducing change.

The change process was difficult to initiate and even more difficult to bring to the point of possessing a degree of momentum. The culture of the organization as represented by its deeply held assumptions viewed customers as incompetent and unable to make proper decisions. Further, the company's products were seen as superior even though their designs were old and they had not been updated to match the capabilities of competitors. Members of the organization behaved as if customers and other outsiders were ignorant and in need of being led by ABX; the employees saw themselves as the source of most of the knowledge regarding the technology in question. A telling aside to this story concerns the company's advertising program which was in effect at the time of the arrival of the new president. The program featured print advertisements in trade publications depicting customers of competitors in various states of distress with bags over their heads. The intended message was that one would be forced to mask their identity as a consequence of making a blind and senseless decision for a competitor's product. While there was some humor associated with the program, the remarkable fact was that many members of the organization believed it, or at least behaved as if they did, in the face of compelling and contradictory evidence.

The changes the new CEO sought to introduce were related to becoming market and customer oriented and undertaking aggressive programs of product enhancement and development. While these initiatives were clearly needed, they were resisted by many members of the organization, both overtly and subtly, from the chairman down. Initiatives of this sort were dramatically at odds with the organization's culture. While the assumptions that have been described were probably more accurate in the past than in the present (the company had in fact been a pioneer in its field), the culture as expressed by these assumptions was out of phase with reality. The chairman and a few others, however, clung to the old assumptions which had found their way into the fabric of the organization. It must be said that many members of the organization, at least on an intellectual level, perceived these assumptions as inaccurate and voiced their support for change. At the level of doing, however, on a day in and day out basis, they continued to be driven by the old assumptions. These assumptions had taken on a life of their own.

A few members of the organization fully and energetically embraced change and some short-term success was achieved; the consequences of the efforts of these people belied their small number. Strong new product marketing and customer relations programs were instituted along with the achievement of significant change in the nature and quality of core products. Market success accompanied these programs, and based on observable changes in financial and market performance, the chairman found it difficult to argue against on-going and more significant change. The CEO was eventually allowed to lead an extensive reshaping of the company from its capital and ownership structure to its core technology and organizational framework. New areas of opportunity were identified, business planning was accomplished, new investment capital was acquired and new leaders were recruited. It could be argued that everything in the company changed — everything, that is, except the essence and effects of its culture.

It seemed at the time that the company had become oriented for long-term success. But the process of change had taken a great deal of time and truly fundamental change had only just then become possible. As defined by its old self, the company and its products were late in their life cycles. The pressures were therefore intense to move quickly within the context of the company's reformulated existence and generate antic-ipated levels of performance. The CEO had burned important bridges, especially with respect to the chairman, and had left himself exposed with other key board members. When performance was slow to materialize, the old assumptions crept back out of the shadows having never really gone away. In the presence of this opportunity, the CEO was ousted and the market and product plans were altered and ultimately abandoned except in rhetorical terms. When the stresses became acute, the old cultural imperatives re-emerged, creating organizational confusion and resulting in the resignation of key leaders. The company survived for a period of time, but it eventually lost financial viability and failed. While certain assets were acquired by other companies, ABX ceased to exist as a corporate entity and the equity of shareholders became worthless.

This story is a complex and multifaceted one. Mistakes were made by the CEO and others, but with the benefit of hindsight, this organization's demise was due to its culture. Irrespective of the efforts of many people, the real change that was enacted and the actions of individuals who knew better, the institutional knowledge — the basic driving assumptions from the past — held sway and drove the company out of existence.

To reiterate, institutional knowledge is not single dimensional. In most organizations, multiple stocks of such knowledge exist and interact with each other for better or for worse. These subcultures, represented by the language, concepts and assumptions unique to them, are associated with disciplines, occupational groupings and other communities of special interest. Information Technology is often cited as a discipline with a very unique subculture. Perhaps in less visible ways, unique stocks of institu-tional knowledge, i.e., unique subcultures, apply to virtually any discipline or occupational grouping such as engineering, marketing, sales, production, administration, etc. These subcultures can be congruent, mutually supportive, interdependent or at odds with each other. When strong subcultures exist in an organization and reconciliation among them around a common cause or purpose does not occur, the organization can find itself in the midst of serious and potentially undermining conflict which can continue indefinitely, largely out of the consciousness of senior leaders.

In the course of our work with a large healthcare organization, we observed the efforts and results connected with attempting to shift from a strong orientation toward autonomous disciplines to one of interdisciplinary clinics and services. Administrative procedures were changed, clerks were trained, physical facilities were redesigned and patient flows were altered. It was assumed that physicians and other professionals would reorient themselves. They did not! These diverse groups of clinicians represented strong subcultures — they spoke differently, they were trained differently and they saw and made sense of the same things in different ways. As conflict over practice and control intensified, they tended to become more entrenched in their own disciplines. Significant cross-cultural work, i.e., reconciliation of the relevant aspects of the interlocking stocks of knowledge, was required but not undertaken. More importantly, the objective rationale for the change was not uniformly clear; to the extent that it was clear, it was not perceived as an overriding cause to change. This case also provides a strong illustration of how espoused values often have no bearing on reality, and if believed, can lead to expectations that are not likely to be realized. Senior managers in this organization seemed to believe and actually spoke about how the organization's culture was one of interdisciplinary focus. Yet, the basic assumptions pertaining to the larger institution and to the relevant subcultures were admittedly and categorically at odds with what the senior leaders espoused.

Institutional knowledge generally operates out of the consciousness of people; it tends to be taken for granted and drives collective perception. The power and grip of institutional knowledge lies in how assumptions become objectified or institutionalized, then become internalized and made subjective by individuals. This process and consequence leads to perceptions of threat and feelings of anxiety when institutional knowledge is challenged. As individuals, and in a mutually reinforcing way in groups, we will go to great lengths to avoid such anxiety. We want reality to be congruent with our assumptions. To make them fit, we engage in distortion, denial, projection and any other psychological processes at hand to mask what may be going on around us. The results of these processes are defensiveness, erroneous perceptions and invalid information — all of which are antithetical to learning, growth and achievement.

8.3   *Freeing Leaders from the Grip and Consequences of Institutional Knowledge*

Leaders have a great deal at stake in enhancing the efficacy of institutional knowledge. Virtually any leader will recognize the frustration and disappointment associated with not being heard and understood. Leaders may flawlessly analyze circumstances, elegantly articulate the need to change and persuasively argue for new directions. Having done these things, many leaders believe that their job is done; they tend to fall under the illusion that there is a direct cause and effect relationship between what they say and what people do. In our experience, however, what people hear and the sense they make of what they hear tends to be more related to the stock of basic assumptions under which they operate than what their leaders say. If institutional knowledge drives perception and perception drives behavior and if purposeful behavior is the aim, a fundamental duty of leadership must be to enhance the relevance and accuracy of institutional knowledge. The process for leaders will begin at a very personal level — building an awareness of how institutional knowledge influences their own perceptions and holding these assumptions up for examination. As we described in Chapter 5 under the heading, "Freeing Individuals from the Grip of Institutional Knowledge", the freeing process is a one person at a time proposition — it must begin with leaders.

The words of the principle itself, *Enhance the Efficacy of Institutional Knowledge*, connote an ongoing and dynamic process. There is no suggestion of an end point or implication that, having once brought about an effective shift in the nature of basic assumptions, the principle is satisfied. As we consider how this principle relates to leaders, we will explore two complementary perspectives on institutional knowledge and change. The first pertains to building continuous learning capacity and not simply trading one set of assumptions for another. The second concerns building the capacity to maintain a balance between acting with economy of effort, within a set of established assumptions, while holding them loosely and questioning their validity when appropriate. Both of these capacities can also be expressed as creating and sustaining the ability to balance modes of learning. Argyris has defined these modes as single-loop learning, which refers to learning within the context of existing assumptions, and double-loop learning, which occurs when governing assumptions are evaluated for relevance and accuracy.[9]

The traditional model for organizational change was articulated by Kurt Lewin and subsequently expanded and embellished by others. "A successful change includes three aspects: unfreezing the present level L1 (of assumptions), moving to a new level L2 (defined by Schein as cognitive restructuring), and freezing group life at the new level (of assumptions)."[10] (Parenthetical comments are those of the authors.) While the insights represented by this model are important, the pace of change and the potential for rapid dislocation render static models such as Lewin's less than fully adequate. A prevalent circumstance illustrates the point. Restructuring, downsizing and re-engineering are terms in current usage that are defined by an orientation to cutting cost, generating perceptions of good performance in the short term and changing the psychological contract between organizations and employees. Many organizations have successfully restructured, which may well have been needed and may have produced good results. The difficulty lies in the fact that many organizations continue to restructure, re-engineer and downsize with Pavlovian-like regularity. Managers in these organizations seem to be addicted to cost cutting interventions. They exhibit no apparent awareness of any other courses of action often resulting in what has been called "corporate anorexia." From the viewpoint of cultural analysis, there will have been a shift in the content of basic management assumptions in such organizations. The old institutional knowledge would have embodied assumptions such as:

"long-term employment and employee loyalty are beneficial to the organization;"
"middle managers provide continuity and long-term stability;"
"keen market awareness and investment in research and development ensure long-term success."

New assumptions include:

"employment relationships are transactional and it is good to achieve the lowest cost in getting work done;"
"the successful long term is simply a rolling out of successful short terms ('... and I probably won't be here in the long term anyway');"
"business activity is given, the value of management therefore is to produce goods and services at the lowest possible cost."

While old assumptions in some organizations were in need of examination and change, what appears to have occurred is that old assumptions were simply traded for new ones. The old assumptions were unfrozen, new assumptions took shape and were then frozen to replace the old ones. In these cases, organizational learning capacity did not change. These organizations are now stuck in a culture of downsizing and restructuring. They are stuck in the new assumptions in the same way as they were stuck in the old ones. When new approaches are indicated, as is currently the case in some organizations, managers don't see them; their perceptions and their actions are now embedded in the new culture.

8.4   *Discovering and Changing Institutional Knowledge*

The conventional wisdom pertaining to change holds that there are risks in analyzing culture, i.e., in seeking to comprehend and evaluate the efficacy of institutional knowledge, and that change to basic assumptions is threatening to people. The risks are seen as associated with destabilization and the possibility of getting the new assumptions wrong; the threats produce anxiety and potential defensiveness. The reasoning continues that given these risks and potential consequences, the motivation to change must be clear and worth the risk and disquiet. Reasons to undertake change are numerous and varied and would generally accompany the presence of any data that disconfirms the attainment of important goals. Examples include declining market share, declining earnings and key balance sheet factors and poor product or service quality. Early indicators might include such factors as diminished gross margins, increasing customer complaints, elevated rates of employee turnover, declining performance standards and indications of fragmentation and disjointedness.

Conventional wisdom aside, it is clear that any purposeful and intentional change or movement from the status quo requires a compelling reason. It is also clear that awareness of internal and external circumstances and discernment of the need to change is a primary requirement of leadership. We believe, however, that in contrast to the image of change as a serial process (a process that incorporates awareness of the need to change, undertaking the hard work of change, bringing it about and then settling back to business as usual within the framework of new assumptions), a more relevant and useful image is one of a continuous orientation to change. This latter image is one of building learning capacity, or more explicitly, creating and embedding an aspect of self-referencing institutional knowledge — an assumption that defines all assumptions (except those pertaining to fundamental purpose) as fluid and continually open to examination, challenge and change. Within the context of building learning capacity, the motivational task for leaders becomes more formidable. Instead of creating motivation to change when either threat or opportunity is imminent or even present, the challenge is to bring about a motivational framework based on anticipation. The aim and the rationale is to avoid aberrations resulting from overreaction, the consequence of which is all too often losing sight of purpose and eventual decline.

Maintaining a clear sense of fundamental purpose, the leader's task is to motivate and bring about change based on the assertion that by the time threat or opportunity is present and observable, it is often too late to change. James O'Toole in his book, *Vanguard Management* [11], argues that effective culture change is virtually always a matter of evolutionary change — change where strengths and fundamentals are held as center posts around which variation and useful change can play out. He argues further that revolutionary change is always painful, frequently bloody and not very frequently successful. Turnaround stories involving revolutionary change are dramatic and interesting but they don't often have happy endings. Evolutionary change requires anticipation and learning and the ability to sustain a culture that embraces these characteristics.

If analysis and change of deeply held assumptions is threatening to people, producing anxiety and defensiveness, an environment that supports a posture of virtually continuous examination of assumptions would be likely to produce continuous and unsustainable anxiety. Paradoxically, such an environment is required for organizational learning and the absence of defensiveness is a precondition to creation of such an environment. In any change effort, an important aspect of the role of leaders is to mitigate the effects of anxiety on the group and, in some cases, to personally assume the anxiety. Further, there is a requirement to maintain grounding in something to sustain a sense of identity and integrity. Having made the case, we hope, for building learning capacity as the basis for enhancing the efficacy of institutional knowledge, it is now necessary to introduce a qualifying thought. We have argued against holding assumptions as frozen and absolute. We must now argue against assuredness in holding that no assumptions are absolute. In other words, the issue is not that there are no non-negotiable assumptions but rather where the line is drawn between those assumptions open for negotiation and those that are not. There are certain governing assumptions, that having been created and while open to examination and widespread awareness, are not subject to negotiation. These assumptions include those related to the fundamental purpose of the organization, the merits and consequences of seeking valid information and discovering the truth in all cases, and holding all other assumptions up for challenge and potential change. Association with any set of assumptions brings about a sense of identity and integrity. The leader's task is to bring about a shift from association with secondary, tertiary and sub-culture related assumptions to association with more fundamental assumptions, i.e., those associated with purpose and truth, thereby maintaining anchors to sustain perceptions of identity and integrity. Leaders seeking to bring about a learning environment must not only make it safe for challenging assumptions but must also reward individuals for responsible questioning and assumption-enhancing behavior. Finally, related to creating comfort with and tolerance for a higher degree of uncertainty, it is not likely that all individuals in any group will be able to productively exist in such an environment. The essence of a leader's task, then, is to build a critical mass of people through recruitment, assimilation and development who are able to thrive and even enjoy environments conducive to learning.

Complex scripts driven by deeply embedded assumptions are resilient and difficult to rewrite. These scripts even embody meanings of conscientious effort and good performance, circumscribing the best efforts of people and further reinforcing the tendency toward inertia. Culture change does occur, however. The content of institutional knowledge does, in fact, shift and creep along in the direction of reality in a natural way in the course of the playing out of an organization's life. But natural change occurs slowly and too frequently not in a manner consistent with the need to change. The requirement leaders face then, in seeking to bring about culture change, is to catalyze and accelerate change where such change can drive success and achievement of potential as well as reverse decline and facilitate survival.

Deliberate culture change is possible. Recent developments in the field of learning and memory affirm that learning is an active, voluntary process not simply a passive one of information assimilation.[12] People learn institutional norms; they can unlearn them. The Dynamic Theme from our model for learning and change as described in Chapter 2 re-emerges here. The pivotal relationship for leaders to comprehend, consider, describe and keep in front of people when undertaking culture change is defined by this dynamic theme. This dynamic relationship concerns that which pertains to institutional forms (objective reality such as culture or institutional knowledge) in contrast to that which pertains to individuals (subjective reality such as motives, imagination, emotion and ways of thinking). The relationship is one of mutual influence and is expressed in the circular argument: Organizations are created by individuals. Organizations (institutions as manifested by their culture) take on the form of objective reality. Individuals are shaped by organizations. In other words, the perceptions and actions of people create institutional knowledge, and while they are clearly affected by it, they have the capacity to recreate it. Leaders can facilitate the process of reformulating basic assumptions. But this doesn't happen automatically as a consequence of rational assessment and logical argument as the President of ABX discovered. It takes conscious and intentional effort, and as previously described, the motivation to change along with a carefully crafted environment to support change.

Leaders are required to inaugurate processes of change. Given that institutional knowledge is usually taken for granted and operates out of consciousness, the first requirement is to bring institutional knowledge into individual and collective awareness. Conflict and contradiction are dramatic and useful constructs to support the process of discovery and the raising of basic assumptions to the level of awareness. Identifying and categorizing observed behavior is a relatively easy and non-controversial way to begin. People may disagree about why they and others behave as they do, but the behavior itself is a fact. Having made explicit the behavior that informs the nature of the relevant culture, the next step is to explore the values that individuals say they hold — both as individuals and as a group. In our experience, it is invariably a straight forward matter to expose the contradictions between what is *espoused* as values and actual behavior. These steps can then lead directly to serious consideration of the assumptions that do, in fact, drive behavior. When both the behavioral and knowledge aspects of existing culture begin to take conscious shape, with persistent orientation to authenticity and veracity, the process can turn to the character of a new culture that individuals want to create. We have found the use of a simple matrix to be helpful. This culture change matrix will describe the characteristics of the existing culture, connecting to the strengths or pillars of culture that should be retained, connecting further, through the pillars, to the characteristics of the new culture. These efforts will necessarily proceed along two dimensions. The first pertains to individuals. The issues associated with individuals have been explored in Chapter 5 under the heading, "The Role of Individuals in Collective Learning". The second dimension pertains to groups which will be the subject of Part Four.

Becoming aware of existing assumptions and identifying new and more relevant ones, however, does not automatically turn the new expressions into "assumptions-in-fact." These new assumptions could become nothing more than new espoused values — sounding good but having little effect in objective existence. Qualified by the notion that the new assumptions are to be held within the framework of an on-going learning capacity, the new assumptions must become operative. The process of their becoming operative is identical to the process that embedded the old assumptions. Essentially, the new assumptions must work — their validity must be borne out in reality. In other words, the behavior spawned by the new assumptions must bring about more effective internal integration resulting in more successful external adaptation. To reiterate, the leader's role is to begin, facilitate and accelerate the process of change. Shein has defined "embedding mechanisms" which usefully spell out how leadership behaviors, when congruent with assumptions, can help make those assumptions operative. Primary embedding mechanisms include: "what leaders pay attention to, measure and control on a regular basis; how leaders react to critical incidents in organizational crises; observed criteria by which leaders allocate scarce resources; deliberate role modeling, teaching and coaching; observed criteria by which leaders allocate rewards and status; observed criteria by which leaders recruit, select, promote, retire and excommunicate organizational members. Secondary mechanisms include: organizational design and structure; organizational systems and procedures; organizational rites and rituals; design of physical space, facades and buildings; stories, legends and myths about people and events; formal statements of organizational philosophy, values and creed."[13] We have seen more often than not, the "cart being placed before the horse" — by focusing on the secondary mechanisms primarily and the primary mechanisms secondarily (or not at all) — in initiating organizational change. One organization in seeking to change its culture embraced virtually all the secondary mechanisms. It redesigned its organizational structure, created new procedures, generated promotional hype around change with posters, glossy brochures, buttons, etc. New physical space was even designed and constructed consistent with the new culture. Virtually none of the primary mechanisms were addressed however. In spite of what was promised, promoted and expected, fundamentally nothing about the culture changed beyond the superficial and cosmetic. In contrast to this "cart before the horse" phenomenon, a Human Resources Director whom we know, is avoiding this common error. Rather than responding to what appear to be red flags in this organization with the usual HR-oriented secondary mechanisms, he is challenging the corporate leaders to ascertain the validity of these early warnings and encouraging them to address the primary mechanisms and drivers of change.

8.5   Creating and Maintaining a Balanced Learning Capacity

To conclude this chapter, a return to the themes of learning capacity and balance is imperative; the greatest challenge to leadership attaches itself to these concepts. We have argued that enhancing the efficacy of institutional knowledge is a dynamic and continuous process. It is fundamentally about creating learning capacity and not about simply replacing a set of old assumptions with new ones. What Lorsh has called, "strategic myopia," the inability to conceive of certain strategic options because they are too out of line with shared basic assumptions, can apply to any set of hardened assumptions, whether old or new.[14] We have seen, for example in our work with healthcare organizations over the past 20 years, how old assumptions about the economics and structure of health services delivery successfully thwarted attempts at timely change and how in the present environment, new (hardened) assumptions about managed care are obscuring other strategic options.

Once culture has been brought into collective awareness — once culture is out of the closet so to speak, the task is to keep it out. An environment is required wherein individuals are relatively comfortable and able to be effective while holding an "interpretative stance." As referenced earlier, Shapiro and Carr argue that such a stance makes it possible to move from "one hypothesis to another hypothesis rather than from uncertainty to certainty." Pertaining to institutional knowledge, there is a profound requirement to create an aspect of institutional knowledge that is self-referencing with respect to the whole of institutional knowledge. An assumption must exist, in other words, that frames virtually all other assumptions as continually unfrozen and open to examination and change. In our experience, such an assumption springs from an orientation to pragmatism as such an orientation pertains to the nature of truth and reality. Pragmatism can be contrasted with perceptions of truth based on authority or dogma or "that's just how it is." Pragmatism maintains a focus on consequences. If outcomes or end results related to purpose become compromised or disconfirmed, basic assumptions become open to scrutiny. A solid grounding is maintained but it is at the level of purpose and reality rather than at the level of assumptions about artifacts.

Challenging and rethinking assumptions consumes energy and time. There are significant benefits associated with assumptions that have been embedded. Problem solving, determining courses of action and acting within the framework of existing institutional knowledge occurs with an economy of effort. Assumptions that account for behavior that produces consequences consistent with goals are assumptions that are best left alone. It would be ludicrous to suggest otherwise (unless the goals themselves are inappropriate goals). The balance to be achieved is one between holding assumptions open for evaluation for the purpose of effectiveness while holding other assumptions relatively stable to bring about efficiency. As we have described, the balance is essentially one of a state of equilibrium between modes of learning, i.e., between single-loop and double-loop learning. The maintenance of this balance is a function of leadership. There is no credible way to argue that achieving and sustaining this balance is a simple task. It requires acute perception, a highly developed sense of perspective and a great deal of knowledge about the operation of the organization in question. The key skill required of leaders is one of anticipation along with the ability to develop the skill in others. In what will be the only sports metaphor in this book, this skill is somewhat analogous to anticipation in tennis. If a player waits until the other player hits the ball and the ball is in flight before beginning to move into position to play the return, the player will not be able to arrive at the right location in time to execute a good return. A good player anticipates. Based on the location of her or his shot and the approach of the other player to the ball, a good player will begin to move into position assuring arrival at the proper spot with time to spare.

We have found the Sigmoid Curve to be a useful tool for framing efforts to achieve balance. The dynamics of the life cycle, or S-curve, provide a framework for thinking about aspects of organizational life from products and services to processes to units of the organization to the organization as a whole. The logic that underlies the notion of the S-curve is that everything has a natural life cycle characterized by slow and halting early growth, followed by rapid and sustained growth, followed by maturity with flattened growth, followed by decline. The shape of the curve that defines life cycle is an elongated S — ⌒. Charles Handy argues, however, that "there is life beyond the curve. The secret to constant growth is to start a new Sigmoid Curve before the first one peters out." For example, ⌒.[15] The point at which the development of a new curve should begin, which is exactly equivalent to saying the point at which new assumptions are required, is when the old curve begins to flatten, *not* when it describes a state of obvious decline. In very general terms, in plotting an S-curve, output is represented on the Y axis while input is shown on the X axis. The important insight from the logic of the S-curve is that as maturity approaches, incremental quantities of input (effort, material, time) are required to produce the same results or output. The S-curve provides a useful, if far from perfect, construct to help frame collective efforts associated with resource allocation, charting of courses of action and executing plans. In seeking to balance modes of learning on an on-going basis, leaders are called upon to foster the skills of anticipation and looking for relevant signals while maintaining an orientation to maximizing the production of results.

References

1. Hassard, J., *Sociology and Organization Theory: Positivism, Paradigms and Postmodernity,* Cambridge University Press, Cambridge, 1993, 26.
2. Schein, E. H., *Organizational Culture and Leadership,* 2nd ed., Jossey-Bass, San Francisco, 1992.

3. Schein, E. H., *Organizational Culture and Leadership*, 2nd ed., Jossey-Bass, San Francisco, 1992, 22.
4. Argyris, C., *Overcoming Organizational Defenses: Facilitating Organizational Learning*, Allyn & Bacon, Boston, 1990.
5. Sheldon, K., *Beyond Counterfeit Leadership: How You Can Become a More Authentic Leader*, Executive Excellence Publishing, Provo, 1997, 215.
6. Legge, K., *Human Resource Management: Rhetorics and Realities*, MacMillan Business, London, 1995, 60.
7. Bethune, G., *From Worst to First: Behind the Scenes of Continental's Remarkable Comeback*, John Wiley & Sons, New York, 1998, 216.
8. Schein, E. H., *Organizational Culture and Leadership*, Jossey-Bass, San Francisco, 1992, 50.
9. Argyris, C., *Overcoming Organizational Defenses: Facilitating Organizational Learning*, Allyn & Bacon, Boston, 1990, 92.
10. Lewin, K., Group Decision and Social Change, *Readings in Social Psychology*, 3rd ed., Holt, Rinehart and Winston, 1947.
11. O'Toole, J., *Vanguard Management: Redesigning the Corporate Future*, Doubleday and Company, New York, 1985.
12. Blackler, F., Formative Contexts and Activity Systems: Postmodern Approaches to the Management of Change, *Rethinking Organization: New Directions in Organizational Theory and Analysis*, Sage Publications, London, 1992, 278.
13. Schein, E. H., *Organizational Culture and Leadership*, 2nd ed., Jossey-Bass, San Francisco, 1992, 231.
14. Lorsh, J. W., Strategic Myopia: Culture as an Invisible Barrier to Change, *Gaining Control of the Corporate Culture*, Jossey-Bass, San Francisco, 1985.
15. Handy, C., The *Age of Paradox*, Harvard Business School Press, Boston, 1994, 50.

GROUPS

IV

Introduction

A critical mass of change at the level of the individual, shaped and molded by leaders and expressed in group action, defines effective organizational change. Our consideration now shifts to the nature and function of groups in organizational life. Groups represent the third dimension of practice as described in our model for learning and change in Chapter 2, and as we have argued throughout this book, change along all three axes or dimensions is required to bring about useful and enduring change. Perhaps in some pure and theoretical sense or in the perception of dogmatic individualists, an organizational model could be described wherein groups, i.e., work groups, teams, etc., would play little part — little part, that is, other than as the group the organization itself would represent. We doubt that such a model exists. We have, without question, never encountered the reality of such an organization even though many organizations are administered as if that contrived reality existed. Specialization and task differentiation are ubiquitous features of life in modern organizations and where collaboration around some common interest is required, purposeful work is accomplished through groups. When individuals meet each other to solve problems and act, the effectiveness of group behavior is a crucial factor. In fact, the character of life in organizations is interdependent and groups representing various job specialties and differentiated tasks are the context for the playing out of such life — whether productively or otherwise.

None of this is to diminish in any way the role of individuals. Three earlier chapters have been devoted to the instrumentality of individuals. Very little happens in organizations, however, based on individuals acting alone and a great deal of what has gone before in previous chapters pertains to the implications of individuals interacting with each other. It is self-evident that groups and group action are important. The only questions at the initial level of analysis are: How important are groups (as groups) and how (i.e., in what manner) are groups important?

These questions unfold to the following question: Do groups have emergent properties, i.e., properties where the whole is greater than or different from the sum of its parts or do groups simply represent the aggregate characteristics of the individuals that comprise them? Rom Harre in his book, *Social Being*[1], states, "The longest running, and perhaps the deepest philosophical issue in the theory of the social sciences has to do with the metaphysics of the groups in which human beings associate." He goes on to assert that any discussion of this perennial area of concern, which lies outside objective experience, must take account of the existence of two extreme positions, the collectivist and the individualist positions. "The extreme collectivist position holds that each human being is wholly constituted as a social person by the collective properties he or she participates in as a member of the society (group)." "Such a theory effectively denies any autonomy or creativity to an individual." On the other hand, "the extreme individualist thesis, that is the theory that each individual is wholly autonomous and could exist as a person wholly independent of the collectives to which he belongs, is a reflection of the theory that the relations which a person has to his collectives are wholly external and consequently quite contingent." In other words, the relations of a person to the groups to which she or he belongs are of little or no significance. In rejecting both extremes, Harre says, "But there is an observable autonomy and creativity shown by individual human beings, so that the collectivist thesis in this form is simply wrong." Further, "it is fairly easy to show, simply by drawing attention to uncontroversial facts available to anyone, that many properties of fully developed human beings are dependent upon that person being a member of a collective."

Harre and his analysis charts a course between these extremes of emergence and nonemergence and our experience in working with individuals and groups in organizations points to the validity of a middle perspective. Individuals do act with autonomy and creativity, yet the dynamics of groups play a significant role in organizational behavior. While individuals make up groups, and perception and action breaks down to the level of the individual, groups themselves bring something extra that contributes to or detracts from the quality of life in organizations. Beyond recognizing aspects of truth in both extreme positions, our practical knowledge of organizations points to the existence of mutual and reciprocal influence between individuals and groups. Effective people can, although they won't necessarily, help create effective groups; conversely, effective group behavior can help individuals become more effective. In a similar manner, ineffective groups can make individuals less effective and vice versa.

The answers to our initial questions are that groups are of vital importance to organizations, and they are vitally important because beyond just representing collections of individuals, they have emergent characteristics. There is a great deal of evidence that groups possess such characteristics. Creativity is widely regarded as a communal affair. Werner Heisenburg, a formulator of the uncertainty principle in modern physics, argued that "science is rooted in conversations."[2] David Bohm, the contemporary quantum theorist, sees thought as largely a collective phenomenon. Cardinal John Henry Newman, in his *Dublin Discourses*, asserted that "truth is wrought out by many minds working together freely."[3] "Truth," said the Scottish philosopher, David Hume, "springs from arguments among friends."[4] Not the least persuasive of such evidence can be observed by anyone at any given time in virtually any organization in terms of the consequences of beneficial or counterproductive group behavior. Who has not wondered how a group of intelligent individuals could collectively produce results suggestive of a mean IQ of about 80? Or, how could a group of knowledgeable people make such an obviously wrong decision when they were all aware they were making it? Conversely, what observer has not witnessed group action that resulted in a transcendent and synergistic solution to a problem — a solution that could not have been produced by the individuals present as simply a collection of individuals?

Schein defines a group in psychological terms. "A psychological group is any number of people who 1) interact with one another, 2) are psychologically aware of one another and 3) perceive themselves to be a group."[5] He goes on to classify groups as formal and informal. Formal groups are deliberately created by managers in organizations for some purpose. Examples include management teams, work units, staff groups providing specialized services, standing committees, and task forces organized to address specific issues. Groups may be vertically oriented, i.e., providing a basis for association within a function, a department or a discipline. Groups may also be horizontally structured, crossing functional boundaries when broadly-based coordination is required as in coordination of engineering, production, sales and marketing in product management. Formal groups may be permanent, or they may come into and go out of existence depending on circumstances. Informal groups arise out of a combination of formal factors and human needs. Informal groupings may coincide with and/or overlap formal ones, or they may exist quite independently from them. Informal groups meet the social needs of individuals and while often ignored by managers, they can wield significant influence on objective achievement in organizations.

The functions of groups encompass a wide range of formal or objective roles and rather more subjective ones related to the individual members of groups. The properties of groups that seem to be emergent, i.e., those that embrace characteristics not derivable by the summation of the characteristics of the individuals that make up the groups, may attach themselves to any group function. Objectively speaking, group functions range from problem solving to executing complex and interdependent tasks to providing coordination for implementation of intricate plans. Subjective functions generally relate to the emotional needs and cognitive processes of individuals and the collective expression of these needs and processes in the groups they form.

If groups possess emergent characteristics, and we believe they do, these characteristics can be useful or harmful. The results of effective group action is purposeful behavior and achievement. The beneficial expression of emergence is perhaps best realized in enhanced learning and creativity. The downside of that "something extra" that can emerge in groups can be observed when the results of group action is lower in quality than the aggregate effects of individuals working alone. Group think, muddled perceptions of accountability, even subversion of formal goals of the organization are examples of the potentially harmful effects of groups. The chapters which follow will explore how the three principles — *Achieve an Operative Balance of Objective and Subjective Factors, Delegate Only Around Purpose,* and *Enhance the Efficacy of Institutional Knowledge,* relate to groups. Specifically, the focus of these chapters will be on maximizing the beneficial effects of the emergent properties of groups and minimizing their potential negative effects.

In organizations, groups come together to form larger groups. For example, the larger group which defines the organization is comprised of groups that represent departments or other units and other groups that overlay departments and functions. As we begin to address the organization as the relevant group, "intergroup dynamics" become progressively more important. These dynamics are often expressed as the interaction of subcultures. Intergroup dynamics are key determinants of organizational performance. Destructive intergroup competition, conflict and working at cross purposes can constrain achievement while intergroup coherence and collaboration can dramatically facilitate it. As a special class of concern related to groups, intergroup dynamics will receive specific and focused attention in the chapters which follow.

References

1. Harre, R., *Social Being: A Theory for Social Psychology*, Basil Blackwell, Oxford, 1979, 83.
2. Heisenberg, W., *Physics and Beyond: Encounters and Conversations*, Harper and Row, New York, 1971.
3. Newman, J. H., *The Living Thoughts of Cardinal Newman*, David McKay Company, New York, 1946.
4. Handy, C., *The Age of Paradox*, Harvard Business School Press, Boston, 1994, 147.
5. Schein, E. H., *Organizational Psychology*, 3rd ed., Prentice-Hall, Englewood Cliffs, 1988, 145.

Chapter 9

Groups: *Achieve an Operative Balance of Objective and Subjective Factors*

Anticipatory Summary

Whenever groups fail to develop and move to a higher plane of achievement, it is usually because of either failing to take into account how people feel, think and perceive or the inability to escape the grasp of how people feel, think and perceive. When objective purpose is clear and consistent with the objective nature of the group, motivation to achieve results pertaining to purpose is the integrating factor; motivation crosses over between objective and subjective realities, connecting purpose with the subjective factors that impel the nature of relationships within the group.

9.1   Bridging from Individuals to Groups

- What individuals bring to groups plays an important role in the nature of the dynamics within their groups and on the character of the groups themselves.

- Individuals can enhance the quality of groups or detract from them; reciprocally, groups can cultivate or diminish the qualities of individuals.
- This level of analysis considers the bridging from individual dynamics to the dynamics of individuals in groups.
- Groups turn back on themselves either "virtuously" or "viciously". Under ideal conditions, the performance of a group would reinforce the positive traits of the individuals leading to a virtuous cycle; under a less than ideal set of conditions, the negative dynamics in a group would reinforce negative subjectivity in the individuals that make up the group thereby creating a vicious cycle.

9.2   Objective and Subjective Functions of Groups

- Objective functions of groups are varied and legitimate to the extent that groups so oriented generate beneficial consequences.
- Groups also provide functions of a more subjective nature.
  - There is a subset of subjective functions that is legitimate in organizations and an embedded subset that is highly beneficial to both organizations and individuals.
  - When legitimate subjective functions are achieved in informal groups within organizations, the effect for organizations is neutral at best.
  - There is a subset of potential subjective functions that is inappropriate and even dangerous.
- As the state of openness to change becomes a way of being in organizations, the requirement to maintain an effective balance between objectivity and subjectivity is intensified.

9.3   Emergent Properties of Groups

- Those characteristics of group behavior and action that are unexpected and not predictable solely from consideration of the characteristics of the individuals that make up the group constitute collective or "emergent" properties.
- Collective or emergent properties are structural properties and represent another dimension beyond the sum of individual characteristics.

- On the positive side of emergence, the collective intelligence and diversity of individuals can be accessed to create a gestalt, something greater than the sum of its parts.
- When the parochial and self-protective aspects of human nature become rooted and reinforced in the behavior of a group, the downside of emergence appears, and a kind of perverse gestalt is created.

9.4 Analysis and Comprehension of Group Dynamics

- If there are no emergent properties associated with the behavior of a group, there are no group dynamics; there are only individual dynamics.
- Any hope of changing the dynamics of a group must be accompanied by an understanding of the emergent dynamics.
- The analysis of group dynamics is approached on three levels: what is observable, what are the consequences of behavior and what are the underlying causes or conditions that spawn behavior.

9.5 Interventions

- Interventions seek to shift the effects of the emergent properties of groups from harmful to beneficial or from beneficial to more beneficial.
- Interventions at this level aim to dismantle old foundations based on defensive structures and patterns of attribution and replace them with new foundations underpinned with non-defensive and learning-oriented norms.

Groups: *Achieve an Operative Balance of Objective and Subjective Factors*

When people come together for the purpose of achieving a set of concrete results, acknowledgment and connection of the objective and subjective realities of their social context is a precondition for both learning and effective action. When a group is created for some objective purpose, the aim of such a creation is to frame the group's existence and actions and to motivate the group for achievement. What is subjective to group members will either facilitate objective achievement by the group or constrain it. We have argued repeatedly that there is a dialectical relationship, a relationship of mutual cause and effect, between objectivity and subjectivity in organizations and that it is important to understand the nature of this relationship. Any collection of individuals continuing as a group over time will naturally evolve an objective reality incorporating such factors as rationale for existence, perceptions of good and bad performance, modes of acceptable behavior, etc. This crystallized reality pertaining to the group will have a life of its own beyond and apart from the individuals that comprise the group. The objective reality associated with any group may or may not have a linkage in reality with the objective purpose for which the group was formed. We have seen that the objective reality of a group will ultimately become internalized by group members thereby becoming subjective to them, merging with whatever other issues of subjectivity these individuals bring to the group. When the group has evolved an objective reality that is not in conformity with its objective purpose, the task of achieving balance must first confront issues of culture and institutional knowledge. These issues pertaining to groups will be taken up in Chapter 11. When, however, the group's objective reality is congruent or at least compatible with the objective purpose for which it was created, the task to satisfy this principle for groups, while not an easy one, is a relatively straightforward one. When objective purpose is clear and consistent with the objective nature of the group, motivation to achieve results pertaining to purpose is the integrating factor. Motivation crosses over between objective and subjective realities, connecting purpose with the subjective factors that impel the nature of relationships within the group. These factors include emotion, perception (including attribution) and ways and patterns of thinking. Maintaining an operative balance between objective purpose and these subjective factors facilitates achievement including beneficial change that will support achievement.

It is undeniable that the success of an organization or any group depends on its ability to perceive reality as it is — to have the capacity to comprehend and deal with truth. The truth is manifested in the whole where the whole pertains to the life of the organization or the group and whatever circumstances confront it. The whole consists of objective and subjective realities and the nature of the relationship between them. The drive to maintain these realities in balance is nothing less than the drive to build the capacity to comprehend reality and deal with truth. The ability to build such capacity is determined by whether or not the group can bring to the surface and deal with issues possessing emotional content and idiosyncratic perceptions, within the framework of objective purpose.

Chris Argyris uses the term, "valid information," to describe the key governing variable around which effective group behavior arises or doesn't. Further, he points to defensiveness as the factor that will inevitably close down communication in valid information.

Incoherence and disconnection between objective and subjective realities invariably leads to failure of effective group action. In our experience, whenever groups fail to develop and move to a higher plane of achievement, it is usually because of either failing to take into account how people feel, think and perceive or the inability to move beyond how people feel, think and perceive. A circumstance which we have encountered on multiple occasions has to do with the now out-of-fashion quality movement. Many of these efforts failed to meet expectations which probably accounts for their passing from favor (irrespective of the inherent merits of the concept). Our involvement was always late in the process and associated with efforts that had, up until that time, produced few if any results. In all cases, the focus had been entirely on objective factors, how to quantitatively analyze performance and measure results, how to redesign physical work processes, etc. In connection with our involvement, we would examine the redesign work of groups that had not been successfully implemented. We were always struck by how the objective work itself seemed straightforward and non-controversial. We found that the most relevant and appropriate question in these circumstances was: "Given that this work is not complex or esoteric, why were these improvements not made before?" The answer to this question, to the extent that groups were able to answer it, not only explained why these improvements had not been made in the past but also why they were not being made in the present and why they would not be made in the future. The answer pointed to issues of subjectivity that were getting in the way of achievement. These issues were best characterized as patterns of defensiveness among individuals and work groups resulting from unresolved conflict, inaccurate perceptions and incongruent ways of seeing the world.

To illustrate the other side of the coin, on at least two occasions, we have encountered groups that could not move beyond subjective issues to be able to address their objective reasons for existence. The first group faced a significant operational problem around which there was so much history, emotion and flawed perception that whenever the objective problem was discussed, degeneration to passive-aggressive behavior or silence occurred. Rather than deal with the emotion associated with this problem, the group eventually refused to discuss it. Indeed, the group colluded around superficial solutions to avoid truthful (and painful) discussions of the issue. Since this group could not move beyond its fixation on subjective issues, it was eventually subsumed by another operating unit of the organization. The group, in effect, relinquished self governance and is now autocractically led.

The second group that could not move beyond subjective issues was attempting to come together as a management team. Among this group of only five people, each person had a separate agenda in addition to at least two subgroups which were operating and set against each other. All of this subterranean activity was overlaid with cordiality, friendship, socializing and expressions of being a team. The group was unable to set a serious and substantive program for itself. Whenever it tried, the underlying subjective dynamics intervened and closed down progress. On one occasion, we facilitated the emergence and confrontation of these subjective issues. Members left in tears and returned, attacked each other, became silent and very nearly lynched us! Months later, one of the team members told us that the team is now working well. He said that as painful as that session was, it had to occur and that they have learned that if they could deal with those issues, anything else looked easy.

9.1   Bridging from Individuals to Groups

What individuals bring to groups plays a significant role in the nature of the dynamics within their groups and on the character of the groups themselves. The observation of how the addition or removal of a single person to a group changes the disposition of a group is a common occurrence. We bring our complete selves to group encounters whether or not we reveal all aspects of ourselves. We bring our objective and subjective selves — our positive traits, our blind spots and our baggage. Individuals can enhance the quality of groups or detract from them. Reciprocally, groups can cultivate or diminish the qualities of individuals. As we will explore later in this chapter, the group itself may evolve a character apart from the sum of the individual traits of the members of the group, i.e., the phenomenon of emergence may occur. If objective purpose is clear and meaningful to members of the group and if some learning has occurred in the pursuit of purposeful achievement, the collective traits arising from the group may mitigate the negative consequences of the faulty perceptions, biases and defenses the individuals bring to the group. If on the other hand, the subjective natures of individuals surface and play out in an unrestrained fashion, the collective traits of the group will probably intensify the negative effects of those very same subjective traits.

Irrespective of potential emergence in groups, our intent at this moment and at this level of analysis is to consider the crossing over or bridging from individual dynamics (as individuals) to the single dimensional dynamics (nonemergent) of individuals in groups. In Chapter 3, we introduced and explored some key concepts related to subjectivity in individuals. We considered how our mental models and attributions act as lenses and filters, largely determining what we see and how we make sense of what we see. We looked into defensiveness and how our defenses frame our patterns of thinking and expressing ourselves. Surrounding these constructs of internalized perception and sense-making, we considered the mechanics of growth and development and argued that while change can be facilitated and helped along in groups, it is essentially a one person at a time process.

Under a set of ideal group conditions, the mental models held by the individuals comprising the group would be objectively accurate or at least held loosely so as to avoid the control they can exert. The attributions made by group members would be routinely tested and understood for what they are, i.e., the results of naturally occurring processes that are systematically and determinedly wrong at least half the time. Non-defensive norms would prevail and productive reasoning would frame the group's collective thought. Motivation, as seen and felt by the individuals in the group, would be congruent with the objective purpose of the group — leading to a reconciliation of objective and subjective meaning. Under such ideal conditions, the performance of the group would reinforce the traits of the individuals leading to a virtuous cycle — at least until the dynamics in the group changed.

At the other end of the group behavior spectrum, under a far less than ideal set of group conditions, the subjective natures of individuals would be in play as well, in an unmitigated way. One member of this group might hold the view that the members of the group representing technical functions, having no operational responsibility, have no legitimate place in the group. These group members would be invisible to the first perceiver. A male member of the group might believe that women are prone to let their emotions rule their actions. This man might send discounting signals whenever women assert themselves. Another member of the group could hold the opinion that those in authority are always right and should not be challenged. Yet another member might hold the attitude that those who always yield to leaders are weak and superficial. The leader of the group could believe that conflict is bad group behavior and a sign of poor leadership and therefore might seek to close down conflict whenever it occurs. All the members of the group might actively distance one member of the group because this person seemed to be out of favor and the cause would be attributed to poor personal characteristics. Two members, having been engaged in unresolved conflict for some time, might believe the conflict is due to just how the other person is.

The members of the group about whom these active patterns of perception and attribution exist, will react defensively. They will hear assertions as affronts whether they are or not. Their responses will be either subdued or argumentative and will trigger defensive responses in others. Those members reasoning defensively will keep their premises and assumptions to themselves and will not test the validity of their inferences and attributions. The members of the group who are certain about the validity of their views (as unverified as they may be) will assert themselves in ways that will close down inquiry into their positions. The information content associated with interactions in this group will be poor. The overall group will evolve patterns of defensiveness. These patterns, called "defensive routines" by Argyris, will insure that the underlying dynamics of this group will be covered up and bypassed to avoid threat and embarrassment.[1] It will be said about this group: "The members all have entrenched positions; no one is confronting the real issues; to outsiders the group looks cohesive but accomplishes nothing; everyone tells the leader what he wants to hear." The negative dynamics in this group reinforce negative subjectivity in the individuals that make up the group thereby creating a vicious cycle.

Having briefly considered the internal dynamics associated with individuals interacting in groups at both ends of the coherence/effectiveness spectrum, we have seen how groups turn back on themselves either "virtuously" or "viciously". Groups also project themselves outwardly and set themselves up for interacting with other groups and with individuals not part of the group.

9.2   Objective and Subjective Functions of Groups

Organizations exist to produce objective results. Objective functions of groups within organizations are varied and legitimate to the extent that groups so oriented generate beneficial consequences. The following list of objective functions is representative although by no means exhaustive.

- Groups of individuals representing various operating and support units of an organization come together to manage the overall enterprise. Such groups, often optimistically referred to as management teams, plan, allocate resources, identify opportunities and respond to threats.
- Operational problem solving groups bring individuals possessing varied skills and experiences together to create solutions beyond the capacity of any single individual.

- Product and service innovation and development requires the stimulation and sounding board character of group activity and the efforts of individuals representing various operating units.
- Groups come together around complex interdependent tasks such as performing cardiovascular surgery. Such a surgical task requires one or more surgeons, anesthesiologists, a scrub nurse, a circulating nurse, and a perfusionist.
- Groups are required to implement complex decisions, such as bringing into operation a new large-scale automated system or converting from a functional organizational format to a format oriented to products or services.

Interleaved with all such group functions are the additional requirements for coordination, development of collective perspectives and consensus, creativity and providing a platform for communication and learning.

Related to the individuals that comprise them, groups may also provide functions of a more subjective nature. Organizations are social systems and the individuals that populate them are social creatures. However, organizations are not social systems that just happen as a result of individuals occupying the same bit of geography or sharing a common biological heritage. Organizations are not like families or communities or countries. Organizations are purposeful and intentional whether or not purpose is achieved or the intent associated with organizing is realized. Out of all the possible subjective functions groups might provide for their members, there is a subset that is legitimate in organizations and an embedded subset thereto that is highly beneficial to both organizations and individuals. Groups can provide an enriching social context for individuals in organizations by meeting affiliation needs and providing a framework for personal growth and development. Groups can enhance the sense that individuals hold of personal identity and self-esteem. Groups can provide a framework for individuals to test their perceptions, to provide reality checks so to speak. Groups can even help individuals reduce anxiety and insecurity by providing a context for thinking about and dealing with fears.

To the extent that these subjective functions are satisfied within the framework of formal groups established for objective purposes, there is mutual benefit for both individuals and organizations. Individuals would have their needs met, as those needs could be reasonably expected to be met in an organizational setting, and organizations would be the beneficiaries of more productive and effective working groups. When what is meaningful to individuals at a subjective level is connected with and finds expression in groups established for objective purposes, the mutual benefit escalates to a higher plane with more profound consequences. When legitimate subjective functions are achieved in informal or ad hoc groups within organizations, the benefits for individuals may be the same but the effect for organizations is at best neutral, and at worst counterproductive. Benefits for individuals derived apart from objectively framed settings may promote self versus organizational interests and behaviors that are contrary to achievement of organizational goals. The leaders of organizations often only have themselves to blame for this circumstance. Robert Merton, in his article, "Bureaucratic Structure and Personality," observed that leaders of organizations usually emphasize reliable and predictable behavior on the part of members of their organizations. One of the consequences of this reductionist emphasis is that personal relationships are reduced. "Bureaucratic actors are considered as role incumbents rather than individuals with personalities. They become the objects of organization, not the subjects."[2] Merton's perspective is from the 1940s. While there is a great deal of espoused difference from this circumstance 50 years later, there is in fact often very little difference.

There is also a subset of potential subjective functions of groups within organizations that is completely inappropriate and even dangerous. Individuals that seek intimacy, love and unconditional regard from objectively driven organizations are setting themselves up for personal disappointment or worse and placing their organizations in the position of having to deal with the consequences. We often hear group members say something like: "We want our team or department or work unit to be like a family!" We usually ask: "Given that there are a lot of different kinds of families, what kind of family do you hope your group will be like?" Further, "Would you want to be a member of a family where the criterion for membership is objective achievement?" There are clearly examples of intimate relationships that exist within work groups that are conducted in responsible and non-damaging ways. In our experience, however, there are far more examples of dysfunctional individual and group relationships resulting from individuals seeking to have their deepest subjective needs met within organizations. It is not our intent to convey the notion that organizations should be cold and sterile places. There are, without question, subjective needs of individuals that can be responsibly and appropriately met by groups within organizations and both individuals and organizations will be better for it. With respect to a standard of behavior between and among individuals within organizations, the best that can be hoped for is one based on treating others in a manner in which we would hope to be treated ourselves. This golden rule, difficult enough to achieve in its own right, is consistent with the objective requirements of any organization, and if achieved even in families, would represent an improvement in many of them.

The subjective functions of groups warrant special attention during periods of change. As the state of change becomes a *way of being* in organizations, the requirement to maintain an effective balance between objectivity and subjectivity is intensified. Individuals experience losses in transitions. Such losses include those related to personal affiliations, autonomy, control, meaning and security. Change also represents opportunity. When the framing of group interactions remains clearly focused on the objective drivers and consequences of change, groups can play a vital role in helping individuals make transitions. In our experience, given sincere encouragement and safety in the expression of feelings around losses, most individuals are able to deal with these losses and move quickly to exploring potential gains and opportunities associated with the change.

9.3   *Emergent Properties of Groups*

Those characteristics of group behavior and action that are unexpected and not predictable solely from consideration of the characteristics of the individuals that make up the group constitute what Rom Harre calls "emergent properties." While arising from natural and logical consequences, such properties represent the something extra to which we have pointed. They relate to newly formed characteristics and qualities. To return to Harre's insights regarding "people in groups," he says: "One way of distinguishing collective from individual properties might be to propose that collective properties are structural properties — that is, they are based upon but not reducible to relations between more than one individual."[3] This assertion is equivalent to one that proposes that collective properties are "object-like" — separate and distinct from the mere collection of individual characteristics. Based on relations driven by subjectivity through the intermediary of a structure (an evolved pattern of relating), qualities attach to the group which are quite separate and apart from the collective qualities of the individuals. Harre further argues that for a structural property to be manifested as a real and causal one, there must be something on which the property has an effect. We have seen, and will subsequently explore in greater detail, that real and observable effects of emergence in groups exist. These effects move between results of group action that beneficially transcend individual capacity to those that reduce group performance to a level far below the capacity of any single individual.

There are important and far reaching implications of the existence of emergent properties on internal group dynamics as well as on inter-group dynamics. On the positive or up side of emergence, the collective intelligence and diversity of individuals can be accessed to create a gestalt — something greater than the sum of its parts.

An example of beneficial emergence or coming forth associated with group action comes from our work with a group of physician-researchers. Each member of the group was a section chief within a large department. The group included the head of the department and his principal associates. Prior to our involvement with the group, the members had been engaged in a process of setting a strategic agenda for the department. The result of the effort had been less than satisfactory. The members had succeeded only in producing what amounted to a wish list. This list was essentially incoherent and included all the initiatives the individual members of the group could conceive of. There was no collective sense of direction for the department and the initiatives were framed as activities without associated objective outcomes. Therefore, there was little ability to discriminate around the relative importance of discrete initiatives. Each section viewed itself as virtually autonomous; as a result, areas of potential collaboration were not identified and explored. Given that resources were limited and all initiatives would consume resources, all proposed initiatives could not be undertaken. Group sessions organized to establish priorities and rationally allocate resources gave way to lobbying by the various section chiefs for their own programs and avoiding anyone's "ox being gored." There were strong, negative, subjective forces at work in the group. Unresolved conflict, lack of trust and an attribution of inappropriate motives to the department head and others had resulted in a general pattern of defensiveness. Whenever attempts to set intermediate or long term outcome goals for the department were made (necessary to effectively discriminate in the allocation of resources), these defensive routines would become engaged and effective work would be closed down. Individuals, perceiving threat to their own programs by other individuals whom they didn't trust, would shut down communication of valid information as such information pertained to external factors, departmental strengths and weaknesses and potential opportunities. The essence of what needed to be communicated was never spoken about directly. They talked, but they didn't really say anything worthwhile about issues that really mattered.

Subjective factors were the initial focus of our work with this group. Having developed a provisional understanding of these factors, the group was presented with an analysis of the dynamics in play and the consequences on objective achievement for the entire department. Individuals and the group validated the assessment. Working with individuals, pairs of individuals and with the group as a group, conflict was surfaced and resolved (or at least mitigated), attributions were tested and more often than not, shown to be inaccurate, and the effects of negative perceptions were minimized. Through these efforts, the defensive dynamics of the group shifted. It would be a stretch of the imagination to suggest that all subjective issues were dealt with and the group lived happily ever after. The effects of the effort, however, are important to consider. The group developed the ability to openly discuss and reflect upon real strategic issues even when individual members would potentially lose status and budget allocations. The group collectively developed a statement of direction which spelled out in objective terms the outcomes or results that would represent significant growth and development for the department. The complete array of proposed initiatives was then evaluated in terms of how each initiative did or did not relate to the objective direction of the department. More importantly, a level of creativity developed in the group wherein collaborative efforts were identified, old initiatives were enhanced and new and more relevant ones were introduced. Because of the altered subjective chemistry of the group, something greater than and different from the sum of the work of the individuals emerged. The work of the group as a group created results that a disconnected collection of individuals simply could not have produced.

When the parochial and self-protective aspects of human nature become rooted and reinforced in the behavior of a group, the downside of emergence appears. A kind of perverse gestalt is created where the whole of the set of defenses and hardened attributions among the individuals assumes an anti-learning and defensive character exceeding the sum of the traits of the individuals in the group. Group performance is reduced to the lowest common denominator or worse, and the very existence of the group becomes counter-productive. The salient feature of such groups is their highly developed ability to obscure reality and deal in less than valid information.

As Harre has suggested, and given that most members of ineffective groups don't intend for their collective efforts to be ineffective, the cause of this circumstance seems to be structural. In other words, the cause appears to be one that operates apart from the conscious motives and actions of the individuals that make up such groups. Argyris argues for the existence of structure as represented in what he calls "defensive routines." His notion of structure is based on a model of socialization which he designates "Model I" and which he believes applies to most of us. Model I instructs us to "seek to be in unilateral control, to win, and not to upset people."[4] According to his analysis, our "Model I governing values" lead us to formulate action strategies for interacting with other people that put us at odds with them (and them with us) and set us (and them) up for potential embarrassment and threat. "Organizational defensive routines are actions or policies (informal rules) that prevent individuals or segments of the organization from experiencing embarrassment or threat. Simultaneously, they prevent people from identifying and getting rid of the causes of the potential embarrassment or threat."[5] (Comments in parentheses are those of the authors.)

The principle casualty of the operation of defensive routines is the truth. When valid information threatens people, invalidates securely held views about control and winning or causes embarrassment for one's self or for other people, methods to avoid it are skillfully enacted. Argyris calls this group phenomenon "skilled incompetence." Numerous examples of skilled group incompetence have been cited in this and other chapters. Without doubt, the reader will be able to bring to mind examples of such incompetence and the unintended consequences of group action. A common example that hardly any of us could have avoided relates to false consensus. When false consensus occurs, group decisions are made in favor of options no one wants. False consensus is humorously illustrated in the classic "Abilene Paradox." Jerry Harvey tells the story of a hot, dusty Sunday afternoon in West Texas and the collective decision of a family to drive 53 miles to Abilene in an unairconditioned car to have dinner in a cafeteria. The story concludes, after the group having made the trip to Abilene, with the discovery that no one wanted to go but had assumed that all the others did.[6]

"Groupthink" represents a special class of group incompetence resulting from too much cohesiveness and conformity. According to Michael Argyle, groupthink occurs when "a group comes to see itself as invulnerable; there is rationalization of blind spots, it ignores ethical issues; stereotyped outgroups are seen as evil, weak or stupid; a lot of pressure is put on dissenters, who are regarded as disloyal; any doubts are not voiced and there is an illusion of unanimity."[7] Well-known examples of groupthink include the decision by the American President and his advisors to back the Bay of Pigs invasion of Cuba in 1961 and the actions of NASA personnel and certain contractors associated with the Challenger space shuttle disaster. To us, in terms of consequences and sheer doggedness, the most profound example of groupthink is connected with America's involvement in Southeast Asia. In the words of historian Barbara Tuchman, "Ignorance was not a factor in the American endeavor in Vietnam pursued through five successive presidencies, although it was to become an excuse. The folly consisted not in pursuit of a goal in ignorance of the obstacles but in persistence in the pursuit despite accumulating evidence that the goal was unobtainable, and the effect disproportionate to the American interest and eventually damaging to American society, reputation and disposable power in the world. The question raised is why did the policy makers close their minds to the evidence and its implications? This is the classic symptom of folly: refusal to draw conclusions from the evidence, addiction to the counter productive."[8]

9.4 Analysis and Comprehension of Group Dynamics

If there are no emergent properties associated with the behavior of a group, there are no group dynamics; there are only individual dynamics. If, however, as is most often the case, certain characteristics of group behavior can be described as emergent, any hope of changing the dynamics of the group must be accompanied by an understanding of those emergent dynamics. Therefore, any useful analysis of group dynamics must bring about comprehension of these emergent properties by members of the group in question. As we have seen, group dynamics or the emergent properties associated with a group tend to be structural. Bearing in mind that an aspect of the structure as represented in patterns of defensiveness brings about behavior designed to cover-up and bypass such patterns and sources, comprehension of group dynamics is easier said than accomplished. In our experience, comprehension only occurs in connection with discovery on the part of group members as in a sort of "aha!" event.

We approach the analysis of group dynamics on three levels. The first level of analysis pertains to that which is observable and includes behavior in the group, actions and decisions taken by the group and assertions made by individual members of the group. The second level relates to the consequences of behavior and action. (There are several orders of consequences where only the first order is usually observable.) The third level of analysis concerns underlying causes or conditions that spawn behavior and tend to be inferential.

Any data that comes our way is grist for analysis. Beyond the direct observation of group behavior and the results of such behavior, the first stage of our analysis includes individual interviews with members of the group. What individuals say in direct response to our questions is important. What is more important is how they make sense of the activity and the results of the efforts of the group — how they attribute causes and motives to circumstances and behavior, how their attributions are formed, i.e., whether based on observation or inference, and what seems to trigger their own defensive responses. The second stage of our analysis yields a set of inferences about causes and the more subtle consequences of the dynamics of the group. The point of the analysis is to bring about an awareness and understanding of how group dynamics are restraining the efforts of the group. That objective is initially pursued through a feedback session, i.e., a presentation of the analysis to the entire group. Questions, comments and challenges to the data are encouraged throughout the presentation, bearing in mind that discovery on the part of individual members is the aim. The presentation begins with a cataloging of what is observable, about which there is little controversy. We then move to causes of behavior and actions. An aspect of what we assert regarding causes will have been inferred, but significantly, an aspect will have been made observable to us through interviews and other encounters but not observable to the group as a whole. Our inferences about causes are publicly tested with the group. However, these inferences usually survive challenges and tend to be quite eye-opening. We conclude the feedback by looking at second and third order consequences, which are also open to challenge, but tend to be seen as logical outcomes assuming the validity of observed behavior, which is self-evident, and the validity of inferred causes of behavior and actions.

We have used two constructs to organize and present feedback to groups. The first of these is based on the metaphor of an iceberg where observable phenomena are above the surface and causes and subtle consequences are below the surface. The image, of course, is one that brings to mind the notion that what we can see is "only the tip of the iceberg," while what is keeping the tip afloat and above water is out of sight. The following illustration comes from our work with a group of managers in an operating division of a large organization. The observable phenomena, i.e., what people said, what people did, operating facts and direct consequences included the following categories: supply and instrumentation issues, staffing issues, facility issues, inconsistent performance, customer dissatisfaction, unresolved conflict, declining volume. The factors below the surface included: culture (a strong sense of looking inward), emotional state (feelings of helplessness, anger and lack of trust), patterns of defensiveness and attribution, systemic issues, leadership issues and strategic issues.

The second construct is an adaptation of the Action Map as described by Chris Argyris. The action map is especially useful because it interprets the structure of group dynamics and illuminates the circular and self sealing nature of such dynamics. The Action Map is a "representation of actions, strategies, consequences and governing conditions and the feedback and feedthrough mechanisms that relate them to one another in a persistent pattern. An Action Map helps actors to think backward and think forward. It is designed to help the actors to find the relevant variables, to link them in a causal chain, and to assess the plausibility of the change."[9]

An Action Map constructed for a group of senior managers with whom we worked is summarized below:

Governing Conditions
Individuals are personally committed to excellence and growth.
Individuals are narrowly focused.
There is qualified (at best) respect and trust for each other as leaders.
There is qualified (at best) interpersonal respect and trust for each other.
Group norms are polite and nonconfronting.
There is little clarity around overall direction.
The environment is reactive and political.
Action Strategies
Make attributions about the motives, intentions and capacities of others.
Craft assertions and attributions in ways that make them untestable.
Rationalize nontesting by exhibiting care for others or attributing blame.
Organize attributions in ways that predict that change is unlikely.
Make these strategies undiscussable.
Make the undiscussability itself undiscussable.
Consequences for Group Dynamics (First Order)
Polarization.
Low confidence in group effectiveness.
Mediocre or no resolution of difficult problems.
Little encouragement of inquiry into one's own position — advocacy over dialogue.
False consensus.
Consequences for the Organization (Second Order)
Maintenance of the status quo.
Territoriality and coalition building.
Nonresolution of conflict.
Cynicism.
Direct and indirect badmouthing.
Maintenance of defensive patterns.

Our feedback to this group began at the level of "Consequences for Group Dynamics" around which there was no disagreement. We proceeded backward to "Action Strategies", which were in part initially inferred, but subsequently confirmed in individual interviews and other observations. We then proceeded back even further to "Governing Conditions" which were challenged but ultimately determined by the group to be valid as were "Consequences for the Organization" which marked the conclusion of the analysis.

As a note regarding methodology to conclude this section, our approach to analysis and understanding is an interpretive one. To summarize the key features of an interpretive approach, the emphasis is on: qualitative rather than quantitative methods; validity, richness and meaningfulness of data rather than their statistical reliability; exploratory, tentative and discovery-oriented investigation rather than on verification-oriented investigation; and explanation through developing understanding rather than predictive testing.[10]

9.5   Interventions

Any reasonable intervention associated with group dynamics, whether undertaken by group leaders or outsiders, would aim to enhance creativity and learning and to bring about purposeful behavior and achievement. It would seek to shift the effects of the emergent properties of the group from harmful to beneficial or from beneficial to more beneficial.

Related to building beneficial consequences of group dynamics, the next chapter addresses the factors surrounding the development of purpose and bringing about purposeful and interdependent thinking and behaving. Chapter 11 will take up the matter of group learning through more effective modes of interaction and the requirement to actively enhance the content of institutional knowledge. These topics come together to bear upon the objectives of well-formed and executed interventions. For the present, however, our concern is with laying down the foundation upon which interventional efforts will build — efforts to change culture, bring about more effective learning and create clarity of purpose and congruent behavior. Creating the foundation relates to nothing less than dismantling the old foundation, often based on a structure of defensive routines and patterns of attribution, and replacing it with a new foundation underpinned with non-defensive and learning-oriented norms. The new foundation must support the development of the skill and the inclination to seek and discover valid information. It must, in other words, support the capacity to interact and ultimately to act within the framework of truth, as nearly as that elusive commodity can be apprehended. Without such a foundation, it makes little sense to pursue any program of change regardless of how good the program sounds or how much change is needed.

As discussed in the section just concluded, the first and often one of the most useful change-oriented interventions is the discovery and analysis of group dynamics and the work in groups to bring about comprehension of those dynamics. It is frequently the case that the process itself of learning about existing dynamics will bring about some change. In any case, understanding where a group is positioned is a prerequisite for moving it to another place. Having established that understanding, our greatest success in change efforts has been when interventions have been pursued along two tracks — one related to the group and one related to the individuals in the group.

Factors pertaining to individual perception and defensiveness are at the core of the hardened patterns of defensiveness and attribution that shape the character of group dynamics. Group settings are appropriate and convenient arenas for bringing about understanding among group members of how the expression of their own individuality produces consequences, related both to other individuals and to the group as a whole. The dynamics of perception and attribution and the processes related to both defensive and productive ways of thinking can be effectively taught in group settings. Group members can also be instructed to use simple techniques to alter and enhance interactions with others; these include use of the "Left-Hand Column," testing attributions and inferences, inviting inquiry and suspending assumptions. These concepts are fully explored in Chapter 3.

The Birkman Method, which has been discussed in earlier chapters related to individuals and leaders, has group dimensions as well. Composite group scores represent the range of differences in style, personality and reactive or defensive behaviors among the members of a group. Based on the proposition that as individuals we are all incomplete and can only become more complete as a collection of individuals, the composite scores can help frame the potential upside of diversity as well as the potential downside of it. Another premise underlying The Birkman is that there are no right or wrong ways of being — only different ways of being. The term diversity is used here in this most basic sense.

Individual settings are the scene for bringing to the surface and taking apart established patterns of flawed perceptions and defensive responses. The application of concepts and tools learned in group settings begins to play out in individual settings. These settings include writing and debriefing cases, preparing for role negotiations, engaging in role negotiations and engaging in other sessions where there is unresolved conflict between and among individuals. These kinds of sessions are fully described in Chapter 3. Within the context of objective reasons for resolving conflict and misunderstanding, subjective factors are actively pursued. Individuals are challenged to make their inferences and bases of attribution explicit, aiming to show where inaccuracies in perception may be at work. "Gunny sack" issues or the residue from events or assertions from the past that trigger defensive reactions are exposed and often set aside. Issues of differences in style and approach may be mitigated through awareness that we are all wired differently and even so, can work together to make our differences an advantage. Based on a variety of factors, many of them subjective, individuals decide whether or not they will become committed to and fully participate in group processes. In connection with all of the above, issues associated with reaching decisions that are in the best interest of the group are pursued in individual settings.

As individuals move back and forth into group settings, the results of the work in individual settings can begin to take hold. With encouragement and reinforcement, the dynamics of the group can change. As groups undertake issues of substance, such as setting direction, allocating resources and solving problems, diminished defensiveness and resolved personal conflict can open the way to greater public candor and an improved ability to deal with objective issues. While the process as we have described it may sound clean and tidy, it usually is not. The process can be quite messy and distinctly non-linear. Addressing long standing issues of subjectivity can be difficult and sometimes painful. Some issues are slow to become resolved; others never reach resolution. Some individuals are unable to move out of their subjective boxes and cannot develop the capacity to function in a more frank and challenging group environment. However, the aim is to improve group dynamics and position the group to deal with real issues and the whole of circumstances, not just pieces and margins, regardless of the emotional implications of doing so. The goal, then, is to bring about a critical mass of changed orientations fueling a shift in group dynamics that will, in turn, enhance group effectiveness and learning potential.

Teambuilding and improving group dynamics is written about and talked about a great deal. The process is often made to sound easy and painless — just get the group together, go through some exercises, go into the backwoods, engage in some bonding activity, or simply agree on some new set of ground rules for working together. In our experience, these superficial and simplistic approaches never work. Without understanding the structure of the dysfunction and systematically and persistently taking it apart, little good will come from these efforts, as popular as they may be.

It is fairly common to observe the language of *being a team* and group effectiveness being taught with group members speaking the new language and behaving no differently. A recent experience with a cross functional work group formed for a specific purpose is illustrative. All of the members of the group knew each other although they represented different departments. As a part of forming the group, the group leader identified a set of ground rules or behavioral norms for the group. The first ground rule stated — "There will be no subgroups or cliques, all issues will be discussed and resolved openly within the whole of the work group." Within hours, at least three subgroups had formed, largely representing political and personal differences. Interestingly, one of the subgroups actually did the objective work and was able to push it through the larger group. While the problem was solved, however, the consequences of non-participation and non-commitment to the solution had significant effects. Regarding wilderness experiences, the typical reactions of participants is something like this — "we were a great team in the woods and on the obstacle course but when we came back to work, all the same problems persisted." The essential point is this — no amount of "forming, storming, norming," etc. or any other pleasantly prescriptive approach to improving group dynamics will bear fruit if the group is systematically unable to deal with the truth.

References

1. Argyris, C., *Knowledge for Action: A Guide to Overcoming Barriers to Organizational Change,* Jossey-Bass, San Francisco, 1994, 49.
2. Hassard, J., *Sociology and Organization Theory: Positivism, Paradigms and Postmodernity,* Cambridge University Press, Cambridge, 1993, 26.
3. Harre, R., *Social Being: A Theory for Social Psychology,* Basil Blackwell, Oxford, 1979.
4. Argyris, C., *Knowledge for Action: A Guide to Overcoming Barriers to Organizational Change,* Jossey-Bass, San Francisco, 1994, 13.
5. Argyris, C., *Knowledge for Action: A Guide to Overcoming Barriers to Organizational Change,* Jossey-Bass, San Francisco, 1994, 25.
6. Harvey, G. B., The Abilene Paradox: The Management of Agreement, *Models for Management: The Structure of Competence,* Teleometrics International, The Woodlands, Texas, 1980.
7. Argyle, M., *The Social Psychology of Work,* 2nd ed., Penguin Books, London, 1989, 145.
8. Tuchman, B., *The March of Folly: From Troy to Vietnam,* Alfred A. Knopf, New York, 1984, 234.
9. Argyris, C., *Knowledge for Action: A Guide to Overcoming Barriers to Organizational Change,* Jossey-Bass, San Francisco, 1994, 92.
10. Legge, K., *Evaluating Planned Organizational Change,* Academic Press, Harcourt, Brace, Jovanovich, 1984.

Chapter 10

Groups: *Delegate Only Around Purpose*

Anticipatory Summary

Among the determinants of beneficial emergence in groups, the foremost is a sense of common cause — a common perception of purpose. Purpose is a primary motivating factor for individuals and frames collective aspiration and shared commitment in groups. A secondary determinant is accountability for collective results leading to interdependent thinking and behaving. This chapter is primarily concerned with the development, translation, interpretation and perception of purpose by groups as a common cause.

10.1   Interdependent Thinking and Behaving

- Groups are the stage for the playing out of interdependent thinking and behaving.
- Interdependent behavior produces beneficial consequences; in the absence of a sense of and working mode of interdependence, the actions of groups can do harm, producing negative leverage.
- Differentiation in function, role, skill and interest is a fact of life in modern organizations.

- The benefits of differentiation set against the requirements for integration define another paradox, one which is becoming increasingly difficult to reconcile.
- When a clear sense of purpose is present, integration of functions, roles and activities driven by interdependent thinking and behaving can develop, reconciling this paradox.
- If a common cause is necessary to bring a group of individuals into thinking and behaving interdependently, that requirement intensifies as issues related to intergroup dynamics begin to be addressed.
- Intergroup dynamics can be understood as the interaction of subcultures; the task of integrating an organization is no less than a problem of integrating subcultures.

10.2 *Bringing About Interdependent Thinking and Behaving*

- How may individuals, working within and through diverse groups, be engaged in the development of organizational purpose in such a way that the larger purpose becomes adopted as their own?
- How can clarity of purpose be sustained over time and the creativity of individuals, in collaboration with others, be fostered and sustained?
- How can the efforts of people within a widely differentiated organization be integrated around accomplishments that matter for the organization?
- Given a clearly articulated purpose at the highest level of the organization, how can purpose be translated, operationalized, executed and evaluated with explicit perceptions of accountability for results related to purpose?
- The Strategy Development and Integration Model addresses the classical organizational problems of strategy development, planning, integration and performance, and more importantly, correlation among all of these concerns.
- Relevance and coherence are the central ideas in the model.
- Relevance for the organization refers to a sustained focus on the results that truly matter for the organization as a whole.
- Relevance for the individuals that make up the groups and the organization refers to a direct and personal connection with those results.

- Coherence relates to the ability to bring about and sustain an orientation to a uniform purpose throughout an organization over time.
- Two major barriers to consistent and purpose-driven execution remain.
  - The first of these is the traditional model of supervision. Effective collaboration is constrained by delegation of tasks passed down the hierarchy.
  - The second barrier relates to managers who are not close enough to problems to be able to make the best operational decisions.
- A peer review concept and model is proposed as a potential route to the mitigation of these concerns.

Groups: *Delegate Only Around Purpose*

Objective purpose is the *why* of organizational existence, but subjective factors either facilitate or inhibit objective achievement. Motivation is the bridge between subjectivity and objectivity. Motivation is the aspect of what is subjective to individuals that crosses over and connects in a real and substantial way with objective reality as expressed in purpose. Purpose is the motivating factor for individuals and frames collective aspiration and shared commitment in groups. Clarity of purpose mitigates the potentially divisive and counterproductive effects of subjectivity and can turn such subjectivity into an effective force for achievement, underpinning and driving purposeful behavior.

The Umbrella Model shown in Figure 1 is a simple representation of how the objective and subjective realities of organizational life can become

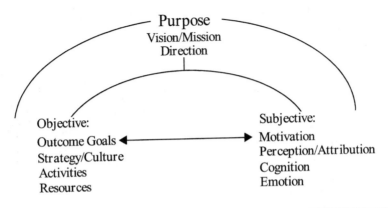

Figure 1   Umbrella Model

reconciled and coexist in a mutually beneficial way. Purpose is what an organization aims to accomplish. Purpose at any organizational level is a distillation of concrete, objective outcome goals, expressed as direction, with vision and mission as its foundation.

This chapter is primarily concerned with the development, translation, interpretation and perception of purpose by groups as a common cause. Outcome goals that have meaning for the organization as a whole are the only kinds of goals that have any meaning in reality. The organization here is defined as the relevant economic unit — the whole as perceived by markets, understood internally and embodying the necessary functional integration. Interdependent thinking and behaving around a common cause (embracing such goals), therefore, is the good that can flow from group action — from collaboration. Interdependence, then, is the theme of this chapter.

10.1   *Interdependent Thinking and Behaving*

As we have seen, in all but the simplest and smallest organizations, groups in some way account for most of the action and achievement in organizations. Within the context of groups, the various perspectives, functions, disciplines and interests that have a bearing on relevant achievement come together for better or for worse. Groups then, are the stage for the playing out of interdependent thinking and behaving. Interdependent behavior produces beneficial consequences: customers are better served, financial performance improves, innovative products make it to the market, patient outcomes are enhanced. Speaking in terms of leverage, groups can create high degrees of leverage consistent with their degree of interdependent behavior. Alternatively, in the absence of a sense of and working mode of interdependence, the actions of groups can do harm, producing negative leverage.

In a very real sense, a strong undercurrent of interdependence and a pattern of acting within that conception defines the most beneficial aspect of emergence in groups. We have defined emergence as the potential of groups emanating from the chemistry of interaction among individuals — the something extra that represents a capacity greater than or different from the sum of the characteristics of the individuals that make up the groups. As we saw in the introduction to groups, there are multiple determinants of beneficial emergence in groups; the foremost of these, however, is a sense of common cause — a common perception of purpose. Differences in personality, interests, training, membership in special occupational groups, world views, etc. are present in any collection of individuals. A clear group purpose, one that has meaning for the individuals that make up the group, is the only factor that will consistently enable individual differences to be transcended. The zero sum game, that mentality that defines human encounters in terms of winning and losing, can only be broken up by a common cause.

Division of labor increases as organizations become more complex. With expanding knowledge, growing technology, discriminating consumers, global markets and workforce diversity, our organizations are clearly becoming more complex. Differentiation in function, role, skill and interest is a fact of life in modern organizations. Differentiation is good; it brings special and finely tuned skills to problems and opportunities. Differentiation also poses a great threat to organizations, a threat that presents itself as a counterforce to integration. The benefits of differentiation set against the requirements for integration define a paradox which is becoming increasingly difficult to reconcile. This paradox, as is most often the case with paradoxes, is colored with irony. The units of an organization cannot exist on their own. Like an arm, or a foot, or a heart in a human body, the units of an organization may be useful, even crucial, to the life of the whole, but they only have meaning and existence as a part of the whole. The irony is that the members of so many units of organizations appear to perceive and behave as if they could exist on their own. Given issues of subjectivity, culture, the interaction of subcultures, and the lack of perception of a common cause, suboptimal behavior may be explainable. It is, however, no less ironic.

When a clear sense of purpose is present, integration of functions, roles and activities driven by interdependent thinking and behaving can develop. Attention can turn to the methods and consequences of collaboration — to the results of group action and the fine tuning of such action to create the greatest leverage. As an illustration, consider a collection of individual managers each responsible for one or more functional units who come together to form what is commonly called a management team. Consider further than this is a top management team where the individuals represent all operating and supporting segments of the organization. Assume that direction for this organization has been established and includes the following components:

1. Maintain market share in two of three market segments
2. Improve market share by some increment in the third market segment
3. Enhance gross margins in all three segments by some factor
4. Improve earnings by some percentage

This simple set of four concrete outcomes represents direction for the organization at the highest level. There are product, service, sales, customer satisfaction, cost and efficiency implications to achieving these outcome goals. The individual managers are each responsible for functional areas that relate to these and other implications throughout the organization. These functional areas must each perform well in order for the outcome goals to be met. More importantly, they must perform well interdependently as an integrated whole for the goals to be achieved. From the perspective of the organization as a whole (which is the only perspective that matters), good performance of individual managers and units is relevant only to the extent that such performance contributes to achievement of organizational outcome goals.

When organizations are subject to market forces, to which virtually all organizations are in some way, organizational success is collective success. The perception of individuals succeeding while their organizations do not is ludicrous. It is analogous to saying "the operation was successful but the patient died." As absurd as this notion is, it is a prevalent one. What lies behind this notion are patterns of delegation and accountability based on tasks or functions. Individual performance can be seen as meaningful in this context even though it is not. It undermines collaboration and interdependent behavior in the most fundamental way. Task-based delegation is the default option when there is no clear sense of purpose. Michael Schrage in his book, *No More Teams! Mastering the Dynamics of Creative Collaboration*, says: "Far too many organizations are so intellectually lazy that they don't define their problems and opportunities in ways that can seduce their people into enthusiastic, unrestrained collaborative efforts. They'd rather manage things the old-fashioned way: divvy up the problem (into tasks) and delegate it."[1] (Parenthetical comments are those of the authors). Perhaps it is not just a matter of intellectual laziness. We know that culture and human subjectivity can be strong obstacles to the development of a clear sense of purpose and to purposeful behavior. Whatever the underlying cause, when a group is not held accountable for collective results — for achievement of outcome goals that relate to the organization as a whole — interdependent behavior and collaboration will not be present.

A clear sense of purpose is necessary to bring a group of individuals into thinking and behaving interdependently. That requirement expands greatly as issues related to intergroup dynamics begin to be addressed to bring about collaboration among multiple groups. Intergroup dynamics can often be understood as the interaction of subcultures, the behavioral effects of which can be quite profound. The task of integrating an organization is no less than a problem of integrating a variety of subcultures. If we return to the illustration involving a hypothetical management team, we'll find that the individual members of this group represent not only functional units, they represent the subcultures associated with those units. For this group to have become aligned and collaborative around purpose, the individual managers will have had to take themselves out of their own occupational or work specialty subcultures. This voluntary and conscious distancing would have to be based on the collective perception that organizational goals are more important than narrow functional ones and that behaving interdependently has a greater payoff than behaving consistently with subculture norms. The task for these leaders is to propel their own developed sense of interdependence into the units they lead. This task encompasses engaging individuals in these units in the process of placing their organizational and occupational subcultures in a position of reduced dominance, moving beyond patterns of internal competition and relating first to organizational purpose.

To reiterate, a clear purpose is required to enable the dynamics of subcultures to be transcended. An organization we know is attempting to align members of multiple departments representing various scientific and technical disciplines into new interdisciplinary teams. Collaboration around new ways to define and address problems is a driving force behind this initiative. The assessments of most people in this organization who are in a position to know are that the initiative is not working. Conflict and hostility exist in some teams while others report little change in either ways of working or results. We asked members of these teams to tell us the purpose behind this change. More specifically, we asked them to identify the improvements in results or outcomes that were expected to come from the new interdisciplinary units. The team members couldn't answer these questions. In their minds, no purpose existed that would enable subculture differences to be transcended.

In the interdisciplinary team illustration just cited, perhaps there was a clear purpose and the team members were unaware of it or didn't agree with it or felt uninvolved in the development of it, and therefore, felt no ownership in it. An engaging purpose is far more likely to emerge when individuals in the relevant groups are able to participate in its definition. In this illustration, virtually no one could disagree with the goal of improving collaboration and serving customers better. This goal, however, had no operative meaning. Consistent with our definition of purpose, if these groups had been engaged in a process of giving meaning to this goal by defining how results or outcomes would be or could be improved, the experience with the initiative would be quite different. At one extreme, if no improvement in outcomes could have been described, the initiative would have correctly been abandoned. At the other extreme, if outcome improvements could have been defined and defended, a clear case for collaboration could have been made and a clear sense of purpose would have emerged. This process itself produces feedback to purpose as perceived at the highest level and affects its character over time. In other words, the process can reinforce or shift the definition and understanding of purpose in the direction of greater clarity and relevance.

10.2   Bringing About Interdependent Thinking and Behaving

Interdependent thinking and behaving around a clear purpose is the foundation of effective collaboration among individuals in groups and among groups within a larger organization. The question to be addressed in the remainder of this chapter pertains to how such thinking and behaving can be brought about. This question opens up additional questions, and the answers all bear directly on achieving interdependence and purposeful behavior.

> How may individuals, working within and through diverse groups, be engaged in the development of organizational purpose in such a way that the larger purpose becomes adopted as their own?
> How can clarity of purpose be sustained over time and the creativity of individuals, in collaboration with others, be fostered and sustained?
> How can the efforts of people within a widely differentiated organization be integrated around accomplishments that matter for the organization?
> Given a clearly articulated purpose at the highest level of the organization, how can purpose be translated, operationalized, executed and evaluated with explicit perceptions of accountability for results related to purpose?

The model in Figure 2, Strategy Development and Integration, relates to applying the principle, *Delegate Only Around Purpose*, to groups — from the group that represents the entire organization through all the groups that comprise the larger organization. The model addresses the classical organizational problems of strategy development, planning, integration, performance, and most importantly, correlation among all of these concerns. The model, however, is not a prescription or a cookbook. There is no assumption that such a neat and tidy clock-like process could be perfectly implemented in any organization at any time. Rather, the model is a conceptual framework for thinking about and developing answers, within a wide variety of organizational settings, to the questions raised in the previous paragraph.

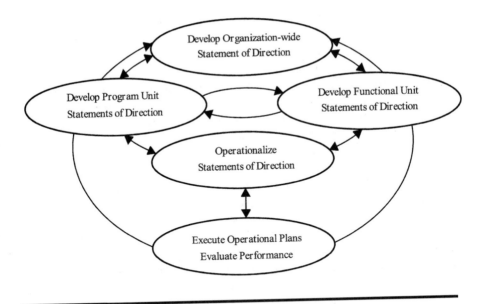

Figure 2   Strategy Development and Integration

Relevance and coherence are the central ideas in the model. Relevance at the level of the organization refers to a sustained focus on the results or outcomes that truly matter for the organization as a whole. Relevance for the individuals that make up the groups and the organization refers to a direct and personal connection with those outcomes. Coherence relates to the ability to bring about and sustain an orientation to a uniform purpose throughout an organization over time (and collaterally, to nurture the awareness that unit performance is meaningless if it doesn't relate to the whole). Specifically, the model is driven by these propositions:

1. Purpose must first relate directly to the concrete aims of the organization at the highest level.
2. The challenge and the payoff is in the translation of purpose throughout an organization without losing the essential meaning of purpose, i.e., without losing direct connection with purpose at the highest level.
3. Purpose at the level of the organization must both provide a framework for meaningful and creative work and reflect the results of a broadly based dialogue around purpose.
4. Purposeful behavior will be cultivated by creating patterns of accountability for operationalizing purpose and producing results that have an impact on organization-wide achievement.

To reiterate, the concern expressed in this model is not with describing yet another highly structured and rigid approach to organizational integration. Such approaches tend to stifle creativity, and worse, create bureaucratic lives of their own that obfuscate purpose even if purpose was ever clearly articulated. When faced with complex and daunting challenges, organizations are disposed to opt for quick fixes and prescriptive undertakings. Such undertakings are prone to reductionism; they call for the production of formal statements of vision, values, core competencies, strategic priorities and key performance indicators. Any or all of these expressions may be useful but to the extent that any process focuses more on the process itself and the accompanying formal artifacts than on integration, on relevance and coherence, it will ultimately become counterproductive.

At the level of specificity addressed in the model, Statement of Direction refers to the only formal construct needed to begin to answer the questions asked earlier. Consistent with our definition of purpose developed throughout this book, a Statement of Direction refers to a distillation of concrete, objective, outcome goals underpinned by vision and mission. The process of translation and integration of purpose with actual achievement is an iterative and never ending one. Information in organizations is imperfect and always incomplete and the implementation of any new process is subject to timing and other circumstances. The process described in the model, therefore, may be thought of as able to be initiated at the level of the organization or at the level of any of the units that make up the organization. Clarity of organizational purpose at the highest level, however, will be the ultimate driving force and must remain the aim.

It should also be borne in mind that while financial planning and budgeting models are important, they should be driven by effective planning of outcome goals and related actions rather than the other way around. There is no attempt to identify how this model connects with budgeting and financial processes. There is also a limited recognition and representation of hierarchy in this model. Hierarchy, as it can be inferred from the model, relates only to organization-wide planning and coordinating and unit-specific planning and doing. Furthermore, to prevent hierarchy from becoming a constraint versus a facilitator in an organization, we need to always treat hierarchy as the servant of purpose.

10.2.1   Develop Organization-Wide Statement of Direction

The organization at this level is defined as the relevant economic unit — the whole as perceived by markets, understood internally and embodying the necessary functional scope. The organization could represent an entire corporate entity or a business or stand alone unit of a larger entity. The Statement of Direction at the level of the organization should incorporate result or outcome goals that relate directly and unambiguously to the core vision and mission of the organization. These outcome goals should have an external focus, addressing markets, customers, communities, etc., and should relate to organizational performance at the highest level. Achievement of these goals must be able to be understood in measurable or otherwise observable terms. The Statement of Direction should not be viewed as a static expression, rather it should be continually under the influence of a broadly-based dialogue regarding purpose and direction. Most importantly, it must reflect choices having been made among a larger set of alternative outcomes based on the principle of potential leverage with respect to vision and mission. This aspect of creating clarity of purpose is without question the most difficult to achieve. Without achieving such discrimination, however, any Statement of Direction is meaningless. The Statement of Direction at the level of the organization defines purpose and sets the direction for all the units of the organization. Given a clear sense of purpose, the units can be freed to interpret, translate, plan and produce results consistent with purpose. Vision and mission of the organization are obvious guideposts in setting direction. Market and organizational assessments are important inputs to the process along with the assessments, perceptions and outcome goals of the units. While this model opens up the process and calls for an on-going dialogue around purpose, it is in no way intended to obscure the reality that ultimate discernment and accountability for performance lies at the senior level of the organization.

The clear intent of the Organization-Wide Statement of Direction is to lay out the way forward for the organization in terms of meaningful results; it is not to identify and describe the actions to be taken by the units of the organization. It is not, in other words, another name for a strategic plan developed by senior managers, professional planners and consultants. The precepts embodied in the Statement of Direction within the context of the process described in Figure 2 are these: 1) direction evolves and is refined based on a systematic, organization wide dialogue, and 2) direction frames the interpretation and planning of the units in something like an improvisational mode.

10.2.2   Develop Program Unit Statements of Direction

The term "Program Unit" applies to organizational units that are specifically focused on some external circumstance or organization-wide endeavor. The most common examples of program units, sometimes called business units, are those concerned with products or services. These units typically cross functional lines to plan, coordinate and execute activities directed toward a market or a segment of the market. Product and service program units are crucial to organizations seeking to effectively integrate themselves, successfully enhance market share and enter new markets. Virtually all successful organizations will have somehow learned how to access the creativity and diverse expertise of their people and direct these attributes to their external constituencies. A program unit may include members of various functional units. A product-based program unit may include people from marketing, engineering, sales, production and finance. A service oriented unit may include representatives of the various disciplines required to enhance or more effectively position a service in the marketplace. Program units may also come into existence to address organization-wide initiatives such as introduction of new technology, quality improvement or process redesign. A Program Unit Statement of Direction will typically incorporate goals pertaining to new product introduction, product and/or service improvement and competitive positioning, gross revenue and market share.

10.2.3　Develop Functional Unit Statements of Direction

If program units are designed to bring about effectiveness in the market place, functional units exist to organize work specialties and disciplines, coordinate practice, develop and enforce standards and bring about efficiency. Functional units include the classical divisions of sales, engineering, production, marketing and finance in industrial organizations, clinical, ancillary and support departments in healthcare organizations, academic departments in universities, etc. Functional units may include information services, accounting, human resources and other internal support services. Functional units may also be program units in some organizations and in some circumstances. For example, the development and implementation of a new information and communication system designed to improve responsiveness to customers could be treated as a program although the effort would be a part of a functional unit. A Functional Unit Statement of Direction is usually a statement of goals relating to such factors as sales volume, cost, production efficiency and availability of financial and other resources.

　　Both Program and Functional Unit Statements of Direction must express objective outcome goals. The goals must describe the expected consequences of work and not the work itself. As in the case of the larger organization, these statements must reflect the results of trade-off decision making. In the case of the units, discrimination should occur around the organization-wide Statement of Direction and the unit's local rendering of vision and mission. Ideally, the unit's outcome goals will be a synthesis of the goals of the individuals in the units and will flow into and influence the goals of the larger organization. There are crucial flows of information and influence between program and functional units. Given that the program units will most often reflect the programmatic focus of the larger organization, the primary flow of influence will be from program to functional units. This will not always be the case, however, and it must be borne in mind that most of the resources required to implement programs will formally reside in the functional units. An extremely market-sensitive organization could turn this aspect of the model inside out and make program units the primary organizational units and functional units the secondary ones.

10.2.4   Operationalize Statements of Direction

The Statements of Direction as formulated by the units must become operationalized or given life in the form of action plans. Program units and functional units must come together to lay out initiatives and coordinate efforts. The outcome goals, as reflected in the Statements of Direction, represent the overriding purpose in this endeavor at this level; planned actions are only relevant in this context. These plans will define how outcome goals will be accomplished, including how work will be organized, what resources will be required, who will be assigned what tasks, what steps are necessary and what milestones are appropriate. The collection of these plans represent what is usually thought of as a "strategic plan." The distinction here, however, is that these plans will have been developed locally (by the units) and solely for the purpose of facilitating achievement of outcome goals. The units will be held accountable for results as defined in their Statements of Direction and not for plans and activities. The form and content of these plans, accordingly, will vary and will not be centrally defined and managed. The level of interaction required to operationalize goals will inevitably bring new information and new insights to the surface. Feedback, or a flow of influence, is therefore required back to the point of outcome goal formulation.

10.2.5   Execute Operational Plans and Evaluate Performance

This point in the model is where the results of the efforts of people meet the world outside the organization. Although focus groups and other means of accessing outside perceptions may be used to help in various assessments, this is the point where products and services meet consumers.

Accountability for achievement of organization-wide outcome goals resides here. There is a connection back to the level of the organization to represent the proposition that execution and performance only have meaning as these relate to organization-wide achievement. The point and the hope, in other words, is that organization-wide goals will have been expressed and translated with consistency throughout the units. The organization as a whole will have acted in such a way as to have brought about achievement of the goals. Effective integration of the organization will have occurred and the central themes of relevance and coherence will have played out.

The recent history of planning processes in a large multinational company illustrates the integrative as well as the disintegrative effects of such processes. At one stage in the life of this company, the business units, corresponding to our program units in Figure 2, were empowered to produce vision and mission statements and to plan within that context. They identified critical success factors, corresponding closely to our out-come goals, and developed strategic action plans for each critical success factor. Each business unit collaborated closely with the functional units to develop their plans and to execute them. The organization seemed coherent to its members and it consistently met its performance objectives.

Some time later, the senior management group developed an over-arching strategic concept and mandated that the concept be integrated with the business units. This was accomplished without a great deal of difficulty since the plans of the units helped shape the character of the overall strategy. For a brief period, the organization was more integrated than it had ever been. The organization was purposefully driven and its approach to planning and execution of its plans looked very much like the model in Figure 2.

Some time later still, there was a change at the level of the CEO and his senior advisors and the simple and effective process for setting and managing direction was replaced. An array of internal planners and external experts brought forth a series of overlapped, labor intensive and often intimidating new planning methodologies. First, a centrally managed and highly detailed cost-based process was introduced. This process demanded that each functional manager break down their cost structure into fine detail and evaluate, essentially in a vacuum, the effect of each activity on the cost structure, line item by line item. Since this process paid little attention to the market performance aspects of the business, another centrally managed process was introduced to overlay the first one. Each manager was required to describe the operational parameters of his or her activity in the terms of an esoteric and rigid construct which was not connected with the cost-based process discussed above.

Finally, the basic planning process was reengineered in a superficial and disconnected manner and put the finishing touches on an overall process which had become completely muddled. To add to the disorder, the new process ignored subjective factors and set up counterproductive human dynamics. Staff members associated with the reengineered process produced massive quantities of paper for each manager in the form of planning charts addressing every conceivable operational variable. Each manager was required to provide information for each variable, make a presentation to a group of senior managers and peers and then to be "roasted" by the group. The managers that came through this process unscathed were the ones who represented stable activities with few challenges, largely irrespective of the quality of their thought and their plans.

This organization had now mutated from purposeful to incoherent, from integrated to cognitively dissonant, from a collective capacity for perspective to reductionism. Because of the quality of its professionals and managers and because of the dynamics of its markets, this company continues to be successful. It does so, however, in spite of itself or at least in spite of its senior leadership. Its business unit and functional managers have reverted to their earlier planning and coordinating processes, at least informally. They tolerate the planning aberrations that have been forced upon them. They play the game, in other words, but they produce results by collaborating with their peers and maintaining a focus on purpose. The cost of this game in terms of energy, dollars and cynicism is a matter of speculation. Whatever the cost, one can be certain that it can ultimately be measured in lost opportunity.

Irrespective of goals, plans and expectations, organizational life, like all life, plays out one day at a time. The degree and quality of collaboration, of interdependent thinking and behaving, day in and day out, will determine whether outcomes that matter for the organization are achieved or not. Conventionally, managers are put in place to monitor and initiate corrective action associated with keeping work focused and productive according to some set of expectations. As we have seen, however, expectations of managers and the units they lead are often not directly related to purpose, a circumstance which leads to organizational dysfunction. If the assumption can be made that purpose has become the basis of delegation to managers, the character of expectation will have changed and the organization will have become better positioned to behave purposefully. Two major barriers to consistent and purpose-driven execution remain. The first of these is the traditional model of supervision. Effective collaboration comes about through the empowerment of groups to produce results not through the delegation of tasks passed down the hierarchy.

The second barrier relates to managers themselves. Managers usually do not know enough and are not close enough to problems to be able to make the best operational decisions. In the face of this ignorance, managers tend to select certain individuals, not necessarily on the basis of objective criteria, to effectually lead them to specific actions. A peer review concept and model is proposed as a potential route to mitigation of these concerns.

Peer review is an accountability concept. It is designed to assist in managing the execution of operational plans and evaluation of performance. Peer review should flow out of the group context within which outcome goals for the group were formulated and accepted. Peer review is a form of self management in groups where collaboration within groups is required to achieve results. It is a framework for sustaining commitment and alignment around purpose. The aims of any peer review process should be to:

1. Empower the people who are in the best position to know what actions and behaviors will contribute the most to producing outcomes.
2. Establish an objective basis for evaluating the performance of the group and the individuals.

The following precepts should always apply:

1. The group must have been involved in the definition of its outcome goals and committed to their achievement.
2. Expectations for group achievement must relate clearly to the outcome goals and not to activities, functions, etc.
3. The perception that the group succeeds or no individual succeeds must be firmly rooted in the minds of the members of the group.
4. The expectations of the leader of the group must mirror the expectations of the group.

Any number of process variations can be applied to peer review. The form of peer review enacted for any setting should be matched to the requirements and character of the setting. In general, any viable process will hold the outcome goals for the group as the primary framework for the activities and efforts of the group. The goals will serve as the standard of performance for the group and its members and the operating agenda for group sessions. Group action will center on how the goals will be met, tracking interim results and modifying initiatives when the need to do so is indicated. Evaluation of individual and group performance will be a feature of peer review.

Two important caveats must be expressed regarding peer review. The first of these pertains to the danger that achievement of objective outcomes could come to be seen as secondary to the process. Any process must, therefore, be as simple and nonburdensome as possible. Forms, documents and any other process trappings should be minimized and the introduction of such artifacts should be guarded against. The second warning concerns the potential misuse or even abuse of the process by individuals seeking to appear superior at the expense of others. Of course in reality, this happens anyway whether or not a formal peer review process is in place. In any case, certain rules must be vigorously enforced. These include:

1. All evaluative submissions must have an objective focus, i.e., no comments can be considered relevant unless they relate to objective achievement.
2. All assertions relating to individuals made by their peers must be illustrated.
3. No negative assertions pertaining to individuals may be formally submitted unless such assertions have been made public in the group in advance.

Interdependent thinking and behaving in general, and peer review in particular, demand that changes be made in certain formal organizational policies and practices. These include performance appraisal, compensation systems and reward and promotion criteria. Fundamentally, the meaning of good performance must shift from successful execution of tasks to successful achievement of results as expressed in relevant outcomes. Perception of leadership performance and associated reward (or lack of it) must be unambiguously linked to group performance and achievement of outcomes. The focus on individual performance must shift to a focus on group performance. Individual rewards, in other words, must be based more on collaboration and contribution to group achievement than on individual achievement. Performance appraisals must incorporate the assessments of peers. Program unit leaders must participate, on at least an equal footing, with functional unit leaders in the performance evaluation of individuals and in the granting of rewards and the imposing of sanctions.

Groups play an indispensable role in organizational achievement. Organizational achievement is by definition group achievement yet organizations often embody and reflect structures, processes and behaviors that work against effective and purposeful group action. These structures, processes and behaviors are aspects of organizational culture undergirded by another aspect of culture, institutional knowledge. The development and implementation of new structures and processes, designed to bring about interdependent thinking and behaving is not enough. As long as culture remains unchanged, any change in behavior will be short lived. The ability to alter deeply held assumptions and the consequential ability to enhance the capacity for learning in groups will be taken up in the next chapter. Application of the principle, *Enhance the Efficacy of Institutional Knowledge*, is the third leg in an integrated strategy to bring about purposeful group behavior and achievement.

References

1. Schrange, M., *No More Teams! Mastering the Dynamics of Creative Collaboration*, Doubleday, New York, 1989.

Chapter 11

Groups: *Enhance the Efficacy of Institutional Knowledge*

Anticipatory Summary

Learning and creativity are largely the result of collective undertakings. Groups provide the framework and the setting for efforts to alter basic assumptions — to enhance the capacity of institutional knowledge to produce desired effects. Attention in this chapter will be brought to bear on the circumstances and methods surrounding learning in groups. The focus will be on the processes that link cognition with social settings, with the ways in which taken-for-granted and crystallized assumptions influence the imagination and ways of thinking of individuals and vice versa.

11.1   The Problem of Learning in Groups

- By and large, the institutional knowledge associated with any group determines the behavior of the group.
- The ability to enhance the efficacy of institutional knowledge is another slant on the definition of organizational learning; comprehension of these basic assumptions is the sine qua non for learning.

11.1.1   Barriers to Comprehension of Basic Assumptions

- Two related barriers to comprehension exist. These barriers pertain to patterns of group dynamics: the first is one of apparent ignorance, the second is one of self-deception.
  - Patterns of ignorance exist when groups systematically close down transmission and reception of valid information. Such groups are unaware of what they don't know and unaware of the need to change.
  - Members of groups practice self-deception when they know they need to change; they know how to behave to bring about improvement, they espouse values consistent with more effective behavior, but they *behave* in an inconsistent manner.
- It can be a greater challenge to shift the unintended behavior of group members when they have begun to believe that their behavior is consistent with what they espouse.
- The common thread that runs through both barriers to learning in groups is the presence of hardened patterns of perception, attribution and defensiveness.

11.2   Building Learning Capacity in Groups

- Any consideration of group effectiveness must take account of the reciprocal effects of individual and group dynamics.
- A necessary step is to discover the gap between what the members espouse as desirable operating theories and how the members actually behave.

11.2.1   A Starting Point — The Quality of Discourse

- Initial efforts to build the learning capacity of groups are most appropriately applied to enhancing the ability to communicate within a standard of valid information. Unhappily, high-quality discourse does not seem to be a feature of life in our times.
- Insofar as certain modes of interaction facilitate critical thought, discovery, accurate perceptions of reality and higher quality solutions to problems, such modes are useful and meaningful to the work of groups.

The Trivium

- The skills to successfully engage in collective discovery and creativity are rooted in the Trivium.

Dialogue — Conversation and Collective Reasoning

- The preconditions for successful dialogue in groups and the steps and skills required to satisfy these preconditions are summarized in Table 1 later in this chapter.

Balancing Dialogue and Advocacy

- As easily as we are drawn to advocacy, our tendency to engage in it is not necessarily coupled with the skill to be good at it. The quality of our arguments can be most improved by mastering the skills for dialogue.

11.3   *Toward a Learning-Oriented Culture*

- The collective and sustained ability to produce relevant, accurate, timely and actionable knowledge is the substance of organizational learning.
- By definition, a learning orientation is a cultural attribute of groups and organizations.
- Culture change is the most significant and far reaching application of group learning in organizations.
- Learning is required to change culture and a learning-oriented culture is the highest aim in any culture change endeavor.

Groups: *Enhance the Efficacy of Institutional Knowledge*

We have argued that the ability to comprehend and change the basic assumptions that drive behavior in organizations is the essence of organizational learning. We have also taken the position, with others, that learning and creativity are largely the result of collective undertakings. Groups, then, provide the framework and the setting for efforts to alter basic assumptions — to enhance, in other words, the capacity of institutional knowledge to produce desired effects. While individuals must be prepared and able to participate in effective group action, and leaders must provide the context for such action, groups represent the stage upon which learning behavior plays out and the scene within which learning actually occurs.

Chapter 9 addressed the issues of understanding and mitigating the subjective barriers to learning; Chapter 10 dealt with motivation in groups to learn. Attention in this chapter will be brought to bear on the circumstances and methods surrounding learning in groups. The focus will be on the processes that link cognition with social settings — with the ways in which taken-for-granted and crystallized assumptions influence the imagination and ways of thinking of individuals and vice versa. The problem of learning in groups will be considered followed by an explanation of the factors associated with building group learning capacity. As we will discover, culture change is the most significant and far reaching application of group learning in organizations. The focus in this chapter will, therefore, shift to the role of groups in culture change. Learning is required to change culture and a learning-oriented culture is the highest aim in any culture change endeavor. Finally then, attention will turn to bringing about a learning oriented culture — one that will facilitate and sustain achievement of organizational potential.

To briefly revisit the meanings of culture and institutional knowledge, "culture exists on two planes or in two dimensions — behavior and the knowledge that sets behavior in motion. Behavior is the aspect of culture that we see. Behavior is what people do and is represented in the symbolic and physical manifestations of deeply held assumptions." Institutional knowledge refers to these assumptions which tend to be highly resistive to change and usually unconscious. According to this perspective, the components of institutional knowledge represent the building blocks of culture. Culture change may, therefore, relate to changing a few or many constituents of institutional knowledge. Any organization will hold certain assumptions that produce useful effects while other assumptions will be incongruent with reality and will produce harmful consequences. The principle, *Enhance the Efficacy of Institutional Knowledge*, defines precisely what we mean by culture change. The intent is to change culture to bring about more desirable and beneficial effects and not simply throw out an existing culture in favor of a new one.

11.1   The Problem of Learning in Groups

We suggested previously that the term "organizational learning" has some appeal for most people in organizations, but when asked to explain what they think it means, they tend to be at a loss to do so. Our definition connects answering a question or solving a problem with action. Simply stated, organizational learning means modification of a behavioral tendency by experience with efficiency and within a relevant period of time. It is confusing and misleading to speak of creating organizational learning as if such a capacity didn't exist. Our meaning, then, is associated with improving the capacity of groups and organizations to learn. In an attempt to provide a short and snappy answer to what organizational learning means, we have asserted that it means thinking and behaving to bring about achievement of organizational potential. Peter Senge has defined a learning organization as one "where people continually expand their capacity to create the results they truly desire."[1] Chris Argyris argues that "learning occurs when we detect and correct error." He further explains, "Error is any mismatch between what we intend an action to produce and what actually happens when we implement that action."[2] We have argued that the set of hardened basic assumptions or institutional knowledge associated with any group largely determines the behavior of the group. As we have asserted previously, it follows that the ability to enhance the efficacy of institutional knowledge is another perspective on the definition of organizational learning.

In Chapter 1, we developed an operative meaning of group and organizational learning on three levels:

1. The ability to comprehend internal and external reality and the connections between these aspects of reality
2. The ability to recognize and understand the basic assumptions operating within the group and the ability to identify the differences between assumptions that are congruent with reality and those that are not
3. The ability to change the assumptions that need to be changed and to leave alone those that do not

The key concepts associated with our perspective on learning in organizations are: reality and our experience of it, assumptions, action and efficacy. The core questions are:

What sense do we make of the circumstances and the playing out of events in the stream of time, both within and outside our groups and organizations?
What actions do we take in response to or in anticipation of these circumstances and events?

In other words, how do we in our groups perceive change and how do we behave within the context of change. The nature of change confronting organizations and groups is, therefore, consequential.

We explored the nature of change in Chapter 1 by looking at how continuous change differs from discontinuous change. Continuous change is linear, incremental, gradual, predictable and controllable. Under continuous change, with minor and fully understood adjustments, reality and our experience of it will play out in approximately the same way in the future as they did in the past. Continuous change suggests that our assumptions will continue to be valid and that the future is a straight line projection from where we are in the present. In contrast, discontinuous change is transformative and disjunctive; it is nonlinear, nonincremental, nongradual, not part of a pattern and not fully predictable. The past is at best only a partial guide to the future. Under discontinuous change, reality and our experience of it will be different. Our assumptions will become incongruent with reality and therefore invalid. We also explored the learning implications associated with change in Chapter 1. We saw how continuous change suggests the appropriateness of single-loop learning while discontinuous change demands double-loop learning.

11.1.1 Barriers to Comprehension of Basic Assumptions

The first requirement for sustaining perspective and balance in modes of learning is a clear sense of purpose and relevant outcomes or results. This theme has been examined in various contexts throughout this book. Beyond clarity of purpose, perspective and balance in groups requires collective comprehension of both the assumptions or institutional knowledge operating within the group and reality, external and internal, bearing upon the life of the organization or group. There are at least two important consequences of collective comprehension of basic assumptions and reality. First, the application of the most appropriate style and mode of learning to various presenting situations will be possible. Second, an opportunity to bring operating assumptions and reality into greater congruence will be created enhancing, in other words, the efficacy of institutional knowledge. Two related but slightly different barriers to comprehension and the desirable consequences of such comprehension exist. These barriers relate to patterns of group dynamics; the first is one of apparent ignorance, the second is one of self-deception.

Patterns of ignorance exist when groups systematically close down transmission and reception of valid information and learning. As described in the previous chapter, members of such groups reason defensively. They keep their premises and assumptions to themselves, and they do not test the validity of their inferences. Group members, certain about the validity of their views, assert themselves in ways that close down inquiry into their own positions. The information content associated with the interactions of this group will be poor. Such groups are unaware of what they don't know and unaware of the need to be different. As Chris Argyris is fond of saying, such groups cover up the truth and cover up the cover-up, sealing their embeddedness in ignorance.

Members of groups practice deception, especially of themselves, when they know they need to elevate their learning potential, they know how to behave to bring about improvement, they espouse values consistent with more effective behavior but they *behave* in an inconsistent manner. IBM's loss of its leadership position in the information technology industry and its status as one of the best companies in the world has been analyzed exhaustively. Without claiming any special knowledge of the IBM story, one salient circumstance stands out in our minds. While IBM was in a state of decline, the company's leaders spoke of a new way of being at IBM. They espoused all the principles that would have enabled them to effectively confront changes in the market. In other words, they espoused perceptions of discontinuity yet they enacted and embedded a new set of assumptions, essentially unthreatening to IBM's culture and behaved as if continuity existed. The consequences for IBM are common knowledge.

When we work with groups, a necessary step is to discover the gap between what the members espouse as values or desirable operating theories and how the members actually behave. One executive group with whom we worked espoused a set of values that included: "openness, collegiality, common purpose, cooperation and mutual respect, directness and risk taking." In individual sessions, the group members were asked to illustrate their own behavior and that of their team members that would show consistency with their espoused values. Failing to accomplish this task, they were asked to identify actual behaviors. These included: "guarded, conservative, deals done behind closed doors, no shared problem solving, work as individuals with own notions of purpose, polite, no questioning or confronting communication." These perceptions were played back to the group and they were acknowledged to be valid. In contrast to working with individuals shielded from the need to change, it can be a greater challenge to shift the explicitly unintended behavior of group members when they have begun to believe that their behavior is consistent with what they espouse. The common thread that runs through both barriers to learning in groups is the presence of hardened patterns of perception, attribution and defensiveness.

11.2   *Building Learning Capacity in Groups*

Earlier in this chapter, we offered a definition of group learning on three levels: the first level pertains to the ability to comprehend internal and external reality and the connections that exist between these aspects of reality. The second level relates to the ability to recognize and understand the basic assumptions operating within the group and the ability to identify those assumptions that are congruent with reality and those that are not. The third level concerns the ability to change the assumptions that need to be changed and to leave in place those that do not. There is a paradox embedded in this definition. To build and sustain learning capacity is to maintain an active openness to new circumstances. "Learning is discovery, Dewey said, but discovery doesn't happen unless you are looking."[3] Connected with discovery is the requirement to change assumptions and behavior when there is a need to do so while sustaining the ability to work with efficiency within a set of existing assumptions when such behavior produces the best results.

A clear sense of purpose is the element around which this paradox may be reconciled. But purpose itself, if purpose is to become the central element or guidepost for decision making and action, will be a result of effective group behavior. In what begins to sound like a "chicken or egg problem," group learning is a prerequisite for development and articulation of purpose. All of this serves to point out that building learning capacity in groups is not simply a serial, step by step process but rather an iterative and multi-dimensional one.

11.2.1   *A Starting Point — The Quality of Discourse*

A starting point is required, however, and the most propitious place to begin is at the level of the basic interactions among the members of the group. The nature and quality of information communicated among the members of a group will determine the potential of the group to learn. As we have seen, patterns of defensiveness, attribution and faulty perception will bring about communication in irrelevant and invalid information. Such patterns of communication will systematically mask the truth. Without the ability to engage in communication that may be threatening and unsettling to some members of the group, the aim of comprehending reality as fully as possible will be hopeless. Efforts to build the learning capacity of groups, then, are most appropriately applied, at least initially, in enhancing the ability of the group to communicate within a standard of valid information.

The pivotal concept in shifting the quality of information communicated in a group lies in understanding the linkage between cognition and the social context of the individuals in question. The key change-enabling factor, in other words, is connected with understanding the ways in which taken-for-granted and crystallized assumptions associated with the group (or social context) influence the imaginations and ways of thinking of individuals and vice-versa. In Chapter 3, "Individuals: *Achieve an Operative Balance of Objective and Subjective Factors,*" we dealt with the topics of individual development, perception, attribution and defensiveness. We argued that the most important question for organizations seeking to learn and change is how able are their people to learn and change. How able, in other words, are the individuals in the organization to perceive a new or changing reality and alter their assumptions to bring them into greater accord with reality. We explored the dynamics of shifting from defensive to productive reasoning and building the faculty for individuals to suspend their assumptions in the interest of more effective learning. The factors associated with bridging between individuals and groups were explored in Chapter 9. It is clear to us that any consideration of group effectiveness must take account of the reciprocal effects of individual and group dynamics. What individuals bring to groups in the form of their mental models, feelings, imaginations and patterns of attribution and defensiveness will shape the group. Conversely, as the individuals internalize the assumptions hardened by the group, their own subjectivity will be altered.

When a group of individuals, through their ability to manage their own idiosyncratic perceptions and patterns of defensiveness, can communicate effectively with each other, a precondition to learning in groups will have been met. Fundamental constraints on collective creativity will have been mitigated and attention may turn to modes of collective thought and discourse. Insofar as certain modes of interaction facilitate critical thought, discovery, accurate perceptions of reality and higher quality solutions to problems, such modes are useful and meaningful to the work of groups. There are such modes of interaction. Unlike discourse framed by autocratic leaders or norms that avoid embarrassment and threat to group members, however, such modes tend to be rather untidy and disorderly. If learning and effective change is the goal, polite models of non-conflict and non-confrontation must be given up as ineffectual. Regarding the practice of management and the role of groups in organizations, Kenneth Gergen suggests in the book *Rethinking Organization* that there is too heavy of a reliance on romantic and modernist forms of discourse. He argues: "The ideal of the organization as a smoothly running machine, clean and austerely effective, becomes dangerous. Rather, from the present perspective, organizational survival depends ultimately on the insinuation of polyglot, immersion in metaphor, and the prevalence of creative confusion. Rather than autonomous, self-directing managers, we find the emphasis on thoroughgoing interdependence, and the quality of relatedness replacing the character of the individual as the centre of concern."[4]

Enhanced group learning and more effective behavior requires an elevation in the quality of discourse in groups. Members of groups bring intelligence, unique perspectives and diverse intellectual and personality styles to their groups. The extent to which this collective intelligence and diversity is accessed and brought to bear on relevant issues determines the relative quality of discourse. Unhappily, high-quality discourse does not seem to be a feature of life in our times. We find examples in virtually all arenas of social life from interactions within organizations to politics to public policy. Conclusions are drawn from untested hypotheses, what passes for debate occurs around incongruent and unchallenged assumptions, faulty attributions are allowed to hold sway, muddled inferences pass for acceptable thought and dilemmas are resolved by the loudest arguments and those that strike some emotional chord. As complexity and interdependence in our collective lives accelerate, we appear to be less and less able to think and interact creatively and effectively. As well educated as we have become in narrow fields of study, our education seems to leave us woefully unprepared to learn in a broader context and from each other. The intellectual skills bestowed upon us by our education are not readily transferable to subjects other than those in which we acquired them. It seems that we have learned almost everything except the art of learning.

The Trivium

The current disappointing state of discourse and collective learning is not surprising to those who view the decline of Liberal Arts and the Humanities as a profound loss to healthy intellectual life. It is also not surprising that the search for a model of learning, relevant to our times and exigencies, should take us back to pre-modern times. The mediaeval syllabus in education consisted of two parts, the Trivium and the Quadrivium. The Trivium pertained to the foundations for learning; the Quadrivium was comprised of subjects. The Trivium itself consisted of three parts; grammar, dialectic and rhetoric, in that order. Dorothy Sayers summarized the Trivium in a paper delivered at Oxford University in 1947. The whole of the Trivium, she said, was intended to teach the pupil the proper use of the tools of learning before he began to apply them to subjects. In grammar, he learned the structure and use of language. Dialectic embraced logic and disputation. In the study of dialectic, the student learned "how to define his terms and make accurate statements, how to construct an argument and how to detect fallacies in arguments (his own arguments and other people's)." In rhetoric, "he learned to express himself in language: how to say what he had to say elegantly and persuasively." Sayers continues, "At this point, any tendency to express himself windily or to use his eloquence so as to make the worse appear the better reason would, no doubt, be restrained by his previous teaching in dialectic. If not, his teacher and his fellow pupils, trained along the same lines, would be quick to point out where he was wrong; for it was they whom he had to seek to persuade."[5]

While it seems that we are masters of rhetoric, and grammar in the service of rhetoric, we have left dialectic behind; therein is our great loss. Without dialectic as a means of creating balance in our rhetoric, our attention is solely on winning arguments and not on accessing the truth. "As the disciplined search for truth, dialectic includes all of logic. It is concerned with every phase of thought: with the establishment of definitions; the examination of hypotheses in the light of their presuppositions or consequences; the formulation of inferences and proofs; the resolution of dilemmas arising from opposition in thought." Dialectic for Augustine, consistent with Plato's original conception in the dialogues, "is the art which deals with inferences, and definitions, and divisions and is of the greatest assistance in the discovery of meaning." Further, "Dialectic, in other words, is divorced from the practical purpose of stating and winning an argument, and given theoretical status as a method of inquiry." "Rhetoric, on the other hand, is not to be used so much for ascertaining the meaning as for setting forth the meaning when it is ascertained."[6] The spirit of learning in the broadest sense as reflected in the Trivium ushered the western mind through the age of discovery to the Enlightenment. The Enlightenment, while underpinning our scientific and technological achievements of the last 250 years, has led us down the path of reductionism. As our specialized fields of study promised answers to all important questions, the fundamental tools of learning were sacrificed with the consequence, in our time, of a general loss of perspective — a loss of a sense of wholes.

To recapitulate, we all learn as individuals and as collections of individuals. Our learning, however, tends to be within the boundaries of subjects. We learn within a framework of institutionalized assumptions surrounding specialized fields of study such as engineering, business, physics, medicine, computer science, etc. Children are exemplary learners in the broadest possible sense, but progressively as we grow into adult-hood, our training and socialization slots us into ever narrower sets of learning options. Therefore, we have few skills in collective learning outside of a fixed frame of reference. Defensive patterns operating within our institutions tend to close down our attempts to rise above our lack of training and circumscribed perceptions. Therefore there should be little mystery surrounding our general lack of ability to grasp and successfully adopt the principles and techniques of organizational learning. Given the motivation to learn, the ability to shift from defensive to productive attitudes and behaviors, and the capacity to hold our perceptions a little less tightly, we can approach the reacquisition of the basic tools of learning or the acquisition of them for the first time.

The spirit of the Trivium is rekindled by modes of collective thought and discourse adapted to enhance learning. The skills to successfully engage in collective discovery and creativity are also rooted in the Trivium. The notion of consciously seeking insights from the past, however, is not especially congenial to late twentieth century minds. The language of the Trivium is also somewhat unnatural and can be seen as off-putting. For the remainder of this chapter, the terms associated with the Trivium will, therefore, be replaced with terms that are friendlier to modern ears and sensibilities. For dialectic, the term dialogue will be substituted; for rhet-oric, advocacy will be used. The term dialogue in current usage is generally and simply taken to mean a conversation between two or more people. However, it should be borne in mind that dialogue and dialectic are from the same Greek root meaning discourse which itself means orderly thought. For our purposes then, the definition of dialogue will more specifically be "conversation and reasoning as a method of intellectual investigation." The common definition of advocacy, the act or process of pleading a cause — of persuasively speaking and writing, serves our purposes. Peter Senge asserts that "most managers are trained to be advocates." "Individuals become successful in part because of their abilities to debate forcefully and influence others." He argues further that "when two advocates meet for an open, candid exchange of views, there is usually little learning — and that advocacy tends to beget more advocacy."[7] The usual mode of interaction for most of us is advocacy. Since our advocacy skills are well developed, we will not specifically address advo-cacy. Our interest in the process of building learning capacity in groups, therefore, will come to bear on dialogue and on the ability to appropriately balance the modes of dialogue and advocacy. However, we will point to the enhancement of advocacy skills resulting from gaining skills in dialogue.

Table 1

Preconditions for Dialogue	Steps to Satisfy Preconditions
• Willingness	• Achieve Motivation Based on Clarity of Purpose and Relevant Outcomes
• Contextual Colleagueship	• Mitigate Defensive Patterns, Suspend Personal Assumptions/Perceptions
• Definition of Terms and Categories • Examination and Qualification of Hypotheses	• Comprehend and Explicitly Define Presuppositions/Assumptions • Invite Inquiry into Own Positions • Explicitly Define Consequences of Actions
• Formulation of Inferences and Proofs	• Make Inferential Steps Explicit and Test Them • Comprehend and Test Attributions
• Reconciliation of Dilemmas Resulting from Opposing Points of View	• Clearly draw distinctions — Use Metaphor, Paradox, Third Perspective

Dialogue — Conversation and Collective Reasoning

Dialogue is the art of seeking the truth, of comprehending reality by logical discussion. In dialogue, we access different perspectives and collective intelligence to gain deeper understanding and a new synthesis. When dialogue is occurring, the opportunity exists to move beyond one person's understanding, to gain insights that wouldn't otherwise be gained and to produce qualitatively better results. In dialogue, we explore complex issues from many points of view and move from contradiction to clarity and reconciliation. Table 1 summarizes the preconditions for successful dialogue in groups and the steps and skills required to satisfy these preconditions.

The initial preconditions to dialogue pertain to the willingness of group members to engage in dialogue and the preparedness of the individuals to grant colleagueship to each other. The requirement for colleagueship relates to context, i.e., the purpose and desired outcomes of the group define the context for colleagueship. Motivation resulting from a clear sense of purpose and the ability to deal with hardened patterns of perception, attribution and defensiveness, as described in previous chapters, represent the steps that satisfy these initial preconditions. Dialogue develops around arguments or propositions. The definition of terms is a universal convention in the crafting of coherent and productive arguments. Defining the terms used in an argument sets the context for the argument and frames it. Without an adequate definition of terms, poor communication, misunderstanding and unintended interpretations will result. Defining terms is a straight forward precondition, yet it is frequently not met. It is the duty of any person presenting an argument in good faith to define the terms pertaining to his or her argument. It is also the duty of others, hearing and becoming engaged in the argument, to ask questions and cause the definitions to be given when they are not. The clear definition of categories or classes of objects, concepts and terms associated with arguments also provides fundamental and crucial building blocks of coherent interaction surrounding those arguments. When opposing arguments are in disagreement concerning the essence of objects or concepts central to the arguments, there can be no basis for common ground — ever! It is an all too common occurrence, in organizations as well as in the public arena, to hear irreconcilable positions debated concerning apples on the one hand and oranges on the other with no attempt having been made to define and reconcile essential classes or categories.

Groups engaged in dialogue are aiming to discover the truth. They are seeking to comprehend reality as completely and accurately as possible. Arguments presented in groups are usually not simple statements of fact but rather take the form of suppositions or hypotheses. A hypothesis is a provisional explanation that may come to be regarded as an acceptable explanation or theory depending on its degree of confirmation. "The term hypothesis has also been used traditionally to refer to the antecedent clause of an 'if — then' statement, the thought being that the consequent clause was conditioned by the assumption of the antecedent clause."[8] (In statements or propositions of the form "If A, then B," A is called the antecedent and B the consequent.) Groups engaged in successful dialogue will be able to examine and qualify hypotheses. They will be able to discriminate between well-formed and flawed arguments and will create high standards and hold such arguments to those standards. Since hypotheses are suppositions and not statements of fact, presenters of arguments must do so in a way that holds them open for inquiry. The choice of words and style of presentation can close down inquiry. We have seen many examples of presentations by leaders and others framed in such a way that challenges could not be made. When this happens, dialogue is thwarted. The quality of an argument is first determined by how clearly and explicitly its assumptions or presuppositions are understood and articulated. Its quality and relevance are further determined by how clearly its consequences have been evaluated and described. The person offering an argument or hypothesis and those hearing it are collaborators in dialogue. Therefore, the presenter has the responsibility to be coherent and unambiguous about presuppositions and consequences and the participants in dialogue are equally responsible to hold the speaker accountable for doing so.

Inference is the process of deriving conclusions from premises. It refers to the steps between presuppositions and conclusions. Some conclusions flow immediately and directly from premises. More often, multiple levels of inference and attribution are involved in the development and presentation of arguments. Inference is the act of passing from one proposition or statement considered as true to another whose truth is believed to follow from that of the former. Attribution is how we explain and give meaning to circumstances and the actions of others. Inference and attribution are tightly linked; inference relates to the act of reasoning while attribution explains causes. Understanding the processes and results of inference and attribution is an important step in the efforts of a group to determine the acceptability of an explanation or theory. Argyris and Schon provide a useful summary of the interplay of inference and attribution in their book *Theory in Practice*.[9] "Anything that claims to be a theory must have *generality* — it must apply to more than one instance; although it may refer to individuals, it must do so in ways that allow similar attributions to be made to other individuals of the same kind." They continue, "A good theory must be *relevant* to its subject matter; if it claims to be about *x*, statements about *x* must be inferable from it." Further, "It should be *consistent*. Simply stated, it should not contradict itself. It must not state in one place that all horses are white and in another that they are not." "A theory should be *complete*. It should contain the full set of propositions required to explain what it sets out to explain. If *y* is to be inferred from *x*, there should be no hidden or unstated component of *x* that is necessary to explain *y*." And finally, "Theories should be *testable*. In order for a theory to be testable, one must be able to infer from its predictions, which can be found to hold or not to hold." Attributions are the product of our perceptions and biases. Our inferences, based on the quality of our reasoning and the content of our attributions, may or may not be congruent with reality. In dialogue, when learning and producing better results is the goal, group members must make the attributions and inferential steps in their arguments explicit. The requirement to make inferences and attributions explicit accomplishes two purposes. It causes the formulator and presenter of the argument in question to become aware of her or his attributions and patterns of inference and it holds these inferences and attributions up for testing and validation (or not) by the group.

There is an analogy between constructing and articulating well-formed and credible arguments for people and programming computers. Computers are devices that make literal interpretations in the extreme and provide a point of unforgiving discipline. Therefore, a successful program must be as close to logically flawless as possible. The steps in writing a program are virtually the same steps as those required to construct and deliver a successful argument. Terms and classes of data, presuppositions and expected consequences must be rigorously defined in programming computers. The logic associated with making inferences from the data and producing results must be carefully crafted. Testing the validity of the output and proving that the output is congruent with the intended consequences is a fundamental and integral aspect of programming computers. The principal difference between arguments constructed for computers and those constructed for humans is that computers will usually fail, unambiguously, if their programs are flawed while flawed human arguments can persist and do damage for long periods of time. When the individual members of a group are able to construct, articulate and evaluate well-grounded and valid arguments, and such standards are able to be sustained, a great deal will have been achieved in the pursuit of dialogue and learning. However, when we remember that most arguments offered in groups are hypotheses and not expositions of fact, opposing points of view will emerge and dilemmas will result from these points of difference. The truth often lies somewhere between opposing points of view. Reconciliation of opposing arguments frequently has the beneficial effects of a more complete and accurate comprehension of reality and higher quality solutions to problems. The focus of attention will now shift to how dilemmas resulting from opposing and apparently incompatible perspectives can be reconciled.

As referenced earlier, Scott Fitzgerald believed that the test of a first class mind is the ability to hold two opposing ideas in the mind at the same time and still retain the ability to function. This is the essential test for individuals seeking to participate in dialogue and group learning. There is an opportunity to convert the conflict encircling opposing points of view to a catalytic force for collective intellectual growth. The requirements for reconciling opposing points of view are the ability to suspend existing assumptions and perceptions, to fully hear and understand different perceptions and to think about the central circumstance in new and different ways. A primary interest in the creation of deeper insights and improved results is the motivation for such behavior. Under the headings "Freeing Individuals from the Grip of Institutional Knowledge" and "The Role of Individuals in Collective Learning" in Chapter 5, we described how individuals must be explicitly aware of their patterns of perception and able to suspend them to be able to participate in dialogue and learning. As partisanship develops around specific arguments in group settings, partisans must be able to suspend their adherence, at least temporarily, in the interest of discovery and producing better results. The rules for defining terms, constructing and examining hypotheses, and formulating and testing inferences will make group members explicitly aware of their assumptions and able to meet the requirement of suspension. Devices in language and storytelling have been used for centuries to alter perceptions and cause events and circumstances to be seen in different ways. Allegory, irony, analogy, parable, metaphor and paradox are examples of such devices. These examples of figurative language provide frames of reference and new ways of making sense of events and experience. We have found three of these constructs to be especially useful, when framed as techniques, in helping to reconcile dilemmas. These techniques are developed around the devices of metaphor, paradox and the third perspective.

Metaphors explain figuratively what could not easily be explained literally. "The man is a rock," "the skies are angry," "the world is a stage" are simple examples. Since metaphors suggest the likeness of one thing to another, a metaphor can sometimes be constructed as a basis or framework of analysis. When the constructed metaphor connects two opposing concepts or apparently incompatible circumstances, similarities and differences between the two sides of the metaphor can be unfolded to point the way to reconciliation. We were introduced to the creative use of the metaphor by David Bohm and F. D. Peat in their book, *Science, Order and Creativity*. They relate the following story: During the 19th century there arose an alternative way of treating the mechanics of moving bodies. Newton had approached motion in terms of the definite paths or trajectories taken by particles. The Hamilton-Jacobi theory, in contrast, developed in the 1860's, presented a new way of treating motion based on waves rather than particles. While the two theories appeared to be radically different, i.e., matter is of a particle nature versus matter is of a wave nature, mathematicians were able to show that the theories generated the same numerical results. This situation suggested the possibility of a metaphorical leap by asserting that: *a particle is a wave!* Such a metaphor connecting the essence of the two theories would have anticipated the modern quantum-mechanical notion of wave-particle duality, i.e., that the same entity behaves under one set of circumstances as a wave and under another set of circumstances as a particle. An unfolding of this metaphor could have led in the mid-nineteenth century to the general outlines of modern quantum theory. Instead, wave theory results were treated as artifacts and the next century turned before scientists were able to seriously consider this new view of reality.[10]

In Chapter 7, we referred to our work with a group of engineers in connection with their company's Continuous Quality Improvement (CQI) program. These engineers were operating in the center of a dilemma. Their managers were promoting CQI, yet the engineers' perceptions were that CQI was extraneous and that they had more real work to do than they could reasonably accomplish. We stated in the earlier chapter that only after the development of a sense of underlying purpose and output or results related to purpose was the group able to achieve some alignment and make progress. Purpose, relevant results and leverage were the key concepts, but a metaphorical leap was achieved to bring about resolution of the opposing points of view. We proposed a metaphor: CQI is Real Work! While the metaphor was initially regarded as an oxymoron, as the group unfolded the similarities and differences between CQI and real work, they realized that in most respects CQI was, in fact, real work. They began to understand how the consequences of CQI initiatives, if well conceived and executed, created leverage in the production of results which is the aim of real work.

Most of the dilemmas we encounter in life are paradoxical. The opposing perspectives that define a dilemma usually define the two sides of a paradox. Paradoxical questions include these: How do we achieve a challenging and rewarding professional life and maintain a satisfying and rich personal and family life at the same time? How do we gratify ourselves in the short term and at the same time postpone gratification? In organizational life, how can we be big in some ways and small in others? How do we sustain differentiated work units yet become integrated around the larger organization? Polarization around opposing points of view tends to be a consequence of paradox-driven dilemmas. Since strong opinions and feelings on the two sides of an issue account for the dilemma in the first place, it is not surprising that polarization develops and restrains creative resolution. Most often, attempts to resolve dilemmas produce winners and losers, i.e., one side of an issue prevails to the detriment of the other. The results of such attempts are frequently worse than the existence of the dilemma itself. Surrounding certain long-standing paradoxes in organizational life, we can observe a kind of oscillation between dominance of firmly established and opposing points of view. A good example pertains to the paradox of how to maintain control and empower organizational units at the same time. Organizational structures cycle back and forth between centralized and decentralized orientations with the sense that neither approach is ever the most efficacious and appropriate one.

Paradoxes tend not to be resolved in ways that make them go away. The best we can hope for in paradox is to reconcile both sides of it — to find a way through the paradox to bring both sides into some degree of congruence where winning and losing doesn't occur. The Third Perspective is a tool for thinking about effective ways through paradox. Charles Handy in the *Age of Paradox* describes how "Trinitarian thinking or third angle thinking is always looking for solutions which can reconcile or illuminate the opposites." Handy reminds us that Adam Smith would have argued that love, or at least the "golden rule," is how markets can be made moral and that "a common humanity is the concept which makes sense of the conflict between male and female."[11] Our strategy development work with organizations points to an example of the third perspective. There is a paradox defined by the need for organizations to be rationally planned, and at the same time, flexible and able to quickly respond to market and technological changes. The third perspective defines a middle path between highly structured, bureaucratic and usually burdensome planning processes and complete flexibility and autonomy. This view sees the development and execution of strategy as a process of defining explicit organization-wide strategic outcome goals and defining congruent unit-specific outcome goals coupled with accountability for achievement of goals in whatever manner is most effective for the units. This planning model is fully described in Chapter 10 under the heading, "Bringing About Interdependent Thinking and Behaving."

There is often a great deal at stake in successfully resolving paradox. There is an important paradox operating for health care providers in the current managed care environment. It defines a dilemma framed by economic interests on the one hand and quality/caring interests on the other. The paradoxical question for hospitals, physicians, other providers and all of us is how can costs be reduced and the delivery system become more efficient while maintaining and improving quality of care and sensitivity to patients? There has been a need to effectively resolve this paradox for at least 25 years. Health care providers could have resolved it. They did not, and by not doing so, they lost a significant degree of self determination and gave up control of the industry to economic interests. Our work with health care organizations has brought us face to face with this paradox on many occasions. We have used the third perspective to help organizations define a new set of operative assumptions leading to a sense of how the paradox can be resolved. The assumption operating on one side of the paradox is "it's all about *cost*;" the assumption on the other side is "its all about *quality*." The insight we aim to bring about is that the two sides of this paradox are not mutually exclusive and can be brought together around a new assumption that declares "it's all about *efficacy* in patient care." The third perspective that emerges from this new assumption is an orientation to objective patient outcomes, and further, that there are economic as well as quality implications in outcomes.

Balancing Dialogue and Advocacy

Advocacy comes naturally to most of us. We are far more inclined to defend our points of view and advocate for them than we are to reconcile them with other perceptions and enhance them for some larger purpose. Chris Argyris believes that most of us are socialized according to a set of social virtues including: "Advocate your position in order to win; hold your own position in the face of the advocacy of others; feeling vulnerable is a sign of weakness; stick to your principles, values and beliefs; do not confront the reasoning and actions of other people."[12] These "Model I Social Virtues" are causes of defensive patterns which Argyris argues are the norm in most organizations and form the basis for his theory of human action and control. While the supposed pervasiveness and consequences of these social virtues are theoretical constructs, it is difficult to deny that interactions in groups seem to be dominated by such governing values as these. Advocacy, then, is a common mode of interaction in groups and most of us are comfortable with it. As easily as we are drawn to advocacy, however, our tendency to engage in it is not necessarily coupled with the skill to be good at it. The quality of our arguments can be most improved by mastering the skills for dialogue — by enhancing our advocacy skills based on the steps for dialogue as expressed in Table 1.

In dialogue, questions are asked, understanding is deepened, options are explored and solutions are enriched. In advocacy, choices are narrowed, alignment is achieved, decisions are made and courses of action are charted. Dialogue is diverging; advocacy is converging. Advocacy is the necessary counterpart of dialogue because learning in organizations, at the core, is concerned with creating actionable knowledge — knowledge that leads to relevant and leverage-producing action. If a group is locked in dialogue, no action will result; if a group is locked in advocacy, thoughtless and inappropriate action will be the result. Achieving an effective balance in these modes of interaction in groups is the key determinant in learning. While this balance is easy to describe, it is difficult to achieve. In our experience, the only way to achieve it is to keep the efforts of the group focused on outcomes or results related unambiguously to a purpose that has meaning for all members of the group.

11.3   *Toward a Learning-Oriented Culture*

Referring again to our multi-level definition of group and organizational learning, the first level pertains to the ability to comprehend internal and external reality and the connections that exist between these aspects of reality; the second level relates to the ability to recognize and understand the basic assumptions operating within the group and the ability to identify those assumptions that are congruent with reality and those that are not. The third level concerns the ability to change the assumptions that need to be changed and to leave in place those that do not. According to this definition, the collective and sustained ability to produce relevant, accurate, timely and actionable knowledge is the substance of organizational learning and is not extraneous in any way to the essential way of being in a group or organization. By definition, then, a learning orientation is a cultural attribute of groups and organizations. The motivation to change or evolve organizational culture comes from the perceived need to solve problems and become more effective and the desire to achieve organizational potential. Culture explains much if not most of the day to day behavior in a group or organization. As we have seen, culture is powerful in its potential to produce effects, whether beneficial or detrimental. If there is great potential leverage in bringing about culture change in organizations, it follows that there is great potential leverage in the application of organizational learning to culture change. Regarding culture, culture change and learning, consistent with the insights and definitions offered in this book, building the capacity to change or evolve culture is exactly equivalent to building the capacity of institutional knowledge to produce desired effects which is exactly the same as building learning capacity. A learning oriented culture is one driven by a clear sense of purpose and a fundamental assumption that holds all assumptions open for evaluation and change within a framework of balance between achieving effectiveness (by challenging assumptions) and efficiency (by holding assumptions constant). This state of balance or equilibrium will exist between modes of learning, i.e., single-loop and double-loop learning, and modes of discourse — dialogue and advocacy.

References

1. Senge, P. M., *The Fifth Discipline: The Art and Practice of the Learning Organization,* Doubleday, New York, 1990, 3.
2. Argyris, C., *Knowledge for Action: A Guide to Overcoming Barriers to Organizational Change,* Jossey-Bass, San Francisco, 1994, 49.
3. Handy, C., *The Age of Unreason,* Harvard Business School Press, Boston, 1989, 59.
4. Gergen, K., Organization Theory in the Postmodern Era, *Rethinking Organization: New Directions in Organization Theory and Analysis,* Sage Publications, London, 1992.

5. Sayers, D., *The Lost Tools of Learning*, Methuen & Co., Ltd., London, 1947.

6. *The Great Ideas: A Syntopicon of the Great Books of the Western World*, 1, Encyclopedia Britannica, Inc., 1952, 347.

7. Senge, P. M., *The Fifth Discipline: The Art and Practice of the Learning Organization*, Doubleday, New York, 1990, 198.

8. Reese, W. L., *Dictionary of Philosophy and Religion: Eastern & Western Thought*, Humanities Press, New Jersey, 1980.

9. Argyris, C. and Schon, D. A., *Theory in Practice: Increasing Professional Effectiveness*, Jossey-Bass Publishers, San Francisco, 1974, 197.

10. Bohm, D. and Peat, F. D., *Science, Order and Creativity*, Phantom, New York, 1987.

11. Handy, C., *The Age of Paradox*, Harvard Business School Press, Boston, 1994, 99.

12. Argyris, C., *Overcoming Organizational Defenses: Facilitating Organizational Learning*, Allyn & Bacon, Boston, 1990, 19.

Index

241

H

Habitualized behavior, 19
Hawthorne studies, 79
Healthcare services, 38
Hierarchy, 28
High leverage change model, 142
Human dynamics, 133
Human potential, 7
Humanities, 228
Hypothesis, examination of, 229

I

Ideal structure, 28
Idiosyncrasy, 48
Ignorance, 220
Illusion of control, 107
Imagination, 50
Incompetence, skilled, 192
Individualist, extreme, 174
Individuals, 47–50
Individuals, achieving operative balance of objective and subjective factors, 51–72
  achieving operative balance of objective and subjective factors, 53–71
  attribution, 59–65
  communication, relationships and preconditions to learning, 68–71
  defensive responses to perceptions and defense of others, 66–67
  insights into defensive behavior, 67–68
  perception, 56–59
  role of defensiveness in perception and cognition, 65–66
  anticipatory summary, 51–53
  attribution, 52
  communication, relationships and preconditions to learning, 53

defensive responses to perceptions and defenses of others, 52
  insights into defensive behavior, 53
  perception, 52
  role of defensiveness in perception and cognition, 52
Individuals, delegating only around purpose, 73–90
  anticipatory summary, 73–75
  delegation as viewed by individuals, 75
  empowerment from perspective of individual, 75
  meaning reconciliation, 74
  motivation, 74
  personal leverage, 75
  purposeful delegation and responses by individuals, 73
  delegating only around purpose, 75–88
  delegation as viewed by individuals, 87–88
  empowerment from perspective of individual, 85–87
  meaning reconciliation, 81–84
  motivation, 77–81
  personal leverage, 84–85
  purposeful delegation and responses by individuals, 76–77
Individuals, enhancing efficacy of institutional knowledge, 91–103
  anticipatory summary, 91–92
  freeing individuals from grip of institutional knowledge, 92
  role of individuals in collective learning, 92
  enhancing efficacy of institutional knowledge, 93–102
  freeing individuals from grip of institutional knowledge, 96–97
  role of individuals in collective learning, 97–102
Inertia, 115
Inference, 233